Tourism, Cyclones, Hurricanes and Flooding

ASPECTS OF TOURISM

Series Editors: **Chris Cooper** *(Leeds Beckett University, UK)*, **C. Michael Hall** *(University of Canterbury, New Zealand)* and **Dallen J. Timothy** *(Arizona State University, USA)*

Aspects of Tourism is an innovative, multifaceted series, which comprises authoritative reference handbooks on global tourism regions, research volumes, texts and monographs. It is designed to provide readers with the latest thinking on tourism worldwide and in so doing will push back the frontiers of tourism knowledge. The series also introduces a new generation of international tourism authors writing on leading edge topics.

The volumes are authoritative, readable and user-friendly, providing accessible sources for further research. Books in the series are commissioned to probe the relationship between tourism and cognate subject areas such as strategy, development, retailing, sport and environmental studies. The publisher and series editors welcome proposals from writers with projects on the above topics.

All books in this series are externally peer-reviewed.

Full details of all the books in this series and of all our other publications can be found on http://www.channelviewpublications.com, or by writing to Channel View Publications, St Nicholas House, 31–34 High Street, Bristol, BS1 2AW, UK.

ASPECTS OF TOURISM: 99

Tourism, Cyclones, Hurricanes and Flooding

Edited by
C. Michael Hall and Girish Prayag

CHANNEL VIEW PUBLICATIONS
Bristol • Jackson

DOI https://doi.org/10.21832/HALL9479
Names: Hall, Colin Michael, editor. | Prayag, Girish, editor.
Title: Tourism, Cyclones, Hurricanes and Flooding/Edited by C. Michael Hall and Girish Prayag.
Description: Jackson: Channel View Publications, [2024] | Series: Aspects of Tourism: 99 | Includes bibliographical references and index. | Summary: "This book explores the relationship between tourism and high-magnitude storm events. It considers the measures available to manage tourism after major storms and floods, examines the means to mitigate the potential impacts of these disasters on tourism, and provides insights into the ethical issues facing tourism after a major flood or storm"—Provided by publisher.
Identifiers: LCCN 2023042485 (print) | LCCN 2023042486 (ebook) | ISBN 9781845419462 (pbk) | ISBN 9781845419479 (hbk) | ISBN 9781845419493 (epub) | ISBN 9781845419486 (pdf)
Subjects: LCSH: Tourism—Environmental aspects. | Tourism—Social aspects. | Natural disasters. Classification: LCC G156.5.E58 .T679 2024 (print) | LCC G156.5.E58 (ebook) | DDC 910.68—dc23/eng/20231024
LC record available at https://lccn.loc.gov/2023042485
LC ebook record available at https://lccn.loc.gov/2023042486

Library of Congress Cataloging in Publication Data
A catalog record for this book is available from the Library of Congress.

British Library Cataloguing in Publication Data
A catalogue entry for this book is available from the British Library.

ISBN-13: 978-1-84541-947-9 (hbk)
ISBN-13: 978-1-84541-946-2 (pbk)

Channel View Publications
UK: St Nicholas House, 31–34 High Street, Bristol, BS1 2AW, UK.
USA: Ingram, Jackson, TN, USA.

Website: https://www.channelviewpublications.com
Twitter: Channel_View
Facebook: https://www.facebook.com/channelviewpublications
Blog: https://www.channelviewpublications.wordpress.com

The policy of Multilingual Matters/Channel View Publications is to use papers that are natural, renewable and recyclable products, made from wood grown in sustainable forests. In the manufacturing process of our books, and to further support our policy, preference is given to printers that have FSC and PEFC Chain of Custody certification. The FSC and/or PEFC logos will appear on those books where full certification has been granted to the printer concerned.

Typeset by SAN Publishing Services.

Contents

Tables and Figures

Figures

Contributors

Bailey Ashton Adie, Visiting Research Fellow, Center for Tourism Research, Wakayama University, Japan & Oulu University, Finland; https://orcid.org/0000-0002-7734-4587

Alberto Amore, Geography Research Unit, University of Oulu, Oulu, Finland; https://orcid.org/0000-0002-8456-8669

Noelia Araújo-Vila, Faculty of Business and Tourism, University of Vigo, 32004 Ourense, Spain; https://orcid.org/0000-0002-3395-8536

Tim Baird, Faculty of Agribusiness and Commerce, PO Box 85084, Lincoln University, Lincoln 7647, Christchurch, New Zealand; https://orcid.org/0000-0002-9169-3564;

Cecilia Bischeri, Griffith University Cities Research Institute, Griffith Architecture and Design, Griffith University, Gold Coast campus, QLD 4222, Australia; c.bischeri@griffith.edu.au

Heidi Chang, Department of Entertainment Management, International College, I-Shou University, No.1, Sec. 1, Syuecheng Rd., Dashu District, Kaohsiung City 84001, Taiwan, R.O.C

Ignatius P. Cahyanto, Department of Marketing and Hospitality, B.I. Moody III College of Business Administration, University of Louisiana at Lafayette, Moody Room 216, PO Box 43661, Lafayette, LA 70504 USA; https://orcid.org/0000-0003-1278-0377

Jennifer M. Fitchett, School of Geography, Archaeology and Environmental Studies, University of the Witwatersrand, South Africa; https://orcid.org/0000-0002-0854-1720;

José Antonio Fraiz-Brea, Faculty of Business and Tourism, University of Vigo, 32004 Ourense, Spain; https://orcid.org/0000-0002-3190-649

C. Michael Hall, Department of Management, Marketing and Tourism, University of Canterbury, Private Bag 4800, Christchurch, New Zealand 8140; Geography Research Unit, University of Oulu, Finland; School of Service Management, Lund University Helsingborg, Sweden; School of Business and Economics, Linnaeus University, Kalmar, Sweden; and Kyung Hee University, Seoul, Korea; https://orcid.org/0000-0002-7734-4587

Gijsbert Hoogendoorn, Department of Geography, Environmental Management and Energy Studies, University of Johannesburg, Corner Kingsway and University Road, Auckland Park, Johannesburg 2006 South Africa; https://orcid.org/0000-0001-7969-7952

Yawei Jiang, Griffith University, Department of Tourism, Sport and Hotel Management, Nathan, Queensland, Australia; Queensland, Australia, 4072; https://orcid.org/0000-0003-3125-3732

Robert Kiss, Department of International Tourism and Hospitality, International College, I-Shou University, No.1, Sec. 1, Syuecheng Rd., Dashu District, Kaohsiung City 84001, Taiwan, R.O.C; https://orcid.org/0000-0003-0209-3004

Simon Milne, Tourism Consultant, Tourismworx Ltd, Auckland, New Zealand.

Cecilia Möller, Geomedia research group, Department of Geography, Media and Communication, Karlstad University, S-65188 Karlstad, Sweden; Myndigheten för samhällsskydd och beredskap, Enheten för utbildningsinriktning (RO-UI), 651 81 Karlstad; https://orcid.org/0000-0002-1918-6701

Girish Prayag, Department of Management, Marketing and Tourism, University of Canterbury, Private Bag 4800, Christchurch, New Zealand 8140; https://orcid.org/0000-0001-6243-2747

Brent W. Ritchie, UQ Business School, The University of Queensland (St Lucia Campus), Brisbane, Queensland, Australia, 4072; https://orcid.org/0000-0003-1540-9389;

Alexander Safonov, Department of Management, Marketing and Tourism, University of Canterbury, Private Bag 4800, Christchurch, New Zealand 8140

Minghui Sun, New Zealand School of Tourism, Auckland, New Zealand; https://orcid.org/0000-0003-1611-1832

Su-Marie van Tonder, Department of Geography, Environmental Management and Energy Studies, University of Johannesburg, Corner Kingsway and University Road, Auckland Park, Johannesburg 2006 South Africa

Diego R. Toubes, Faculty of Business and Tourism, University of Vigo, 32004 Ourense, Spain

Acknowledgements

Girish would like to thank a number of colleagues with whom he has undertaken disaster management research in the past few years for sharing their knowledge and insights. In particular, thanks go to Caroline Orchiston, Mesbahuddin Chowdhury, Lucie Ozanne, Sam Spector, Peter Fieger, Alberto Amore, Deborah Blackman, Hitomi Nakanishi, Ben Freyens, Joerg Finsterwalder, Alistair Tombs, Chris Chen and Sussie Morrish. Also, Girish would like to thank family and friends who have supported him over the years.

Michael would like to thank colleagues and friends with whom he has had relevant conversations or conducted research with over the years in relation to this work, some of which are also contributors. In particular, thanks go to Bailey Adie, Alberto Amore, Tim Baird, Dorothee Bohn, Chris Chen, Tim Coles, Hervé Corvellec, David Duval, Martin Gren, Stephan Gössling, Johan Hultman, Myung Ja Kim, Tyron Love, Dieter Müller, Yael Ram, Jarkko Saarinen, Anna Dóra Sæþórsdóttir, Daniel Scott and Siamak Seyfi for their thoughts on disasters, resilience and tourism, as well as to Linnaeus University, Lund University and the University of Oulu for their support in undertaking related research in the Nordic countries. Michael would like to also thank Jody and Cooper for their support over so many years and especially during the time that this book was developed. The proofreading by Jody Cowper-James and Émilie Crossley of chapters in this book is also gratefully acknowledged.

Finally, we would like to thank our authors for dealing with COVID and life-related delays to this book and to all at Channel View for continuing to support this project despite the stresses of the last few years.

1 Introduction: The Threat from Flooding and Cyclones

C. Michael Hall and Girish Prayag

Introduction

Flooding, and the impact of high magnitude low frequency storm events (known variously as cyclones, hurricanes and typhoons), which have long posed a threat to tourism destinations, such as the Caribbean, East Asia, northern Australia and the islands of the Pacific and the Indian Oceans, are becoming an increasingly significant concern for the tourism industry at a global scale. Flooding and large storm events, such as cyclones, are expected to get worse as a result of global heating. As July 2023 became the hottest month recorded in the world since historical records have been kept (Badshah, 2023), and wildfires affected the Mediterranean and Hawaii, at the same time China, Korea, northern Europe, and the north-eastern United States experienced intense flooding (Hulton, 2023). A warmer world is also one that will experience more flooding and intense weather events (Ajjur & Al-Ghamdi, 2022; Alifu et al., 2022; Cea & Costabile, 2022; Corringham et al., 2022).

As a result of the climate crisis, cyclones (the collective name used here to describe cyclones, hurricanes and typhoons, see Box 1) that make landfall are taking longer to weaken, meaning that they take more moisture inland and are consequently also more destructive (Li & Chakraborty, 2020; IPCC, 2021). This situation is only going to get worse given that the world's oceans keep getting hotter (Cheng et al., 2021; IPCC, 2021). Warmer seas also mean more energy and moisture for cyclones and storms, making them stronger and contributing to more severe winds, storm surges, rainfall and flooding. In 2020, the annual record for the number of major storms forming in the Atlantic was broken in November, with Subtropical Storm Theta becoming the 29th named event (storms are named by the US Hurricane Center once they hit a wind speed of 39mph) (Milman, 2020). More than 90% of the heat trapped by carbon emissions is absorbed by the world's oceans and seas. Just as seriously, the rate of heating of the oceans is increasing. The hottest years for the oceans have occurred since 2015, and the rate of heating since 1986 has been eight times higher than that between 1960 and 1985 (Cheng *et al.*, 2021).

This chapter is designed to provide an introduction to the seriousness of floods and cyclones as global weather events, as well as the use of the various specialist terminology that is used to describe such events and which is used throughout the book. This introduction also discusses some of the language used to describe disaster management in a tourism context as well as related terms, such as resilience and vulnerability.

The Impacts of Weather Events

The effects of weather events are substantial with their impacts exacerbated by inappropriate urbanisation practices, such as building in flood plains, and the sheer growth of the size of cities. The seriousness of such events is only being exacerbated by climate change. In addressing the question of whether climate change has altered the probability of extreme river flood events, Alifu *et al.* (2022) found that for the period 1951–2010 anthropogenic climate change altered the probabilities of 20 of the 52 analysed flood events. And where urbanisation occurs in already flood-prone areas the results may be catastrophic in the long-term (Deng *et al.*, 2022; Gao *et al.*, 2022). As the IPCC (2021, C.2.6) reported, urbanisation

> increases mean and heavy precipitation over and/or downwind of cities (*medium confidence*) and resulting runoff intensity (*high confidence*). In coastal cities, the combination of more frequent extreme sea level events (due to sea level rise and storm surge) and extreme rainfall/riverflow events will make flooding more probable (*high confidence*).

Rentschler *et al.* (2022a) estimates that 1.81 billion people (23% of global population) face significant flood risk worldwide. Of these, 89% live in low- and middle-income countries. Overall, 780 million flood-exposed people live on less than $5.50 a day, and 170 million live in extreme poverty (less than $1.90 a day). This means that four in every 10 people that are exposed to flood risk globally live in poverty (Rentschler *et al.*, 2022b), highlighting their extreme vulnerability to flooding.

In terms of spatial coverage, every country in Rentschler *et al.*'s (2022a) study (188 countries) was affected by flood risk. Their research suggests that almost 70% (1.24 billion) of flood-exposed people live in South and East Asia, with China and India accounting for over one third of global exposure. East Asia has 668 million flood-exposed people, corresponding to about 28% of its total population (Rentschler *et al.*, 2022b; see also Global Flood Database, https://global-flood-database.cloudto-street.ai). Such data is also important because it highlights the challenges that floods may pose to tourism as a tool for encouraging poverty reduction.

The number of recorded flood and storm disasters has been increasing over time (Centre for Research on the Epidemiology of Disasters (CRED), 2022). CRED (2022) defines a disaster as 'a situation or event that overwhelms local capacity, necessitating a request at the national or international level for external assistance; an unforeseen and often sudden event that causes great damage, destruction and human suffering'. Only disasters attributed to natural hazards (excluding biological hazards) are included in their database, and requires at least one of the following criteria to be met:

- 10 or more people reported killed;
- 100 or more people reported affected;
- declaration of a state of emergency;
- call for international assistance.

Floods and storms are the most recorded disaster events by CRED both over the 2001–2020 period and in 2021 (Table 1.1). In 2021, over half (223) of the 432 catastrophic events recorded were floods, up from an average of 163 annual flood disaster events in the 2001–2020 period. The most significant of these events were the monsoon season (June to September) floods in India that claimed 1282 lives. The Henan Flood in China in July resulted in 352 deaths, 14.5 million people affected, and a cost of US$16.5 billion. Also in July, the Nuristan floods in Afghanistan resulted in 260 fatalities while floods in Central Europe and subsequent landslides resulted in $40 billion economic costs in Germany alone (CRED, 2022). Storms were the second most recorded type of disaster event in 2021 with 121 events recorded, over double the 2001–2020 average of 102 entries per year. Among the most notable was Typhoon Rai in the Philippines, which resulted in at least 457 deaths and affected 10.6 million people in December. In April, Tropical Cyclone Seroja claimed 226 lives in Indonesia. In the USA, which has some of the highest economic costs arising from storms and floods, a North American winter storm in February killed at least 235 people and cost more than $30 billion, while Hurricane Ida caused 96 deaths and $65 billion in economic costs, and tornadoes in December caused 93 deaths and $5.2 billion in economic costs (CRED, 2022). Between 2001 and 2021, seven of the ten greatest disasters with respect to economic losses in the world were flood or storm events (Table 1.2).

Box 1. Hurricane and Cyclone terminology

- Hurricane/Typhoon: A tropical cyclone with sustained winds of 74mph or 119km/h is classified as a *hurricane* in the North Atlantic, central and eastern North Pacific (east of the

Table 1.1 Overview of disasters by type 2001–2022

Type of disaster	Occurrence			Total deaths		Total affected (mn)		Economic losses (bn)	
	2021	2022	annual average 2001–2021	2021	annual average 2001–2021	2021	annual average 2001–2021	2021	annual average 2001–2021
Drought	15	22	16	0	1059	52.7	67.5	12.1	6.7
Earthquake	28	31	27	2742	37,942	1.1	6.2	11.3	35.4
Extreme temperature	3	12	21	1044	8684	0	5.1	5.6	3.1
Flood	223	176	163	4143	5185	29.2	82.7	74.4	34.1
Landslide	14	17	18	474	884	0	0.2	0.5	0.3
Mass movement (dry)	0	0	1	0	37	0	0	0	0
Storm	121	108	102	1876	10,442	17.6	37.4	137.0	77.0
Volcanic activity	9	5	5	85	89	0.5	0.3	1.3	0.1
Wildfire	19	15	11	128	77	0.7	0.7	9.2	5.0

After CRED, 2022, 2023; For comparison purposes, all economic damages are adjusted using the Consumer Price Index (CPI), OECD (2022), Inflation (CPI) (indicator). doi: 10.1787/eee82e6e-en.

International Dateline to the Greenwich Meridian), while called a *typhoon* in the Northwest Pacific (north of the Equator west of the International Dateline).
- Tropical cyclone: A generic term describing a rotating and organised system of clouds and thunderstorms that originates over tropical or subtropical waters and has closed surface wind circulation about a well-defined centre. The term is used in the South Pacific and Indian Ocean regardless of wind strength associated with the weather system.
- Tropical depressions: Weakest tropical cyclone with the maximum sustained wind speed of 38mph or 62km/h or less.
- Saffir-Simpson Hurricane Wind Scale: 1 to 5 categorisation based on the hurricane's intensity at the indicated time. The scale provides examples of the type of damage and impacts in the United States associated with winds of the indicated intensity (Table 1.3).

Source: National Hurricane Center and Central Pacific Hurricane Center (2022), United Nations General Assembly (2016)

The association between economic loss and the United States noted in Table 1.2 highlights not so much the frequency of weather-related disasters in the country, but more the strength of its economy and the insurance costs associated with such events. Tables 1.4 to 1.6 report on the substantial insurance costs of such events over the period 1980–2022 (Natural Centers for Environmental Information (NCEI), 2022). The NEIC note that there is inconsistency in available data, and that the uncertainty of loss estimates differ by different disaster event type and reflect the quality and completeness of data sources. Nevertheless, they suggest that their comprehensive public and private sector sources data represents a relatively accurate estimated total of the direct costs (both insured and uninsured) of these events. The costs included cover: 'physical damage to residential, commercial, and municipal buildings; material assets (content) within buildings; time element losses such as business interruption or loss of living quarters; damage to vehicles and boats; public assets including roads, bridges, levees; electrical infrastructure and offshore energy platforms; agricultural assets including crops, livestock, and commercial timber; and wildfire suppression costs, among others' (NCEI, 2022). However, losses such as 'natural capital or environmental degradation; mental or physical healthcare related costs, the value of a statistical life (VSL); or supply chain, contingent business interruption costs' (NCEI, 2022) are not included. Therefore, overall the NCEI (2022) regard their estimates as conservative.

Table 1.2 Economic losses associated with greatest economic disasters from storms and floods 2001–2021

Event	Country	Date	Economic cost (US$ billions)
Hurricane Katrina	USA	2005	173
Monsoon floods	Thailand	2012	48
Hurricane Sandy	USA	2013	59
Hurricane Ima	USA	2017	63
Hurricane Maria	Puerto Rico	2017	75
Hurricane Harvey	USA	2017	105
Hurricane Ida	USA	2021	65

After CRED, 2022; For comparison purposes, all economic damages are adjusted using the OECD (2022) Consumer Price Index (CPI).

Table 1.3 Saffir-Simpson Hurricane Wind Scale

Category	Sustained Wind*	Types of Damage
1	74–95mph (119–153km/h)	Very dangerous winds will produce some damage: Well-constructed frame homes could have damage to roof, shingles, vinyl siding and gutters. Large branches of trees will snap and shallowly rooted trees may be toppled. Extensive damage to power lines and poles likely will result in power outages that could last a few to several days.
2	96–110mph (154–177km/h)	Extremely dangerous winds will cause extensive damage: Well-constructed frame homes could sustain major roof and siding damage. Many shallowly rooted trees will be snapped or uprooted and block numerous roads. Near-total power loss is expected with outages that could last from several days to weeks.
3 (major)**	111–129mph (178–208km/h)	Devastating damage will occur: Well-built framed homes may incur major damage or removal of roof decking and gable ends. Many trees will be snapped or uprooted, blocking numerous roads. Electricity and water will be unavailable for several days to weeks after the storm passes.
4*** (major)**	130–156mph (209–251km/h)	Catastrophic damage will occur: Well-built framed homes can sustain severe damage with loss of most of the roof structure and/or some exterior walls. Most trees will be snapped or uprooted and power poles downed. Fallen trees and power poles will isolate residential areas. Power outages will last weeks to possibly months. Most of the area will be uninhabitable for weeks or months.
5*** (major)**	157mph or higher (252km/h or higher)	Catastrophic damage will occur: A high percentage of framed homes will be destroyed, with total roof failure and wall collapse. Fallen trees and power poles will isolate residential areas. Power outages will last for weeks to possibly months. Most of the area will be uninhabitable for weeks or months.

*mph: winds maximum 1-min
**hurricanes rated Category 3 and higher are known as 'major hurricanes'
***typhoons equivalent of a Category 4 or Category 5 hurricane are called 'super-typhoons'
Source: National Hurricane Center and Central Pacific Hurricane Center (2021)

Table 1.4 Major flooding affecting the US 1980–2022

Name	Year	Total Unadjusted Cost (in millions)	Deaths
Gulf States Storms and Flooding	1982	$ 1536	45
Western Storms and Flooding	1983	$ 1500	50
Virginia, West Virginia, Pennsylvania and Maryland Flooding	1985	$ 1400	62
Southern Flooding	1990	$ 1007	13
Midwest Flooding	1993	$ 20,961	48
Texas Flooding	1994	$ 1000	19
California Flooding	1995	$ 2500	27
Pacific Northwest Severe Flooding	1996	$ 1008	9
West Coast Flooding	1997	$ 3017	36
Northern Plains Flooding	1997	$ 3677	11
Northeast Flooding	2006	$ 1522	20
Midwest Flooding	2008	$ 9958	24
Northeast Flooding	2010	$ 1844	11
East/South Flooding and Severe Weather	2010	$ 2266	32
Mississippi River flooding	2011	$ 2986	7
Missouri River flooding	2011	$ 2002	5
Illinois Flooding and Severe Weather	2013	$ 1077	4
Colorado Flooding	2013	$ 1509	9
Michigan and Northeast Flooding	2014	$ 1032	2
Texas and Oklahoma Flooding and Severe Weather	2015	$ 2500	31
South Carolina and East Coast Flooding	2015	$ 1998	25
Texas and Louisiana Flooding	2016	$ 2295	5
Houston Flooding	2016	$ 2676	8
West Virginia Flooding and Ohio Valley Tornadoes	2016	$ 969	23
Louisiana Flooding	2016	$ 10,000	13
California Flooding	2017	$ 1500	5
Missouri and Arkansas Flooding and Central Severe Weather	2017	$ 1659	20
Missouri River and North Central Flooding	2019	$ 10,727	3
Arkansas River Flooding	2019	$ 3025	5
Mississippi River, Midwest and Southern Flooding	2019	$ 6169	4
California Flooding and Severe Weather	2021	$ 1095	2
Louisiana Flooding	2021	$ 1319	5

Source: Natural Centers for Environmental Information (NCEI) (2022).

Table 1.5 Major severe storms affecting the US 1980–2022

Name	Year	Total Unadjusted Cost (in millions)	Deaths
Midwest/Plains Tornadoes	1994	$ 985	3
South Plains Severe Weather	1995	$ 5487	32
Mississippi and Ohio Valley Severe Weather and Flooding	1997	$ 978	67
Western/Eastern Severe Weather and Flooding	1997	$ 1005	132
Minnesota Severe Storms/Hail	1998	$ 1631	1
Northern Plains and Great Lakes Derecho, Tornadoes	1998	$ 1138	20
Oklahoma and Kansas Tornadoes	1999	$ 2012	55
Midwest/Ohio Valley Hail and Tornadoes	2001	$ 3095	3
Severe Storms and Tornadoes	2002	$ 2094	7
Severe Storms/Hail	2003	$ 2006	3
Severe Storms/Tornadoes	2003	$ 4128	51
Southern Derecho and Eastern Severe Weather	2003	$ 1008	7
Severe Storms, Hail, Tornadoes	2004	$ 1014	4
Severe Storms and Tornadoes	2006	$ 1338	10
Midwest/Southeast Tornadoes	2006	$ 1604	10
Midwest Tornadoes	2006	$ 2424	27
East/South Severe Weather and Flooding	2007	$ 2508	9
Western, Central and Northeast Severe Weather	2008	$ 982	12
Southeast Tornadoes and Severe Weather	2008	$ 1212	57
Southeast Tornadoes	2008	$ 1131	5
Southern Severe Weather	2008	$ 1040	2
Midwest Tornadoes and Severe Weather	2008	$ 3030	13
Midwest/Mid-Atlantic Severe Weather	2008	$ 1636	18
Southeast/Ohio Valley Severe Weather	2009	$ 1740	10
Midwest/Southeast Tornadoes	2009	$ 1641	0
South/Southeast Severe Weather and Tornadoes	2009	$ 1430	6
Midwest, South and East Severe Weather	2009	$ 1328	0
Colorado Hail Storm	2009	$ 1000	0
Oklahoma, Kansas, and Texas Tornadoes and Severe Weather	2010	$ 3334	3
Arizona Severe Weather	2010	$ 3800	0
Midwest/Southeast Tornadoes and Derecho	2011	$ 2775	9

(Continued)

Table 1.5 (Continued)

Name	Year	Total Unadjusted Cost (in millions)	Deaths
Southeast/Midwest Tornadoes	2011	$ 2179	0
Midwest/Southeast Tornadoes	2011	$ 2059	38
Ohio Valley Derecho and Southern Tornadoes	2011	$ 1038	0
Southeast/Ohio Valley/Midwest Tornadoes	2011	$ 10,222	321
Midwest/Southeast Tornadoes	2011	$ 9097	177
Midwest/Southeast Tornadoes and Severe Weather	2011	$ 1537	3
Rockies and Midwest Derecho	2011	$ 1235	2
Midwest/Southeast Severe Weather	2011	$ 1151	0
Southeast/Ohio Valley Tornadoes	2012	$ 3129	42
Texas Tornadoes	2012	$ 1015	0
Midwest Tornadoes	2012	$ 1124	6
Midwest/Ohio Valley Severe Weather	2012	$ 3276	1
Southern Plains/Midwest/Northeast Severe Weather	2012	$ 2304	1
Rockies/Southwest Severe Weather	2012	$ 2598	0
Plains/East/Northeast Derecho	2012	$ 2888	28
Southeast Severe Weather	2013	$ 2020	1
Midwest/Plains Severe Weather	2013	$ 1444	1
Midwest/Plains/East Tornadoes	2013	$ 2400	27
Midwest/Plains/Northeast Tornadoes	2013	$ 1814	10
Midwest Severe Weather	2013	$ 1042	0
Ohio Valley Tornadoes	2013	$ 1091	8
Plains Severe Weather	2014	$ 1424	0
Midwest/Southeast/Northeast Tornadoes and Flooding	2014	$ 1736	33
Rockies/Midwest/Eastern Severe Weather	2014	$ 3713	0
Rockies/Central Plains Severe Weather	2014	$ 1919	2
Rockies/Plains Severe Weather	2014	$ 1400	0
Midwest/Ohio Valley Severe Weather	2015	$ 1556	2
South/Southeast Severe Weather	2015	$ 1284	0
Southern Plains Tornadoes	2015	$ 1272	4
Central and Northeast Severe Weather	2015	$ 1172	1
Texas Tornadoes and Midwest Flooding	2015	$ 1962	50
Southeast and Eastern Tornadoes	2016	$ 1040	10

(Continued)

Table 1.5 (Continued)

Name	Year	Total Unadjusted Cost (in millions)	Deaths
Southern Severe Weather	2016	$ 1210	1
North Texas Hail Storm	2016	$ 2065	0
North/Central Texas Hail Storm	2016	$ 3499	0
South/Southeast Tornadoes	2016	$ 2395	6
Plains Tornadoes and Central Severe Weather	2016	$ 1720	2
Rockies/Central Tornadoes and Severe Weather	2016	$ 1146	0
Rockies and Northeast Severe Weather	2016	$ 1466	0
Southern Tornado Outbreak and Western Storms	2017	$ 1105	24
Central/Southeast Tornado Outbreak	2017	$ 1806	6
Midwest Tornado Outbreak	2017	$ 2176	2
South/Southeast Severe Weather	2017	$ 2695	0
Southeast Severe Weather and Tornadoes	2017	$ 976	1
Colorado Hail Storm and Central Severe Weather	2017	$ 3350	0
Minnesota Hail Storm and Upper Midwest Severe Weather	2017	$ 2350	0
Midwest Severe Weather	2017	$ 1509	0
Midwest Severe Weather	2017	$ 1425	0
Southeastern Tornadoes and Severe Weather	2018	$ 1452	0
Southern and Eastern Tornadoes and Severe Weather	2018	$ 1318	3
Central and Northeastern Severe Weather	2018	$ 1390	0
Central and Eastern Severe Weather	2018	$ 1370	5
Texas Hail Storm	2018	$ 1300	0
Colorado Hail Storm	2018	$ 955	0
Colorado Hail Storm	2018	$ 2223	0
Central and Eastern Tornadoes and Severe Weather	2018	$ 1585	0
Rockies and Plains Hail Storms	2018	$ 1025	0
Southeast, Ohio Valley and Northeast Severe Weather	2019	$ 1238	2
Texas Hail Storm	2019	$ 1535	0
Southern and Eastern Tornadoes and Severe Weather	2019	$ 1252	7
South and Southeast Severe Weather	2019	$ 1514	0
Central Severe Weather	2019	$ 973	0
Rockies, Central and Northeast Tornadoes and Severe Weather	2019	$ 4498	3

(Continued)

Table 1.5 (Continued)

Name	Year	Total Unadjusted Cost (in millions)	Deaths
Colorado Hail Storms	2019	$ 1008	0
Texas Tornadoes and Central Severe Weather	2019	$ 1718	2
Southeast Tornadoes and Northern Storms and Flooding	2020	$ 1149	10
South, East and Northeast Severe Weather	2020	$ 1256	3
Tennessee Tornadoes and Southeast Severe Weather	2020	$ 2336	25
Midwest and Ohio Valley Severe Weather	2020	$ 2558	0
North Central and Ohio Valley Hail Storms and Severe Weather	2020	$ 2881	0
Southeast and Eastern Tornado Outbreak	2020	$ 3444	35
Southern Severe Weather	2020	$ 1350	3
Central, Southern and Eastern Severe Weather	2020	$ 1027	1
Central and Eastern Severe Weather	2020	$ 2113	2
South, Central and Eastern Severe Weather	2020	$ 1584	2
South Texas Hail Storms	2020	$ 1400	0
Central Severe Weather	2020	$ 1196	0
Central Severe Weather - Derecho	2020	$ 11027	4
Southeast Tornadoes and Severe Weather	2021	$ 1677	6
Eastern Severe Weather	2021	$ 1346	8
Texas Hail Storms	2021	$ 1475	0
Texas and Oklahoma Severe Weather	2021	$ 3149	0
Southern Tornadoes and Southeast Severe Weather	2021	$ 1264	4
Ohio Valley Hail Storms	2021	$ 1707	0
Central Severe Storms	2021	$ 1253	0
Central Severe Storms	2021	$ 1080	0
North Central Severe Weather	2021	$ 1284	2
Southeast, Central Tornado Outbreak	2021	$ 3915	93
Midwest Derecho and Tornado Outbreak	2021	$ 1782	1
Southern Tornado Outbreak	2022	$ 1254	2
Southeastern Tornado Outbreak	2022	$ 1262	3
Southern Severe Weather	2022	$ 2207	1
North Central Hail Storms	2022	$ 1148	0
North Central Severe Weather	2022	$ 1310	1

(Continued)

Table 1.5 (Continued)

Name	Year	Total Unadjusted Cost (in millions)	Deaths
North Central Hail Storms	2022	$ 1306	0
Central Severe Weather	2022	$ 1378	0

Source: Natural Centers for Environmental Information (NCEI) (2022).

Table 1.6 Major severe hurricanes affecting the US 1980–2022

Name	Year	Total Unadjusted Cost (in millions)	Deaths
Hurricane Alicia	1983	$ 3000	21
Hurricane Elena	1985	$ 1297	4
Hurricane Juan	1985	$ 1497	63
Hurricane Hugo	1989	$ 9000	86
Hurricane Bob	1991	$ 1503	18
Hurricane Andrew	1992	$ 27,000	61
Hurricane Iniki	1992	$ 3100	7
Tropical Storm Alberto	1994	$ 999	32
Hurricane Marilyn	1995	$ 2100	13
Hurricane Opal	1995	$ 4689	27
Hurricane Fran	1996	$ 5007	37
Hurricane Bonnie	1998	$ 980	3
Hurricane Georges	1998	$ 5985	16
Hurricane Floyd	1999	$ 6491	77
Tropical Storm Allison	2001	$ 8522	43
Hurricane Lili	2002	$ 1105	2
Tropical Storm Isidore	2002	$ 1150	5
Hurricane Isabel	2003	$ 5484	55
Hurricane Charley	2004	$ 16,000	35
Hurricane Frances	2004	$ 9800	48
Hurricane Ivan	2004	$ 20,501	57
Hurricane Jeanne	2004	$ 7497	28
Hurricane Dennis	2005	$ 2495	15
Hurricane Katrina	2005	$ 125,030	1833
Hurricane Rita	2005	$ 18,500	119
Hurricane Wilma	2005	$ 19,000	35
Hurricane Dolly	2008	$ 1267	3

(Continued)

Table 1.6 (Continued)

Name	Year	Total Unadjusted Cost (in millions)	Deaths
Hurricane Gustav	2008	$ 5997	53
Hurricane Ike	2008	$ 29,999	112
Hurricane Irene	2011	$ 13,494	45
Tropical Storm Lee	2011	$ 2513	21
Hurricane Isaac	2012	$ 2764	9
Hurricane Sandy	2012	$ 65,040	159
Hurricane Matthew	2016	$ 10,000	49
Hurricane Harvey	2017	$ 125,000	89
Hurricane Irma	2017	$ 50,000	97
Hurricane Maria	2017	$ 90,000	2981
Hurricane Florence	2018	$ 24,000	53
Hurricane Michael	2018	$ 24,975	49
Hurricane Dorian	2019	$ 1610	10
Tropical Storm Imelda	2019	$ 5000	5
Hurricane Hanna	2020	$ 1075	0
Hurricane Isaias	2020	$ 4757	16
Hurricane Laura	2020	$ 23,215	42
Hurricane Sally	2020	$ 7274	5
Hurricane Delta	2020	$ 2867	5
Hurricane Zeta	2020	$ 4352	6
Tropical Storm Eta	2020	$ 1460	12
Tropical Storm Elsa	2021	$ 1213	1
Tropical Storm Fred	2021	$ 1277	7
Hurricane Ida	2021	$ 73,572	96
Hurricane Nicholas	2021	$ 1016	0

Source: Natural Centers for Environmental Information (NCEI) (2022).

Flooding, Cyclones and Extreme Weather Events and their Challenge to the Tourism Industry

Flooding, cyclones and other extreme weather events all pose threats to tourism (Möller *et al.*, 2018). The scale of these disasters is not only costly in terms of lives lost but also in terms of damage to existing tourism infrastructure. Disasters can also have a hidden cost, which is the harm done to the reputation of tourist destination (Brown *et al.*, 2017; Möller *et al.*, 2018; Williams *et al.*, 2017). The difference between a crisis and a disaster is often a point of contention. Faulkner (2001) argued that a crisis is usually related to failure at an organisational level, whereas a disaster is where an unpredictable or unexpected event occurs. Both can have significant consequences. However, much of the tourism literature is also engaged with the different states of disaster management: prevention, preparedness, response, and recovery (Shurland & de Jong, 2008), often within a broader context of resilience (Annarelli & Nonino, 2016; Brown *et al.*, 2017; Hall, 2017; Linnenluecke, 2017; Williams *et al.*, 2017; Möller *et al.*, 2018; Gao *et al.*, 2022; Hall *et al.*, 2023; Scott *et al.*, 2023). However, as Scott at al. (2023) highlight in their review of the Sixth Assessment Report (AR6) of the IPCC, there are many knowledge gaps in relation to tourism and climate change by region; there is also limited discussion of many impacts and very limited understanding of integrated impacts and the effectiveness of adaptation strategies at the destination scale. In terms of the IPCC report, for example, this means that while there is general awareness of the threat of flooding and high magnitude storm events on tourism, particularly in cyclone affected small island developing states (SIDS), there is a substantial knowledge gap with respect to short- and long-terms impacts on tourism and related systems and the capacity of destinations to adapt to and mitigate climate change threats.

Vulnerability

When considering tourism and the effects of natural disasters, it is important to note that *resilience* and *vulnerability are two sides of the same issue*. Although a destination might appear to be able to recover well from a natural disaster and therefore appear to possess resilience, this does not change the fact that the destination itself might still be vulnerable to future unexpected events (Espiner & Becken, 2014), the occurrence of which may also lead to resilience declining over time. Adger *et al.* (2003) identified this distinction by examining vulnerability caused by sudden climate-induced changes and found that vulnerability primarily centred on three aspects. In tourism destination terms, they can be understood as the physical environment of the destination, how exposed the destination is to factors in its environment, and also how sensitive a destination is to sudden changes in its economic, social and physical make-up. Espiner and Becken (2014) also argued that adaptive governance, capacity building, community participation, social and cultural factors, and perception management of the tourist destination were important when considering how vulnerable a destination could be to the effects of a disaster. Djalante *et al.* (2011) similarly noticed how adaptive governance, disaster risk reduction and resilience were vital in terms of helping destinations to address their own unique vulnerabilities. For example, research by Calgaro and Lloyd (2008) on the effects of the 2004 tsunami on Khao Lak in Thailand, found that vulnerability was shaped by factors relating to social norms, local and national governance processes, and linkages within the tourism industry itself.

Risk perception

The increasing body of literature which examines the link between the risk of natural disasters and the effects on tourism development (Hughey & Becken, 2016; Wang, 2009) has seen greater attention being given to risk perception. This concept can be viewed from multiple perspectives: from the perspective of tourists and their level of safety experienced at a destination; through the lens of tourism organisations responsible for providing the tourism product; and from the perspective of the local community and how they perceive risk (Espiner & Becken, 2014; Gurtner, 2016; Sun *et al.*, 2017). Although Sun *et al.* (2017) suggest that the latter is a relatively under researched area.

Sitkin and Pablo (1992) suggest that risk perception is a reflection of decision makers' evaluation of the situation or scenario that they are in, and the level of uncertainty that is being dealt with. Existing frameworks of learned knowledge on the part of the individual concerned informed Xie's (1994) view of risk perception as the individual's recognition and evaluation of the amount of objective risk that they face. Significantly, past experiences therefore inform whether a situation is viewed as a risk or not (Slovic, 1987). Frewer (2001) suggests that social and cultural constructs from an individuals' upbringing also inform their view of risk, which is greatly influenced by an individuals' values and the amount of trust that they are willing to place in others. The Intergovernmental Panel on Climate Change (IPCC) (2007) expanded on the approach by Frewer (2001) by arguing that those who are not in the position to be able to respond and adapt easily to a natural disaster, i.e. those with high levels of vulnerability, would also have a heightened level of risk perception dependent on whether or not they had a degree of control over the situation or scenario that they found themselves in. Therefore, vulnerability reinforces the interplay that exists between flood and weather event threats, resilience, vulnerability and perception of risk.

Outline of the Book

The contents of this book are broadly organised according to the different states of a disaster: prevention, preparedness, response, and recovery. This chapter provides an introduction to some of the technical terminology and definitions that are used throughout this book. The following chapter by Baird *et al.* (Chapter 2) provides a review of some of the relevant literature on flooding and high magnitude storm events to also help contextualise the following chapters.

Chapter 3 by Bischeri discusses the importance of design strategies for fostering community resilience in Far North Queensland, Australia as part of disaster prevention and preparedness. In Chapter 4, Cahyanto focuses on understanding the needs of visitors during hurricane advisory warnings, while in Chapter 5, Kiss and Chang explore the hazard management of typhoons and their impact on tourism in Taiwan.

Chapter 6 by Fitchett *et al.* looks at the impacts of weather events on tourism with reference to tropical cyclones in the South-West Indian Ocean, while in Chapter 7, Sun and Milne discuss the impact of such cyclones on tourist behaviour and demand in Vanuatu, in the South Pacific, with respect to the case of Cyclone Pam. Issues of impact and response are also examined in Chapter 8 with respect to collaborative structure and actions in tourism disaster management in the case of Cyclone Marcia in Central Queensland, Australia, by Jiang and Ritchie; in Chapter 9 by Möller in terms of Tropical Cyclone Winston in Fiji; and in Chapter 10 by Toubes *et al.* with respect to flood damage and its effects on tourism in Galacia, Spain.

Chapters 11 and 12 provide a more extended perspective on recovery from weather events. Chapter 11 by Adie discusses the effects of Hurricane Sandy on second-home tourism on Fire Island, New York, USA, and decision-making regarding the retention of summer houses in light of both recovery and the prospect of future weather events. In Chapter 12, Amore takes an even longer-term perspective in his analysis of the recovery of the Cinque Terre in Italy following the October 2011 floods, and uses this case to raise issues regarding resilience and sustainability in relation to weather events. The book then concludes with a forward-looking chapter and review from the editors.

As tourism continues its recovery from COVID-19 it faces significant new challenges, not least of which is climate change (Scott *et al.*, 2019). The IPCC (2021) makes clear that global heating, to which tourism substantially contributes (Lenzen *et al.*, 2018), presents a direct threat to destinations and the tourism sector with respect to flooding and the extreme weather events that are the subject of this book. It is already recognised that 'human influence has likely increased the chance of compound extreme events since the 1950s. This includes increases in the frequency of compound flooding in some locations (*medium confidence*)' (IPCC, 2021, A.3.5), and that a 'warmer climate will intensify very wet and very dry weather and climate events and seasons, with implications for flooding or drought (*high confidence*)' (IPCC, 2021, B.3.2). In terms of the future: 'At 1.5°C global warming, heavy precipitation and associated flooding are projected to intensify and be more frequent in most regions in Africa and Asia (*high confidence*), North America (*medium to high confidence*) and Europe (*medium confidence*)' (IPCC, 2021, C.2.2). However, current predictions have us looking beyond 1.5°C:

> At 2°C global warming and above, the level of confidence in and the magnitude of the change in droughts and heavy and mean precipitation increase compared to those at 1.5°C. Heavy precipitation and associated flooding events are projected to become more intense and frequent in the

Pacific Islands and across many regions of North America and Europe (*medium to high confidence*). These changes are also seen in some regions in Australasia and Central and South America (*medium confidence*). (IPCC, 2021, C.2.3)

Given these scenarios, it is vital for the future of many tourism destinations and attractions that the tourism sector seeks not only to adapt to and mitigate climate change overall but also floods and extreme weather events. We hope that this book and the collective efforts of its authors makes such a contribution.

Acknowledgements

The authors would like to thank Youri Oh and Sara Naderi Koupaei for their assistance with some of the data provided in this chapter.

References

Adger, W.N., Huq, S., Brown, K., Conway, D. and Hulme, M. (2003) Adaptation to climate change in the developing world. *Progress in Development Studies* 3 (3), 179–195.

Ajjur, S.B. and Al-Ghamdi, S.G. (2022) Exploring urban growth–climate change–flood risk nexus in fast growing cities. *Scientific Reports* 12 (1), 12265.

Alifu, H., Hirabayashi, Y., Imada, Y. and Shiogama, H. (2022) Enhancement of river flooding due to global warming. *Scientific Reports* 12 (1), 20687.

Annarelli, A. and Nonino, F. (2016) Strategic and operational management of organizational resilience: Current state of research and future directions. *Omega* 62, 1–18.

Badshah, N. (2023) July was world's hottest month on record, climate scientists confirm. *The Guardian,* 8 August, https://www.theguardian.com/environment/2023/aug/08/july-2023-worlds-hottest-month-climate-crisis-scientists-confirm

Brown, N.A., Rovins, J.E., Feldmann-Jensen, S., Orchiston, C. and Johnston, D. (2017) Exploring disaster resilience within the hotel sector: A systematic review of literature. *International Journal of Disaster Risk Reduction* 22(Supplement C), 362–370.

Calgaro, E. and Lloyd, K. (2008) Sun, sea, sand and tsunami: Examining disaster vulnerability in the tourism community of Khao Lak, Thailand. *Singapore Journal of Tropical Geography* 29 (3), 288–306.

Cea, L. and Costabile, P. (2022) Flood risk in urban areas: Modelling, management and adaptation to climate change. A review. *Hydrology* 9 (3), 50.

Centre for Research on the Epidemiology of Disasters (CRED) (2022) *2021 Disasters in numbers.* CRED, Institute Health and Society UCLouvain.

Centre for Research on the Epidemiology of Disasters (CRED) (2023) Disasters year in review 2022. *CRED Crunch,* Issue 70, April.

Cheng, L., Abraham, J., Trenberth, K.E. *et al.* (2021) Upper Ocean Temperatures Hit Record High in 2020. *Advances in Atmospheric Scien*ce, https://doi.org/10.1007/s00376-021-0447-x

Corringham, T.W., McCarthy, J., Shulgina, T., Gershunov, A., Cayan, D.R. and Ralph, F.M. (2022) Climate change contributions to future atmospheric river flood damages in the western United States. *Scientific Reports* 12 (1), 13747.

Deng, Z., Wang, Z., Wu, X., Lai, C. and Zeng, Z. (2022) Strengthened tropical cyclones and higher flood risk under compound effect of climate change and urbanization across China's Greater Bay Area. *Urban Climate* 44, 101224.

Djalante, R., Holley, C. and Thomalla, F. (2011) Adaptive governance and managing resilience to natural hazards. *International Journal of Disaster Risk Science* 2 (4), 1–14.
Espiner, S. and Becken, S. (2014) Tourist towns on the edge: Conceptualising vulnerability and resilience in a protected area tourism system. *Journal of Sustainable Tourism* 22 (4), 646–665.
Faulkner, B. (2001) Towards a framework for tourism disaster management. *Tourism Management* 22 (2), 135–147.
Frewer, L.J. (2001) Public risk perceptions and risk communication. In P. Bennett and K. Calman (eds) *Risk Communication and Public Health* (pp. 21–34). Oxford: Oxford University Press.
Gao, M., Wang, Z. and Yang, H. (2022) Review of urban flood resilience: Insights from scientometric and systematic analysis. *International Journal of Environmental Research and Public Health* 19 (14), 8837.
Global Flood Database, https://global-flood-database.cloudtostreet.ai
Gurtner, Y. (2016) Returning to paradise: Investigating issues of tourism crisis and disaster recovery on the island of Bali. *Journal of Hospitality and Tourism Management* 28, 11–19.
Hall, C.M. (2017) Resilience in tourism: Development, theory, and application. In A. Lew and J. Cheer (eds) *Tourism, Resilience and Sustainability* (pp. 18–33). New York: Routledge.
Hall, C.M., Safonov, A. and Koupaei, S.N. (2023) Resilience in hospitality and tourism: Issues, synthesis and agenda. *International Journal of Contemporary Hospitality Management* 35 (1), 347–368.
Hughey, K.F.D. and Becken, S. (2016) Value-engaged evaluation of a tourism-specific disaster management plan. *Tourism Management Perspectives* 19, 69–73.
Hulton, F. (2023) Weather tracker: Floods, storms and wildfires in Europe. *The Guardian*, 11 August, https://www.theguardian.com/environment/2023/aug/11/weather-tracker-floods-storms-and-wildfires-in-europe
Intergovernmental Panel on Climate Change (IPCC) (2007) *Summary for policymakers of climate change 2007: The physical science basis.* (Contribution of Working Group to the Fourth Assessment Report of the Intergovernmental Panel on Climate Change) Cambridge University Press.
IPCC (2021) *Summary for Policymakers. In Climate Change 2021: The Physical Science Basis. Contribution of Working Group I to the Sixth Assessment Report of the Intergovernmental Panel on Climate Change* (Eds. V. Masson-Delmotte, P. Zhai, A. Pirani, S.L. Connors, C. Péan, S. Berger, N. Caud, Y. Chen, L., Goldfarb, M.I. Gomis, M. Huang, K. Leitzell, E. Lonnoy, J.B.R. Matthews, T.K. Maycock, T. Waterfield, O. Yelekçi, R. Yu and B. Zhou). Cambridge: Cambridge University Press.
Lenzen, M., Sun, Y.Y., Faturay, F., Ting, Y.P., Geschke, A. and Malik, A. (2018) The carbon footprint of global tourism. *Nature Climate Change* 8 (6), 522–528.
Li, L. and Chakraborty, P. (2020) Slower decay of landfalling hurricanes in a warming world. *Nature* 587, 230–234. https://doi.org/10.1038/s41586-020-2867-7
Linnenluecke, M.K. (2017) Resilience in business and management research: A review of influential publications and a research agenda. *International Journal of Management Reviews* 19 (1), 4–30.
Milman, O. (2020) Devastating 2020 Atlantic hurricane season breaks all records. *The Guardian*, 10 November, https://www.theguardian.com/world/2020/nov/10/devastating-2020-atlantic-hurricane-season-breaks-all-records
Möller, C., Wang, J. and Nguyen, H.T. (2018) # Strongerthanwinston: Tourism and crisis communication through Facebook following tropical cyclones in Fiji. *Tourism Management* 69, 272–284.

National Centers for Environmental Information (NCEI) (2022) *U.S. Billion-dollar Weather and Climate Disasters.* https://www.ncei.noaa.gov/access/billions/, DOI: 10.25921/stkw-7w73

National Hurricane Center and Central Pacific Hurricane Center (2021) *The Saffir-Simpson Hurricane Wind Scale.* https://www.nhc.noaa.gov/pdf/sshws.pdf

National Hurricane Center and Central Pacific Hurricane Center (2022) *Glossary of NHC Terms.* https://www.nhc.noaa.gov/aboutgloss.shtml#s

OECD (2022) *Inflation (CPI) (indicator)* doi: 10.1787/eee82e6e-en

Rentschler, J., Salhab, M. and Jafino, B. (2022a) Flood exposure and poverty in 188 countries. *Nature Communications* 13, 3527.

Rentschler, J., Salhab, M. and Jafino, B. (28 June, 2022b) Flood risk already affects 1.81 billion people. Climate change and unplanned urbanization could worsen exposure. World Bank, https://blogs.worldbank.org/climatechange/flood-risk-already-affects-181-billion-people-climate-change-and-unplanned

Scott, D., Hall, C.M. and Gössling, S. (2019) Global tourism vulnerability to climate change. *Annals of Tourism Research* 77, 49–61.

Scott, D., Hall, C.M., Rushton, B. and Gössling, S. (2023) A review of the IPCC Sixth Assessment and implications for tourism development and sectoral climate action. *Journal of Sustainable Tourism*, https://doi.org/10.1080/09669582.2023.2195597.

Sitkin, S. and Pablo, A. (1992) A reconceptualizing the determinants of risk behavior. *Academy of Management Review* 17 (1), 9–38.

Slovic, P. (1987) Cognition of risk. *Science* 236 (17), 280–285

Sun, Y., Zhou, H., Wall, G. and Wei, Y. (2017) Cognition of disaster risk in a tourism community: An agricultural heritage system perspective. *Journal of Sustainable Tourism* 25 (4), 536–553.

Williams, T.A., Gruber, D.A., Sutcliffe, K.M., Shepherd, D.A. and Zhao, E.Y. (2017) Organizational response to Adversity: Fusing crisis management and resilience research streams. *The Academy of Management Annals* 11 (2), 733–769.

United Nations General Assembly (1 December 2016) *Report of the open-ended intergovernmental expert working group on indicators and terminology relating to disaster risk reduction*, Res 69/284, UN GAOR, 71st sess, Agenda item 19(c), UN Doc A/71/644, 7.

Xie, X. (1994) *Psychology Research on Risk Cognition.* Beijing: Institute of Psychology, Chinese Academy of Sciences.

2 Flooding and High Magnitude Storm Events in Tourism

Tim Baird, Alexander Safonov and C. Michael Hall

Introduction

Disasters are an increasingly important issue in tourism. Although there is a substantial literature on economic crises and disasters such as earthquakes, there is now also growing awareness of the impacts of flooding as well as high magnitude storm events, such as hurricanes, typhoons, and cyclones. These latter events are also becoming more significant because of the effects of climate change and the subsequent effects of intensity, frequency, and location of occurrence (Colette, 2007; Rentschler *et al.*, 2022a, 2022b). While the immediate effects of natural disasters are dreadful, flooding represents long-term risks to resident populations, tourism infrastructure and destination image as it contaminates the environment and freshwater, affects tourism resources and infrastructure, and leaves debris (Pathak *et al.*, 2021). Flooding can be caused by various events, such as sea-level rise, tsunamis, freshets, cyclones, and intense rainfalls, with the winds associated with cyclones and hurricanes also causing immense damage, which can affect impacted locations in physical, social, and cultural ways (Colette, 2007; Dube *et al.*, 2023; Rutty *et al.*, 2023).

Climate related disasters and tourism relationships are characterised by their complexity (Gössling & Hall, 2006; Hall & Higham, 2005; Scott *et al.*, 2023) and reciprocal influence (Gössling, 2002). While disasters are hard to predict or avoid, their aftermath can be substantially influenced by implementing planning and management actions (Faulkner, 2001). The literature on the ability of the tourism industry to respond to and recover from unexpected events speaks volumes regarding the current state of play in terms of risk assessment, governance and preparedness. Although the industry itself is two decades on from Faulkner's (2001) framework for dealing with natural disasters and their effects on tourism, there is a wider problem at play. Much research has tended to focus on the national levels and has often overlooked the regional dimensions of disasters (Schmude *et al.*, 2018). Since tourist destinations are vulnerable to different types of disasters, consideration of various actions and responses is vital to mini-mise the consequent impacts (Faulkner, 2001). While floods present a severe risk, much disaster management and preparedness stay relatively reactive, ignoring the proactive view with its anticipatory management practices (Raikes *et al.*, 2019). The importance of preparedness is also emphasised in the *Global Assessment Report on Disaster Risk Reduction,* which acknowledges the rising level of investments in disaster manage-ment (UNDRR, 2015). However, integrating these new forms of manage-ment with existing systems of governance within the context of new destination developments that are designed to be less vulnerable to flood-ing has been problematic (Raikes *et al.*, 2019).

Unexpected flash flooding events pose a real threat to tourism activi-ties not only due to the high risk of lives being lost (Jonkman, 2005), but also due to the direct impact on existing infrastructure (Chen *et al.*, 2020). Environmental disasters also have direct and indirect impacts on tourism dependent economies (Aliperti *et al.*, 2019). The interrelationships between tourism and communities raise the question of vulnerability and the challenges destination communities face in the light of climate change and tourism development (Lew, 2014). For example, following the devel-opment of tourism and changes in land use, the risks of freshets occurring increased by 28% in the Juma River area of China (Chen *et al.*, 2020). Rain-induced flash floods on Madeira Island, Portugal resulted in signifi-cant property loss of 210 million Euros (Fragoso *et al.*, 2012). In Zhejiang, China, flash flood events caused an estimated loss of 180 million Chinese Yuan (Chen *et al.*, 2020). Even though these destinations were clearly vul-nerable to the risk of such events occurring, detailed risk assessments had not been carried out (Chen *et al.*, 2020). Not only was key infrastructure lost as a result, but also the perceived relative safety of these destinations was affected, causing undesirable social and economic impacts (Chen *et al.*, 2020; Fragoso *et al.*, 2012).

The resilience of business entrepreneurs has also emerged as a key theme when considering the impact of flooding on tourism activities. In a study of tourism related micro-businesses situated in Kratie, Cambodia, Ngin *et al.* (2020) found that either temporary or reactive responses were adopted by businesses as opposed to long-term systematic measures. It was also discovered that preparation for flooding events and the ability to adapt in such situations would be greatly enhanced by the quality of infor-mation which was made available to the businesses by the government (Ngin *et al.*, 2020). However, this ability to adapt to change is something which differs according to the situation tourism businesses find themselves in. For example, adapting to climate-induced change in the Great Barrier Reef involves navigating an established ecosystem of services which support mainly smaller tourism-related businesses in the area, something to which Marshall *et al*. (2013) attest as being down to the formal business networks and the degree of place attachment which businesses exhibit. These factors have been shown to dictate exactly how much of an impact flooding events have had on commercial fishing operations and marine-based tourism in the Great Barrier Reef region (Marshall *et al*., 2013).

Flooding in Coastal Areas

Coastal ecosystems are increasingly affected by global climate change and coastal development (Hernández-Delgado, 2015). Papageorgiou (2016) notes that coastal tourism represents one of the largest segments of the global tourism industry; its importance is not just in terms of job creation but also as a significant contributor to economic performance. Tourism tends to overwhelm many coastal and marine ecosystems, especially when wetlands and mangroves are removed (Papageorgiou, 2016), making them more susceptible to storms and other flooding events. For example, Lynett *et al*. (2013) show how the tsunami-induced flooding affected coastal areas of the Galapagos Islands causing structural damage. In the Caribbean, Barbados suffers from sea-level rise causing beach erosion and coral reef degradation, which exposes the island to hurricanes and storms that increase flooding risks (Pelling & Uitto, 2001). Reguero *et al*. (2019) also demonstrate that coral reefs in Quintana Roo, Mexico are a natural protection from flooding. Both climate change and coastal development increase the risks of flooding, erosion, and extreme weather events (Reguero *et al*., 2019). However, increasing degradation of coastal ecosystems in some tourist destinations (Gopalakrishnan & Kumar, 2020) is potentially adversely affecting the reputation of many formerly popular resorts as tourists move on to seek out 'pristine environments where the aesthetic aspects are undamaged by excessive touristic development' (Lithgow *et al*., 2019: 44).

Coastal flooding has also threatened destination tourism product offerings in relation to their competitors. These are expected to get worse as a result of climate change (Perch-Nielsen, 2009; Priego *et al*., 2014). Priego *et al*. (2014) contend that the threat of flooding and coastal erosion coupled with changing temperatures has seen parts of northern Spain become increasingly popular with tourists at the expense of their southern Spanish counterparts who would normally be enjoying the economic benefits of this patronage. Windupranata *et al*. (2019) showed the vulnerability of tourism infrastructure in Pangandaran Beach, West Java to tsunami threats. Based on the analysis, all tourism related infrastructure appears to be highly vulnerable to tsunamis as well as to high magnitude storms due to its beach location. In South Africa, three floods changed the position of the mouth, the structure of the flood-tidal deltas and flow channels in the Keurbooms Estuary (Schumann, 2021). The

Keurbooms lagoon and beach are part of the attractive scenery of Plettenberg Bay. Not only was the infrastructure heavily damaged, but the inaccessibility to the washed away beach impacted tourism attractiveness (Schumann, 2021). Nevertheless, such examples are useful as they highlight that it is the inappropriate location of tourism infrastructure rather than flooding and storm events per se which can make them more vulnerable to loss or destruction.

Flooding can also impact tourism businesses that rely on the use of natural resources for their products. Jones and Berkelmans (2014) investigate how tropical cyclones 'Tasha' and 'Yasi' brought severe rainfall and flooding along the Queensland coast. Low salinity floodwater negatively affects reef ecosystems, thereby affecting their attractiveness to tourists. Jones and Berkelmans (2014) estimated that the recovery would probably take 10–15 years based on the historical examples in this area, impacting visitor numbers. However, they also stress that predictions of climate change, lower rainfall and higher-intensity summer rain events in the coastal regions of Australia and anthropogenic influences on water quality will likely slow reef regeneration. As a result of damage to reef systems, water-related activities, such as snorkelling, scuba diving and coral viewing, may shift to undamaged areas and put even more pressure on recovery from other impacts on reef ecology such as bleaching. As a result, they suggest that it may be necessary to consider human intervention to support the regeneration of coral reefs after major floods (Jones & Berkelmans, 2014). Obviously, it is not only the tourists who lose out if action is not taken with respect to flood impacts, but all the actors who make up the local tourism ecosystem if the problems of coastal flooding and land erosion are not addressed. However, the unpredictability of coastal flooding hazards means that each case also brings its own unique set of challenges for local communities (Zscheischler et al., 2018). Inland tourism businesses should not be treated as less susceptible to natural disaster events, but the complex nature of these threats should be acknowledged (Hyman, 2014).

Coastal tourism around the world is coming under increased threat from sea level rise [SLR] related issues. Scott et al. (2012) contend that a variety of SLR problems exist, which include (but are not limited to) the erosion of coastal habitats and beaches. A process that is termed as 'coastal squeeze', where there is a boundary such as a sea wall or road in the beach space between the sea and the boundary, is also an issue. This, coupled with blocked drainage systems and poor maintenance, can adversely affect the stability of coastal tourism infrastructure (Scott et al., 2012). Coastal erosion is another threat and is defined by the Ministry for the Environment [MFE] (2020: 1) as 'when the shoreline retreats, either temporarily or permanently. Erosion becomes a hazard when it threatens people's activities or settlements or other things they value.' However, unless there is a major disaster, 'most coastal tourism destinations seem to have remained remarkably blasé about rising sea levels, even though these are one of the best-documented aspects of global change' (Buckley *et al.*, 2013: 72). Nevertheless, as the IPCC (2021, C.2.6) observed, 'In coastal cities, the combination of more frequent extreme sea level events (due to sea level rise and storm surge) and extreme rainfall/riverflow events will make flooding more probable (*high confidence*)'.

Assessment of Impacts

The significance of risk assessment becomes even more evident when the role of tourism in small and rural communities is taken into account. Small nations are dependent on natural and environmental resources, which means that flooding triggers severe disruptions to the local economies relying on rural tourism activities (Berred & Berred, 2021). Climate-linked natural disasters not only damage infrastructure but also bring job losses and decrease tourist numbers, affecting rural economies the most (Madzivhandila & Niyimbanira, 2020). Berred and Berred (2021) stress that tourism is almost the only income generator in the Region of Tata, Morocco. However, high temperatures in summer and flooding in winter make the region vulnerable and unsustainable and affect the livelihood of the local population (Berred & Berred, 2021).

Lorenz and Dittmer (2021) argue that perceiving tourism as a development strategy rarely touches upon the vulnerabilities it brings. The Indian Himalayas is a region highly dependent on pilgrimage tourism. In 2013, the 'Himalayan Tsunami' occurred in the Indian Himalayas. Heavy rain created flooding, landslides and flash floods which caused severe damage. The over-dependence on tourism affected the long-term recovery of the region given the lack of a diverse economic base. The study also underlines that the secondary effects of a disaster can last longer than the immediate damage (Lorenz & Dittmer, 2021). Thus, there is a strong need for assessment frameworks in place to understand the risks and possible impacts, especially in locations that are highly prone and vulnerable to flooding.

There are direct and indirect impacts of flood events on tourist activities with effects being both tangible, i.e. physical, and intangible, i.e. social, cultural and perceptual (Araújo Vila *et al.*, 2019). Direct impacts are the most visible in terms of damage to tourist facilities and infrastructure, while indirect impacts are the after-effects which can last long after the event itself has occurred (Araújo Vila *et al.*, 2019). Evaluation of the impact of flood events on tourist activities related directly to whether the flood occurred during periods of peak tourism demand and the duration of the flooding (Araújo Vila *et al.*, 2019; Merz *et al.*, 2005). One of the current challenges which exists when measuring the impacts of coastal tourism risk assessments is the lack of a standardised approach in terms of measuring the impacts of flooding (Fang *et al.*, 2016). This is not to say that attempts to provide some direction have not been attempted. For example, a five-step climate change vulnerability assessment methodology for coastal tourism was proposed by Moreno and Becken (2009), while work on a vulnerability framework grounded in the IPCC's vulnerability concept for the beach tourism sector was the focus of Perch-Nielsen's (2009) work based around adaptive capacity, sensitivity and exposure.

Hyman (2014) has addressed the effects of rising sea levels and climate change on coastal beach environments in Jamaica based around the themes of technological, physical, economic, institutional and social factors. Presently, a rapid natural disaster risk assessment model considering the physical characteristics of the flood events which focuses on disaster prevention and relief is the main way that the impacts of such events are measured (Tsai *et al.*, 2016). Toubes *et al.* (2017) developed a framework for flood risk assessment at beach locations in Galicia, Spain and discovered that 10% of the 724 beaches were at risk of flooding. When this figure is considered within the context of the ongoing effects of climate change, they suggested that flooding events may continue to increase in both frequency and intensity, thereby increasing levels of risk (Toubes *et al.*, 2017).

Resilience of Tourism Businesses

Resilience provides a new perspective on development and socioecological adaptation (Lew, 2014; Hall *et al.*, 2022). Research into the resilience which exists within tourism organisations and destinations has only really been explored over the last decade (Hall, 2017; Hall *et al.*, 2017; Möller *et al.*, 2018; Orchiston *et al.*, 2016). This comes at a time when the tourism industry is being told that much more effort is required in terms of disaster preparedness and, ultimately, disaster prevention (Brown *et al.*, 2017; Hystad & Keller, 2008). Brown *et al.* (2017: 365) examined resilience within the hotel sector and suggested that the fundamental elements of a successful approach towards navigating an unexpected event lay in individual businesses being able to 'assess, innovate, adapt and overcome possible disruptions'. The importance of tourism organisations being able to deal effectively with the impact of a natural disaster led to the notion that organisations which are resilient then go on to influence others through their planning, thereby creating further resilience within the wider community (Orchiston *et al.*, 2016).

Although it appears to be a relatively obvious idea to state that greater degrees of pre-planning and preparedness will lead to higher degrees of resilience within tourism, it is important to remember that many sectors within the industry are still reactive in their approach towards natural disasters (Filimonau & De Coteau, 2020; Ghaderi *et al.*, 2021). An example of this is seen in research by Filimonau and De Coteau (2020) into the effect of the 2017 hurricanes on the Caribbean island of Grenada, which caused widespread damage to tourism infrastructure. It was found in this instance that the failure of tourism industry stakeholders in Grenada to collaborate in any form of pre-planning had exacerbated the impacts of the event on the island (Filimonau & De Coteau, 2020). As previous research into disaster management by Jiang and Ritchie (2017) and Waugh and Streib (2006) has highlighted, stakeholder collaboration and disaster resilience are two concepts where a lack of either can ultimately cripple any tourism-reliant community.

The ability of tourism businesses to respond to the effects of a natural disaster is not just solely down to the business owners themselves; a complex web of stakeholders, including those in positions of governance, those who design disaster management policy, and local communities affected, must all be considered in this process as well (Cheng & Zhang, 2020). The formation of robust plans which demonstrate preparedness and aim to encourage business recovery have been shown to be vital in the recovery of tourism-based economies (Dogru & Bulut, 2018; Zhang & Cheng, 2019). Cheng and Zhang (2020: 2602) point out that one direction for future research in this area is how economic resilience can be better mapped to incorporate what the authors terms as the 'synthetic characteristics' of a destination. Another area that is noted as being understudied within the extant research into the resilience of tourism businesses is whether the development of social capital and knowledge sharing are also important factors which could potentially impact overall business survival (Biggs *et al.*, 2012).

Disaster Management

The way in which the response to a disaster is managed can have lasting effects not only on the area where the disaster itself occurred, but also on other areas outside of the immediate area of impact (Estevão & Costa, 2020). The physical damage caused by a disaster not only has the capacity to cause physical damage to a tourism destination, but if a lack of disaster management planning is prevalent, then a long tail of economic repercussions can also be experienced (Bhati *et al.*, 2016; Estevão & Costa, 2020; Loayza *et al.*, 2012). It is cheaper to include risk management practices at the design stage rather than to repair infrastructure after it has been unnecessarily damaged (Saverimuttu & Varua, 2016). In examining the consequences of hurricanes and storms, Challender (2016) argues that infrastructure needs to be built by design rather than rebuilt by design. Therefore, having an established plan in place to help deal with problems when they occur is prudent. This is also reflected in research that suggests that many rural and peripheral area tourism destinations that have borne the brunt of severe impacts from natural disasters have found finding a pathway towards recovery difficult (Sanders *et al.*, 2015).

Destination image and reputational impacts are cited by Ritchie and Jiang (2019) as being a key reason as to why a number of studies focus on marketing in the post-crisis phase (Möller *et al.*, 2018; Zhai *et al.*, 2020). However, reflection on the part of tourism business owners during this phase has been found to be an under-researched area in relation to flooding and the impact of storm events (Prayag *et al.*, 2018). Although COVID-19 has brought focus to the topic, the transferability of such information from one crisis situation to another is unknown (Hall *et al.*, 2022). Ritchie and Jiang (2019) believe that this is largely because of the number of small to medium enterprises which exist within the tourism industry, and this has made documenting learning in the wake of disasters a difficult process.

Ensuring that a destination is able to provide a sustainable tourism offering means that there needs to be forward planning for unexpected events should they ever eventuate (Estevão & Costa, 2020; Sanders *et al.*, 2015). Management, and therefore the planning for such situations, needs to be viewed from not only the perspective of those in positions of governance or responsibility for local tourism businesses, but must also be inclusive of the needs of the community (Prideaux *et al.*, 2003). Tsai *et al.* (2016: 153) note that the absence of policies around disaster preparedness means that 'disaster-affected areas may experience negative impacts as tourists' intentions to travel are lowered and residents suffer from a slow recovery or even a permanent decline'. However, particularly in the case of island destinations, it has been noted that that tourists' acceptance of the risk and unpredictability posed by natural hazards can also add to the excitement of visitation (Ghaderi *et al.*, 2015; Granville *et al.*, 2016; Kennedy *et al.*, 2020). In fact, Kennedy *et al.* (2020) even state that islands that are reliant on tourism in order to bolster their economy have a higher propensity towards being unaware of their vulnerability to disasters. This observation is also echoed by Becken *et al.* (2014) who add that this can also serve to destabilise the reputation of the tourism offering itself through a lack of foresight and management of potential hazards.

The lack of reliable information for tourists based around the risks posed by local hazards (Kennedy *et al.*, 2020) is problematic. Ensuring that the multiple stakeholders involved in the management of tourism activities are held accountable for managing the level of risk that visitors encounter has been shown to be affected by the resources available to tourism organisations (Hughey & Becken, 2016). The risk of natural disasters could also be underestimated. Main *et al.* (2018) point out that international rankings of disaster exposure position Malta in a low-risk zone that could potentially mislead the public. Malta is exposed to a variety of extreme natural events. While groundwater storming from high tides, storm waves and heavy rainfalls occur to a limited extent, flash flooding caused by sudden rainfall presents a high risk. This, coupled with placing tourists in an unfamiliar environment where there may also be significant language barriers, has led to a situation whereby tourists may be less informed regarding the risks posed by hazards simply because those tasked with managing these elements are under-resourced (Bird *et al.*, 2010; Nguyen *et al.*, 2016). However, this situation has found itself under the spotlight due to the implementation of disaster risk reduction (DRR) frameworks becoming more prevalent in the tourism industry (Kennedy *et al.*, 2020).

Disaster risks, and the uncertainty that such conditions can create not only for the natural environment but also for the associated tourist infrastructure, have been the subject of a growing area of research (Mistilis & Sheldon, 2006; Williams & Baláž, 2013, 2015). From the perspective of individual tourists, perception is everything when it comes to considering the risks associated with visiting a particular destination (Williams & Baláž, 2013). Individual perceptions of what constitutes a hazard, and how these perceptions influence the consumer decision making process of tourists when it comes to factoring in safety to their travel plans, are an important consideration in terms of risk management (Pizam *et al.*, 2004; Williams & Baláž, 2013). Liu *et al.* (2019: 857) even argue that the 'levels of perceived risk, in the individuals mind, determine the competitiveness of a destination'.

Effective governance concerning disaster risk management has been found to have a strong relationship with maintaining tourism competitiveness (Gooroochurn & Sugiyarto, 2005; Liu *et al.*, 2019). The ease with which governments are able to implement policies around risk management has been identified as a critical factor in ensuring the ongoing safety of visitors (Liu *et al.*, 2019; Zuo *et al.*, 2017). However, Liu *et al.* (2019) note that the level of effectiveness achieved through robust governance dissipates as the level of exposure that a destination has to natural hazards is heightened. This means that the destination itself becomes vulnerable through not only not being able to cope with the effects of a natural disaster, but also through the absence of any form of capacity to adapt to events which threaten the tourism system (Liu *et al.*, 2019).

Adaptation and Mitigation Strategies

Hall *et al.* (2015) state that although there is substantial evidence that the threat of climate change on tourism activities is very real, there exist many points of contention around how to adapt to, and potentially mitigate, such threats. Adaptation strategies to circumvent climate change related disasters have occurred in assessments designed to highlight the vulnerability of destinations and address resilience to climate change (Dogru *et al.*, 2019).

Satellite images and modelling techniques are widely used in research and practice to address issues of climate change, especially in relation to flooding. For instance, Pradjoko *et al.* (2021) use bathymetric data and topography to investigate development of the Mandalika tourism area in Indonesia in the tsunami inundation area. Through the use of modelling,

Hernandez-Mora *et al.* (2021) suggest adapting existing dunes by adding vegetation and increasing height in Tossa del Mar, Spain, where 82% of the city's income comes from tourism. Therefore, degradation and erosion of the coast is a severe risk to the sustainability and livelihood of the city. Stressing that floods, storms, hurricanes and droughts have substantially increased, Olivera and Heard (2019) propose to employ the Weibull distribution to predict climatic events and demonstrate the extreme precipitation trends in the western part of Mexico. They argue that the correct assessment of probabilities is important for tourism as well. Cuca (2017) utilises satellite images to observe areas that are prone to submerging during great floods. The before and after images indicate the usefulness of remote sensing imagery to monitor cultural heritage landscapes. The use of such approaches could inform decision making in the management of these territories as well as during the emergency situation.

Psarra *et al.* (2021) propose several approaches to climate adaptation design strategies that could be implemented in the high flood risk areas of the Lake District, UK. The area is a UNESCO World Heritage Site that is prone to flooding, sea-level rise and storm surges. The project proposed infrastructural change, a tourist attraction change, and a trail with cultural attractions that would allow interaction with the natural events when they happen. Ciampa *et al.* (2021) discuss various mitigation solutions in the Mediterranean coastal areas. Many types of flooding, such as flash floods, river, lake and coastal flooding, pose high risks to the coastal infrastructure and population. Coastal areas are attractive to personal construction and tourism development. The authors discuss flooding prevention systems, including coastal barriers in Portugal, infrastructural drainage systems in urban areas of Barcelona, Spain, mechanical wetlands in Thessaloniki, Greece, and mobile dams in Venice, Italy. Each of these systems has advantages and disadvantages which also need to be considered.

There are also other perspectives, such as that put forward in a Greek case study by Michailidou *et al.* (2016), who state their belief that the use of renewable energy and the construction of dams would help to offset climate change effects. Caramel (2014) discussed how the island of Kiribati had actually purchased land in Fiji to escape escalating climate change effects. The latter two case studies also show that practical versus seemingly impractical solutions to climate change also rest on whether the solution put forward is, in fact, feasible in the first place (Dogru *et al.*, 2019).

Disaster management strategies to deal with climate change also fall victim to a lack of long-term planning, and as Hoogendoorn *et al.* (2016) point out, it is often not until the effects of climate change are experienced by destinations that anything is actually done. The notion that climate change can directly threaten the economic and social benefits derived from tourism has created a need for further research in this area (Hoogendoorn *et al.*, 2016). As this idea becomes a reality for more governments and tourism-related organisations around the world, a growing stream of literature is exploring these issues (Hoogendoorn *et al.*, 2016; March *et al.*, 2014; Scott *et al.*, 2004). These effects are dependent on the type of tourism market, and can also be multi-faceted; for example, coastal beach tourism not only faces rising sea levels as a threat, but also higher temperatures (Fitchett *et al.*, 2016; Sagoe-Addy & Appeaning Addo, 2013). Such situations have long been projected for many popular Mediterranean tourist destinations (Amelung *et al.*, 2007; Demiroglu *et al.*, 2020).

Pathak *et al.* (2021) emphasise the dependence of Small Island Developing States (SIDS) on tourism. They demonstrate direct and indirect impacts of climate change on the Bahamas island of New Providence and adjacent Paradise Island. Relying on satellite images to analyse the exposure of tourism infrastructure to the flooding, they stress that sea level rise threatens only a small portion of properties, but in combination with various storm categories the impact drastically increases in respect to the category of storm. Reefs are important as a natural barrier of the coastline from storm events. Flooding also brings disaster debris and sediment and contaminates freshwater. Also, even when hurricanes do not affect some parts of the islands, the whole area falls under the tourists' perception of a damaged and dangerous area. The authors call to diversify the economy of the Bahamas as its tourism industry is particularly climate sensitive.

Additionally, small nations are becoming more vulnerable in the face of natural disasters because of the more 'developed' nations' interference in post-disaster assistance. Saverimuttu and Varua (2016) argue that adaptive systems need to be carefully considered and combined with local knowledge. The Pacific nations are very dependent on tourism, which pays for the imports that support development of small island nations. The region is subject to cyclone activity during November and April, with strong winds and rainfall generating damage and destruction by flooding. Vanuatu was affected by a cyclone in 2015, and Australia provided help and support. However, the authors argue that such aid impacts the indigenous knowledge on how to survive and cope with these events, which create dependency and vulnerability of island inhabitants. Indigenous adaptive systems and local knowledge need to be combined with modern adaptive systems and knowledge to reduce risks, while avoiding the replacement and loss of indigenous knowledge (Saverimuttu & Varua, 2016). Tourism is a valuable part of economies in many countries, including small island nations. So the threat to coastal tourism from climate change cannot, and should not, be underestimated.

Conclusion

Research into the effects of flooding and climate-based events on the tourism industry demonstrates that there is a concerning level of unpreparedness at a regional level, while there is a somewhat reluctant move towards tourism stakeholder collaboration at a national scale. However, the main problem that underpins what is reflected in the extant literature is one of pace; coastal erosion, sea-level rise, extreme weather events, and climate change are occurring at a speed and intensity that the tourism industry, as well as many governments, appear to be failing to keep up with (see Chapter 1 for details of weather events and their costs). The end result of this are policies which largely appear to be reactive, rather than well prepared and proactive (Jarratt & Davies, 2020). If this current situation continues, many popular destinations and attractions will be adversely affected or even lost, and the economic survival of many tourism businesses and those employed in the industry will hang in a perilous balance.

Acknowledgement

Thanks to Sara Naderi Koupaei for her assistance with the chapter.

References

Aliperti, G., Sandholz, S., Hagenlocher, M., Rizzi, F., Frey, M. and Garschagen, M. (2019) Tourism, crisis, disaster: An interdisciplinary approach. *Annals of Tourism Research* 79. https://doi.org/10.1016/j.annals.2019.102808

Amelung, B., Nicholls, R. and Viner, D. (2007) Implications of global climate change for tourism flows and seasonality. *Journal of Travel Research* 45 (3), 285–296. https://doi.org/10.1177/0047287506295937

Araújo Vila, N., Toubes, D.R. and Fraiz Brea, J.A. (2019) Tourism industry's vulnerability upon risk of flooding: The Aquis Querquennis Complex. *Environments* 6 (12) https://doi.org/10.3390/environments6120122

Becken, S., Mahon, R., Rennie, H.G. and Shakeela, A. (2014) The tourism disaster vulnerability framework: An application to tourism in small island destinations. *Natural Hazards* 71 (1), 955–972. https://doi.org/10.1007/s11069-013-0946-x

Berred, S. and Berred, K. (2021) Climate change issues, challenges, and impacts in terms of rural geo-biological and cultural tourism activity development in semiarid areas: A case study from Tata, Bani Geopark (Anti-Atlas, South Morocco) *Geoheritage* 13 (4) https://doi.org/10.1007/s12371-021-00640-1

Bhati, A., Upadhayaya, A. and Sharma, A. (2016) National disaster management in the ASEAN-5: an analysis of tourism resilience. *Tourism Review* 71 (2), 148–164. https://doi.org/10.1108/TR-12-2015-0062

Biggs, D., Hall, C.M. and Stoeckl, N. (2012) The resilience of formal and informal tourism enterprises to disasters: Reef tourism in Phuket, Thailand. *Journal of Sustainable Tourism* 20 (5), 645–665. https://doi.org/10.1080/09669582.2011.630080

Bird, D.K., Gisladottir, G. and Dominey-Howes, D. (2010) Volcanic risk and tourism in southern Iceland: Implications for hazard, risk and emergency response education and training. *Journal of Volcanology and Geothermal Research* 189 (1), 33–48. https://doi.org/10.1016/j.jvolgeores.2009.09.020

Brown, N.A., Rovins, J.E., Feldmann-Jensen, S., Orchiston, C. and Johnston, D. (2017) Exploring disaster resilience within the hotel sector: A systematic review of literature. *International Journal of Disaster Risk Reduction* 22, 362–370. https://doi.org/10.1016/j.ijdrr.2017.02.005

Buckley, G.L., Whitmer, A. and Grove, J.M. (2013) Parks, trees, and environmental justice: Field notes from Washington, DC. *Applied Environmental Education & Communication* 12 (3), 148–162.

Challender, J. (2016) Storm surge impact to subterranean areas by Hurricane Sandy, and lessons for Japan's storm surge countermeasures. *Journal of Disaster Research* 11 (2), 274–284. https://doi.org/10.20965/jdr.2016.p0274

Chen, Y., Wang, Y., Zhang, Y., Luan, Q. and Chen, X. (2020) Flash floods, land-use change, and risk dynamics in mountainous tourist areas: A case study of the Yesanpo Scenic Area, Beijing, China. *International Journal of Disaster Risk Reduction* 50. https://doi.org/10.1016/j.ijdrr.2020.101873

Cheng, L. and Zhang, J. (2020) Is tourism development a catalyst of economic recovery following natural disaster? An analysis of economic resilience and spatial variability. *Current Issues in Tourism* 23 (20), 2602–2623. https://doi.org/10.1080/13683500.2019.1711029

Ciampa, F., Seifollahi-Aghmiuni, S., Kalantari, Z. and Ferreira, C.S.S. (2021) Flood mitigation in Mediterranean coastal regions: Problems, solutions, and stakeholder involvement. *Sustainability* 13 (18) https://doi.org/10.3390/su131810474

Colette, A. (2007) *Climate Change and World Heritage: Report on Predicting and Managing the Impacts of Climate Change on World Heritage and Strategy to Assist States Parties to Implement Appropriate Management Responses.* Retrieved 04/04, 2022, from https://unesdoc.unesco.org/ark:/48223/pf0000160019

Cuca, B. (2017) The contribution of earth observation technologies to monitoring strategies of cultural landscapes and sites. *International Archives of the Photogrammetry, Remote Sensing and Spatial Information Sciences, XLII-2/W5* 135-140. https://doi.org/10.5194/isprs-archives-XLII-2-W5-135-2017

Dogru, T. and Bulut, U. (2018) Is tourism an engine for economic recovery? Theory and empirical evidence. *Tourism Management* 67, 425–434. https://doi.org/10.1016/j.tourman.2017.06.014

Dogru, T., Marchio, E.A., Bulut, U. and Suess, C. (2019) Climate change: Vulnerability and resilience of tourism and the entire economy. *Tourism Management* 72, 292–305. https://doi.org/10.1016/j.tourman.2018.12.010

Dube, K., Nhamo, G., Kilungu, H., Hambira, W.L., El-Masry, E.A., Chikodzi, D. ... and Molua, E.L. (2023) Tourism and climate change in Africa: Informing sector responses. *Journal of Sustainable Tourism*, https://doi.org/10.1080/09669582.2023.2193355.

Estevão, C. and Costa, C. (2020) Natural disaster management in tourist destinations: A systematic literature review. *European Journal of Tourism Research* 25, 2502–2502. https://doi.org/10.54055/ejtr.v25i.417

Fang, Y., Yin, J. and Wu, B. (2016) Flooding risk assessment of coastal tourist attractions affected by sea level rise and storm surge: A case study in Zhejiang Province, China. *Natural Hazards* 84 (1), 611–624. https://doi.org/10.1007/s11069-016-2444-4

Faulkner, B. (2001) Towards a framework for tourism disaster management. *Tourism Management* 22 (2), 135–147. https://doi.org/10.1016/S0261-5177(00)00048-0

Filimonau, V. and De Coteau, D. (2020) Tourism resilience in the context of integrated destination and disaster management (DM2) *The International Journal of Tourism Research* 22 (2), 202–222. https://doi.org/10.1002/jtr.2329

Fitchett, J.M., Grant, B. and Hoogendoorn, G. (2016) Climate change threats to two low-lying South African coastal towns: Risks and perceptions. *South African Journal of Science* 112 (5/6), 9. https://doi.org/10.17159/sajs.2016/20150262

Fragoso, M., Trigo, R.M., Pinto, J.G., Lopes, S., Lopes, A., Ulbrich, S. and Magro, C. (2012) The 20 February 2010 Madeira flash-floods: Synoptic analysis and extreme rainfall assessment. *Natural Hazards and Earth System Sciences* 12 (3), 715–730. https://doi.org/10.5194/nhess-12-715-2012

Ghaderi, Z., King, B. and Hall, C.M. (2021) Crisis preparedness of hospitality managers: Evidence from Malaysia. *Journal of Hospitality and Tourism Insights* 5 (2), 292–310. https://doi.org/10.1108/JHTI-10-2020-0199

Ghaderi, Z., Mat Som, A.P. and Henderson, J.C. (2015) When disaster strikes: The Thai floods of 2011 and tourism industry response and resilience. *Asia Pacific Journal of Tourism Research* 20 (4), 399–415. https://doi.org/10.1080/10941665.2014.889726

Gooroochurn, N. and Sugiyarto, G. (2005) Competitiveness indicators in the travel and tourism industry. *Tourism Economics* 11 (1), 25–43. https://doi.org/10.5367/0000000053297130

Gopalakrishnan, T. and Kumar, L. (2020) Potential impacts of sea-level rise upon the Jaffna Peninsula, Sri Lanka: How climate change can adversely affect the coastal zone. *Journal of Coastal Research* 36 (5), 951–960. https://doi.org/10.2112/JCOASTRES-D-19-00155.1

Gössling, S. (2002) Global environmental consequences of tourism. *Global Environmental Change* 12 (4), 283–302. https://doi.org/10.1016/S0959-3780(02)00044-4

Gössling, S. and Hall, C.M. (eds) (2006) *Tourism and Global Environmental Change: Ecological, Social, Economic, and Political Interrelationships*. Abingdon: Routledge. https://doi.org/10.4324/9780203011911

Granville, F., Mehta, A. and Pike, S. (2016) Destinations, disasters and public relations: Stakeholder engagement in multi-phase disaster management. *Journal of Hospitality and Tourism Management* 28, 73–79. https://doi.org/10.1016/j.jhtm.2016.02.001

Hall, C.M. (2017) Resilience in tourism: Development, theory and application. In J.M. Cheer and A.A. Lew (eds) *Tourism, Resilience and Sustainability: Adapting to Social, Political and Economic Change* (pp. 18–33). New York: Routledge. https://doi.org/10.4324/9781315464053

Hall, C.M., Amelung, B., Cohen, S., Eijgelaar, E., Gössling, S., Higham, J., Leemans, R., Peeters, P., Ram, Y. and Scott, D. (2015) On climate change skepticism and denial in tourism. *Journal of Sustainable Tourism* 23 (1), 4–25. https://doi.org/10.1080/09669582.2014.953544

Hall, C.M. and Higham, J. (2005) Introduction: Tourism, recreation and climate change. In C.M. Hall and J. Higham (eds) *Tourism, Recreation and Climate Change* (pp. 3–28). Clevedon: Channel View Publications.

Hall, C.M., Prayag, G. and Amore, A. (2018) *Tourism and Resilience: Individual, Organisational and Destination Perspectives*. Bristol: Channel View Publications.

Hall, C.M., Safonov, A. and Koupaei, S.N. (2022) Resilience in hospitality and tourism: Issues, synthesis and agenda. *International Journal of Contemporary Hospitality Management*, https://doi.org/10.1108/IJCHM-11-2021-1428.

Hernández-Delgado, E.A. (2015) The emerging threats of climate change on tropical coastal ecosystem services, public health, local economies and livelihood sustainability of small islands: Cumulative impacts and synergies. *Marine Pollution Bulletin* 101 (1), 5–28. https://doi.org/10.1016/j.marpolbul.2015.09.018

Hernandez-Mora, M., Meseguer-Ruiz, O., Karas, C. and Lambert, F. (2021) Estimating coastal flood hazard of Tossa de Mar, Spain: A combined model – data interviews approach. *Natural Hazards* 109 (3), 2153–2171. https://doi.org/10.1007/s11069-021-04914-3

Hoogendoorn, G., Grant, B. and Fitchett, J.M. (2016) Disjunct perceptions? Climate change threats in two-low lying South African coastal towns. *Bulletin of Geography* 31 (31), 59–71. https://doi.org/10.1515/bog-2016-0005

Hughey, K.F.D. and Becken, S. (2016) Value-engaged evaluation of a tourism-specific disaster management plan. *Tourism Management Perspectives* 19, 69–73. https://doi.org/10.1016/j.tmp.2016.03.003

Hyman, T.-A. (2014) Assessing the vulnerability of beach tourism and non-beach tourism to climate change: A case study from Jamaica. *Journal of Sustainable Tourism* 22 (8), 1197–1215. https://doi.org/10.1080/09669582.2013.855220

Hystad, P.W. and Keller, P.C. (2008) Towards a destination tourism disaster management framework: Long-term lessons from a forest fire disaster. *Tourism Management* 29 (1), 151–162. https://doi.org/10.1016/j.tourman.2007.02.017

Jarratt, D. and Davies, N.J. (2020) Planning for climate change impacts: Coastal tourism destination resilience policies. *Tourism Planning & Development* 17 (4), 423–440.

Jiang, Y. and Ritchie, B.W. (2017) Disaster collaboration in tourism: Motives, impediments and success factors. *Journal of Hospitality and Tourism Management* 31, 70–82. https://doi.org/10.1016/j.jhtm.2016.09.004

Jones, A.M. and Berkelmans, R. (2014) Flood impacts in Keppel Bay, Southern Great Barrier Reef in the aftermath of cyclonic rainfall. *PLoS ONE* 9 (1), Article e84739. https://doi.org/10.1371/journal.pone.0084739

Jonkman, S.N. (2005) Global perspectives on loss of human life caused by floods. *Natural Hazards* 34 (2), 151–175. https://doi.org/10.1007/s11069-004-8891-3

Kennedy, V., Crawford, K.R., Main, G., Gauci, R. and Schembri, J.A. (2020) Stakeholder's (natural) hazard awareness and vulnerability of small island tourism destinations: A case study of Malta. *Tourism Recreation Research* 47 (2), 160–176. https://doi.org/1 0.1080/02508281.2020.1828554

Lew, A.A. (2014) Scale, change and resilience in community tourism planning. *Tourism Geographies* 16 (1), 14–22. https://doi.org/10.1080/14616688.2013.864325

Lithgow, D., Martínez, M.L., Gallego-Fernández, J.B., Silva, R. and Ramírez-Vargas, D.L. (2019) Exploring the co-occurrence between coastal squeeze and coastal tourism in a changing climate and its consequences. *Tourism Management* 74, 43–54. https://doi.org/10.1016/j.tourman.2019.02.005

Liu, Y., Cheng, P. and OuYang, Z. (2019) Disaster risk, risk management, and tourism competitiveness: A cross-nation analysis. *The International Journal of Tourism Research* 21 (6), 855–867. https://doi.org/10.1002/jtr.2310

Loayza, N.V., Olaberría, E., Rigolini, J. and Christiaensen, L. (2012) Natural disasters and growth: Going beyond the averages. *World Development* 40 (7), 1317–1336. https://doi.org/10.1016/j.worlddev.2012.03.002

Lorenz, D.F. and Dittmer, C. (2021) Disasters in the 'abode of gods'—Vulnerabilities and tourism in the Indian Himalaya. *International Journal of Disaster Risk Reduction* 55. https://doi.org/10.1016/j.ijdrr.2021.102054

Lynett, P., Weiss, R., Renteria, W., De La Torre Morales, G., Son, S., Arcos, M.E.M. and MacInnes, B.T. (2013) Coastal Impacts of the March 11th Tohoku, Japan Tsunami in the Galapagos Islands. *Pure and Applied Geophysics* 170 (6–8), 1189–1206. https://doi.org/10.1007/s00024-012-0568-3

Madzivhandila, T.S. and Niyimbanira, F. (2020) Rural economies and livelihood activities in developing countries: Exploring prospects of the emerging climate change crisis. *International Journal of Economics and Finance Studies* 12 (1), 239–254. https://doi.org/10.34109/ijefs.202012115

Main, G., Schembri, J., Gauci, R., Crawford, K., Chester, D. and Duncan, A. (2018) The hazard exposure of the Maltese Islands. *Natural Hazards* 92 (2), 829–855. https://doi.org/10.1007/s11069-018-3227-x

March, H., Saurí, D. and Llurdés, J.C. (2014) Perception of the effects of climate change in winter and summer tourist areas: The Pyrenees and the Catalan and Balearic coasts, Spain. *Regional Environmental Change* 14 (3), 1189–1201. https://doi.org/10.1007/s10113-013-0561-0

Marshall, N.A., Tobin, R.C., Marshall, P.A., Gooch, M. and Hobday, A.J. (2013) Social vulnerability of marine resource users to extreme weather events. *Ecosystems* 16 (5), 797–809. https://doi.org/10.1007/s10021-013-9651-6

Merz, B., Thieken, A. and Kreibich, H. (2005) Quantification of socio-economic flood risks. In A.H. Schumann (ed.) *Flood Risk Assessment and Management* (pp. 229–247). Cham: Springer.

Michailidou, A.V., Vlachokostas, C. and Moussiopoulos, N. (2016) Interactions between climate change and the tourism sector: Multiple-criteria decision analysis to assess mitigation and adaptation options in tourism areas. *Tourism Management* 55, 1–12. https://doi.org/10.1016/j.tourman.2016.01.010

Ministry for the Environment. [MFE] (2020) Coastal erosion. https://www.mfe.govt.nz/sites/default/files/media/MFE_Coastal_Fact%20Sheet%201.pdf

Ministry for the Environment. [MFE] (2020) Coastal erosion. https://www.mfe.govt.nz/sites/default/files/media/MFE_Coastal_Fact%20Sheet%201.pdf

Mistilis, N. and Sheldon, P. (2006) Knowledge management for tourism crises and disasters. *Tourism Review International* 10 (1–2), 39–46. https://doi.org/10.3727/154427206779307330

Möller, C., Wang, J. and Nguyen, H.T. (2018) Strongerthanwinston: Tourism and crisis communication through Facebook following tropical cyclones in Fiji. *Tourism Management* 69, 272–284. https://doi.org/10.1016/j.tourman.2018.05.014

Moreno, A. and Becken, S. (2009) A climate change vulnerability assessment methodology for coastal tourism. *Journal of Sustainable Tourism* 17 (4), 473–488. https://doi.org/10.1080/09669580802651681

Ngin, C., Chhom, C. and Neef, A. (2020) Climate change impacts and disaster resilience among micro businesses in the tourism and hospitality sector: The case of Kratie, Cambodia. *Environmental Research* 186, 109557–109557. https://doi.org/10.1016/j.envres.2020.109557

Nguyen, D., Imamura, F. and Iuchi, K. (2016) Disaster management in coastal tourism destinations: The case for transactive planning and social learning. *International Review for Spatial Planning and Sustainable Development* 4 (2), 3–17. https://doi.org/10.14246/irspsd.4.2_3

Olivera, S. and Heard, C. (2019) Increases in the extreme rainfall events: Using the Weibull distribution. *Environmetrics* 30 (4) https://doi.org/10.1002/env.2532

Orchiston, C., Prayag, G. and Brown, C. (2016) Organizational resilience in the tourism sector. *Annals of Tourism Research* 56, 145–148. https://doi.org/10.1016/j.annals.2015.11.002

Papageorgiou, M. (2016) Coastal and marine tourism: A challenging factor in marine spatial planning. *Ocean & Coastal Management* 129, 44–48. https://doi.org/10.1016/j.ocecoaman.2016.05.006

Pathak, A., van Beynen, P.E., Akiwumi, F.A. and Lindeman, K.C. (2021) Impacts of climate change on the tourism sector of a Small Island Developing State: A case study for the Bahamas. *Environmental Development* 37. https://doi.org/10.1016/j.envdev.2020.100556

Pelling, M. and Uitto, J.I. (2001) Small island developing states: Natural disaster vulnerability and global change. *Global Environmental Change. Part B, Environmental Hazards* 3 (2), 49–62. https://doi.org/10.1016/S1464-2867(01)00018-3

Perch-Nielsen, S.L. (2009) The vulnerability of beach tourism to climate change—an index approach. *Climatic Change* 100 (3–4), 579–606. https://doi.org/10.1007/s10584-009-9692-1

Pizam, A., Jeong, G.-H., Reichel, A., van Boemmel, H., Lusson, J.M., Steynberg, L., State-Costache, O., Volo, S., Kroesbacher, C., Kucerova, J. and Montmany, N. (2004) The relationship between risk-taking, sensation-seeking, and the tourist behavior of young adults: A cross-cultural study. *Journal of Travel Research* 42 (3), 251–260. https://doi.org/10.1177/0047287503258837

Pradjoko, E., Setiawan, A., Wardani, L. and Hartana (2021) The impact of mandalika tourism area development on the Kuta village, centre Lombok, Indonesia based on tsunami hazard analysis point of view. *IOP Conference Series: Earth and Environmental Science* 708 (1). https://doi.org/10.1088/1755-1315/708/1/012010

Prayag, G., Chowdhury, M., Spector, S. and Orchiston, C. (2018) Organizational resilience and financial performance. *Annals of Tourism Research* 73, 193–196. https://doi.org/10.1016/j.annals.2018.06.006

Prideaux, B., Laws, E. and Faulkner, B. (2003) Events in Indonesia: Exploring the limits to formal tourism trends forecasting methods in complex crisis situations. *Tourism Management* 24 (4), 475–487. https://doi.org/10.1016/S0261-5177(02)00115-2

Priego, F.J., Rosselló, J. and Santana-Gallego, M. (2014) The impact of climate change on domestic tourism: A gravity model for Spain. *Regional Environmental Change* 15 (2), 291–300. https://doi.org/10.1007/s10113-014-0645-5

Psarra, I., Genel, Ö.A. and van Spyk, A. (2021) A research by design strategy for climate adaptation solutions: Implementation in the low-density, high flood risk context of the lake district, UK. *Sustainability* 13 (21). https://doi.org/10.3390/su132111847

Raikes, J., Smith, T.F., Jacobson, C. and Baldwin, C. (2019) Pre-disaster planning and preparedness for floods and droughts: A systematic review. *International Journal of Disaster Risk Reduction* 38, 101207. https://doi.org/10.1016/j.ijdrr.2019.101207

Reguero, B.G., Secaira, F., Toimil, A., Escudero, M., Díaz-Simal, P., Beck, M.W., Silva, R., Storlazzi, C. and Losada, I.J. (2019) The risk reduction benefits of the mesoamerican reef in Mexico. *Frontiers in Earth Science* 7. https://doi.org/10.3389/feart.2019.00125

Rentschler, J., Salhab, M. and Jafino, B. (2022a) Flood exposure and poverty in 188 countries. *Nature Communications* 13, 3527. https://doi.org/10.1038/s41467-022-30727-4

Rentschler, J., Salhab, M. and Jafino, B. (28 June, 2022b) Flood risk already affects 1.81 billion people. Climate change and unplanned urbanization could worsen exposure. World Bank, https://blogs.worldbank.org/climatechange/flood-risk-already-affects-181-billion-people-climate-change-and-unplanned

Ritchie, B.W. and Jiang, Y. (2019) A review of research on tourism risk, crisis and disaster management: Launching the annals of tourism research curated collection on tourism risk, crisis and disaster management. *Annals of Tourism Research* 79. https://doi.org/10.1016/j.annals.2019.102812

Rutty, M., Hewer, M., Knowles, N. and Ma, S. (2022) Tourism & climate change in North America: Regional state of knowledge. *Journal of Sustainable Tourism*, https://doi.org/10.1080/09669582.2022.2127742.

Sagoe-Addy, K. and Appeaning Addo, K. (2013) Effect of predicted sea level rise on tourism facilities along Ghana's Accra coast. *Journal of Coastal Conservation* 17 (1), 155–166. https://doi.org/10.1007/s11852-012-0227-y

Sanders, D., Laing, J. and Frost, W. (2015) Exploring the role and importance of post-disaster events in rural communities. *Journal of Rural Studies* 41, 82–94. https://doi.org/10.1016/j.jrurstud.2015.08.001

Saverimuttu, V. and Varua, M.E. (2016) Seasonal tropical cyclone activity and its significance for developmental activities in Vanuatu. *International Journal of Sustainable Development and Planning* 11 (6), 834–844. https://doi.org/10.2495/SDP-V11-N6-834-844

Schmude, J., Zavareh, S., Schwaiger, K.M. and Karl, M. (2018) Micro-level assessment of regional and local disaster impacts in tourist destinations. *Tourism Geographies* 20 (2), 290–308. https://doi.org/10.1080/14616688.2018.1438506

Schumann, E.H. (2021) Floods, sedimentation and tidal exchanges in the Keurbooms Estuary, South Africa. *Geo-Marine Letters* 41 (3). https://doi.org/10.1007/s00367-021-00709-4

Scott, D., Hall, C.M., Rushton, B. and Gössling, S. (2023) A review of the IPCC Sixth Assessment and implications for tourism development and sectoral climate action. *Journal of Sustainable Tourism*, https://doi.org/10.1080/09669582.2023.2195597.

Scott, D., McBoyle, G. and Schwartzentruber, M. (2004) Climate change and the distribution of climatic resources for tourism in North America. *Climate Research* 27 (2), 105–117. https://doi.org/10.3354/cr027105

Scott, D., Simpson, M.C. and Sim, R. (2012) The vulnerability of Caribbean coastal tourism to scenarios of climate change related sea level rise. *Journal of Sustainable Tourism* 20 (6), 883–898.

Toubes, D., Gössling, S., Hall, C. and Scott, D. (2017) Vulnerability of coastal beach tourism to flooding: A case study of Galicia, Spain. *Environments* 4 (4), 83. https://doi.org/10.3390/environments4040083

Tsai, C.-H., Wu, T.-c., Wall, G. and Linliu, S.-C. (2016) Perceptions of tourism impacts and community resilience to natural disasters. *Tourism Geographies* 18 (2), 152–173. https://doi.org/10.1080/14616688.2016.1149875

UNDRR (2015) *Global Assessment Report on Disaster Risk Reduction*. Retrieved 04/04, 2022, from https://www.undrr.org/publication/global-assessment-report-disaster-risk-reduction-2015

Waugh, W.L. and Streib, G. (2006) Collaboration and leadership for effective emergency management. *Public Administration Review* 66 (s1), 131–140. https://doi.org/10.1111/j.1540-6210.2006.00673.x

Williams, A.M. and Baláž, V. (2013) Tourism, risk tolerance and competences: Travel organization and tourism hazards. *Tourism Management* 35, 209–221. https://doi.org/10.1016/j.tourman.2012.07.006

Williams, A.M. and Baláž, V. (2015) Tourism risk and uncertainty: Theoretical reflections. *Journal of Travel Research* 54 (3), 271–287. https://doi.org/10.1177/0047287514523334

Windupranata, W., Aristawati, G., Hanifa, N.R. and Nusantara, C.A.D.S. (2019) Vulnerability mapping of tsunami inundation hazard at the tourism area of pangandaran, West Java. *Proceedings of 2019 IEEE Asia-Pacific Conference on Geoscience, Electronics and Remote Sensing Technology: Understanding and Forecasting the Dynamics of Land, Ocean and Maritime* 79–85. https://doi.org/10.1109/AGERS48446.2019.9034458

Zhai, X., Luo, Q. and Wang, L. (2020) Why tourists engage in online collective actions in times of crisis: Exploring the role of group relative deprivation. *Journal of Destination Marketing & Management* 16, 100414. https://doi.org/10.1016/j.jdmm.2020.100414

Zhang, J. and Cheng, L. (2019) Threshold effect of tourism development on economic growth following a disaster shock: Evidence from the Wenchuan Earthquake, P.R. China. *Sustainability* 11 (2), 371. https://doi.org/10.3390/su11020371

Zscheischler, J., Westra, S., Van Den Hurk, B.J.J.M., Seneviratne, S.I., Ward, P.J., Pitman, A., Aghakouchak, A., Bresch, D.N., Leonard, M., Wahl, T. and Zhang, X. (2018) Future climate risk from compound events. *Nature Climate Change* 8 (6), 469–477. https://doi.org/10.1038/s41558-018-0156-3

Zuo, W., Zhu, W., Wang, F., Wei, J. and Bondar, A. (2017) Exploring the institutional determinants of risk governance: A comparative approach across nations. *International Journal of Disaster Risk Reduction* 24, 135–143. https://doi.org/10.1016/j.ijdrr.2017.05.022

3 Fostering Communities' Resilience in Far North Queensland Tourist Destinations: Design Strategies for the Foreshore[1]

Cecilia Bischeri

Introduction

Together with agricultural and mining activities, tourism constitutes a primary economic resource for communities in Queensland, Australia (Queensland Treasury, 2017). The Far North Queensland (FNQ) region is nationally and internationally renowned for its natural attractions. Natural beauty, aquatic, coastal and wildlife experiences are the leading drivers for the tourism industry in FNQ (Tourism Australia, 2016). Four of the twelve Australian UNESCO World Heritage Sites are located in FNQ. Among those, the Great Barrier Reef (GBR) is of paramount importance to the pivotal role of the natural environment for the Australian tourist market. According to a recent report delivered by Deloitte, 'the total value of the significant tourist activity associated with the GBR in 2015–16 is estimated to contribute around \$5.7 billion to the Australian economy' (2017: 20). In quantifying these resources from a mere monetary perspective, it becomes clear that the natural environment constitutes a conspicuous source of economic wealth for the FNQ coastal communities. Yet every year cyclonic activities and related flooding events not only threaten the lives of the local population but undermine their economic security, damaging the natural and anthropic environments of this territory. Mitigating the effects of destructive events with the aim of protecting communities and the source of their economic stability becomes, therefore, a priority. Within this broad and multifaceted scope, this chapter aims to showcase an architect's perspective on the issue concerning tourism and natural disasters, and it specifically focuses on the outline of design strategies for fostering communities' full recovery in FNQ tourist destinations.

In recent years, an increasing number of architectural projects have addressed the issue of recovery in centres devastated by natural disasters. Generally, however, the architectural contribution has been limited to the provision of post-disaster housing projects for the local community. Needless to say, a safe shelter constitutes an urgent matter in the aftermath of a disaster; this, however, does not constitute a substantial step forward in achieving a successful recovery for the community or at least does not guarantee a positive outcome. It seems evident that in current disaster resilience practice the architectural discipline has a very limited scope. Architects, in fact, have been consulted with the intent of providing disaster relief interventions in the aftermath of a destructive event and only at the time of reconstruction. With the intention of breaking the confinement of the architectural discipline, this study aspires to redefine the value of architecture into the community's recovery process. The study proposes to rethink the potential strategic role of the foreshore as an active edge between the community and water.

The ambitious task of outlining design strategies able to prompt full recovery of the FNQ local communities located in tourist destinations draws its aim from a central gap in the research of post-disaster recovery. According to Mair *et al.* (2016: 22), while a significant effort has been put into the understanding of post-disaster marketing and promotion, 'less attention' has been given to other 'aspects of recovery for the destination as a whole'. Therefore, this study aspires to promote a more holistic approach able to benefit and accelerate the resumption of tourist activities via prioritising the local community's recovery. Foregrounding local communities and their capacity to recover brings to the discussion the concept of resilience. Becken and Khazai (2017: 97) cast light on the importance of resilience to 'reduce tourism's vulnerability to a range of hazards and enhance the sector's ability to recover from crises and disasters'. Becken and Khazai (2017) identify communities as actors who need to be included in a comprehensive strategy to be able to enhance the adaptive capacities and resilience of the tourism sector.

The structure of the chapter is divided into two parts. In the first part, the concepts of 'resilience' and 'recovery' are discussed. The creation of a common ground becomes of great importance to underpin the centrality of the local community resilience to achieve a quick and full recovery of the tourist destination. The second part focuses on the specificity of the approach provided by the architectural discipline which, via the promotion of design strategies, supports the process of strengthening community resilience while mitigating the impact of cyclonic events on the natural environment. In this section, the specific competence that architects can claim and differentiates them from allied professionals, such as engineers, are clarified. Case studies are then presented. The conclusion presents the benefits that a more holistic approach can bring to the tourism industry. This chapter contributes to the promotion of more proactive engagement in addressing disaster risks from public and private stakeholders, assuring a positive impact to both the tourism industry and local communities.

What Makes a Full Recovery Successful for Tourists and Locals? A Focus on Resilience

The concepts of resilience and recovery are constantly recurring when investigating a post-disaster scenario. It is therefore central to build a common understanding of the two terms to avoid misinterpretations.

Resilience

Defining resilience is not a simple task. The concept acquires different meanings according to the field of study. An increasing number of scholarly publications from disparate disciplines are investigating the concept of resilience. According to Scopus, Elsevier's abstract and citation database, in 2010 3199 peer-reviewed publications included the term resilience in their titles. In 2017, the figure reached 8973, and by mid-2023 it had reached over 53,000. This section does not have the ambition of determining the ultimate meaning of resilience, rather to highlight the fundamental difference between two opposite trends. Definitions of resilience can be grouped into two main categories: it can be considered as a *restorative action* or, alternatively, as a *proactive process* (Paton, 2001). The former, which is mainly adopted by engineering disciplines, conceptualises resilience as a process aiming to recreate the state prior to the shock, deemed as stability. The latter, which is attributable to ecological–focused subjects, recognises resilience as a proactive process. The system is here assessed against its capacity to adapt, overcome a disruptive event, and reach a new stability which does not necessarily recreate the identical set of characteristics present before the impact of the shock. In this study, the definition of resilience aligns itself with this second category.

The definition of resilience as a proactive process was first used by Holling (1973: 14) who defined it as the 'measure of the persistence of systems and their ability to absorb change and disturbance and still maintain the same relationships between populations or state variables'. In 1999, Mileti offered a definition of resilience focused on the capacity of a community to cope with natural disasters. Resilience 'means that a locale is able to withstand an extreme natural event without suffering devastating losses, damage, diminished productivity or quality of life and without a large amount of assistance from outside the community' (Mileti, 1999: 32–33).

In 2005, the Hyogo Framework for Action 2005–2015 describes resilience as:

the capacity of a system, community or society potentially exposed to hazards to adapt, by resisting or changing in order to reach and maintain an acceptable level of functioning and structure. This is determined by the degree to which the social system is capable of organising itself to increase this capacity for learning from past disasters for better future protection and to improve risk reduction measures. (Hyogo Framework for Action, 2005: 9)

At stake, therefore, it is the active response of the local community to the disruptive event with a clear emphasis on endogenous resources and the capacity of the 'social system' to 'learn' and 'improve' to reach a new, ameliorated stability. This change of perspective surpasses the positivist approach very often adopted in response to natural disasters, where disaster proofing a community consists of the adoption of engineering solutions that aim to preserve pre-disaster stability rather than the identification of the aspects that play a role in equipping communities with built-in resilience strategies.

It is widely accepted by scholars of the disaster field that the basic parameters to measure the level of resilience of a system/community to a particular threat has to be formulated through the evaluation of three fundamental aspects of the community's environmental, economic and social spheres (Mileti, 1999; Christopherson et al., 2010). Often, however, a major level of articulation of the three key factors is suggested and other important indicators of community resilience, such as social networks and infrastructure, are claimed as independent (Cutter et al., 2008; Kapucu et al., 2013) instead of being aggregated to one of the three key factors. It is within this scenario that the definition of community competence emerges. Cutter (2008: 604) identifies in community competence 'another form of resilience', which (1) through places fosters 'population wellness, quality of life and emotional health' and (2) assesses the performance of the community in pre- and post-disaster scenarios, 'including a sense of community and ideals as well as attachment to place and the desire to preserve pre-disaster cultural norms and icons'. High importance has been accorded to this factor because of the possibility of defining an active role for architecture in enhancing community resilience which is not just limited to the provision of cyclone-proof buildings and infrastructure but also establishes its determinant role in shaping spaces and places capable of fostering community resilience at a local and social level.

Before concluding, a final aspect of the resilience concept must be tackled: the relationship between resilience and recovery. In generalising the concept of resilience, the two components that identify a resilient community are: being prepared to face the disaster and being able to quickly recover (Norris et al., 2008; Haigh & Amaratunga, 2010). Thus, recovery could be considered either a component of resilience or an ex-post instrument to verify the level of resilience of a community. Having recognised the central role played by social systems and their functional performance, particular attention will be paid to the potential for architecture to contribute to the enhancement of community resilience through communitarian places as catalysts for social networks and strategic means in fostering recovery.

Recovery

The term 'recovery' is associated with the process embedding 'the combination of activities – generally, restoration and reconstruction – that enables structures, facilities, and their contents to again satisfy the functions and aesthetics for which they were first installed or constructed' (Rapp, 2007: 262). Therefore, the full recovery of a community implies a more elaborate process than rebuilding homes. Studying communities in an extreme scenario becomes strategically important for indicating the endogenous resources which facilitate the success of community recovery. The literature investigating the effects of natural disasters on human systems analyse a wide range of aspects related to the impacted community. However, being able to renew proper social functions constitutes a major thread among the cases of fully recovered communities. For example, Norris (2008: 133), from a mental health perspective, argues that a community has recovered when 'considerable distress' or 'dissatisfaction' have been surpassed by members of the community and when they resume 'adequate role functioning at home, school, and/or work'. In addition, Norris (2008: 135) specifies how resilience fails when 'resilience-resources', such as 'social connections', are damaged or severed, 'leaving survivors feeling isolated and alone'. Tobin (1999: 15), from the geographic arena, says that 'recovery does not entail simple clean-up and restoration operations to get a community back on its feet, but requires long-term rehabilitation processes that are affected by prevailing socio-economic conditions and structural constraints'. Vale and Campanella (2005: 12), from an urban design and planning perspective, identify recovery as the process that 'entail[s] some sort of return to normalcy in the human terms of social and economic relations' of a city. Again, Campanella (2006: 142) states, 'to enable total recovery, familial, social and religious networks of survivors ... must be reconnected'. Even though distant disciplines emphasise different aspects, in the definition of an accomplished recovery the social dimension of the community holds a fundamental spot. Therefore, it is widely agreed that the resilience of a community is greatly influenced by the performance of its social networks. Cutter's (2008) definition of community competence and the role held by places indicate the possibilities for architecture to acquire a strategic role in the enhancement of community resilience through the application of disciplinary instruments that evade the limiting structural/functionalistic sphere where it is often consigned.

The specific character of buildings, spaces and places, and their related symbolism, have been broadly recognised (Gupta & Ferguson, 1997; Gordon, 2004a, 2004b; Vale & Campanella, 2005; Campanella, 2006; Berke & Campanella, 2006; Norris et al., 2008; Cutter et al., 2008) in their capacity to beneficially contribute to the process of enhancing community resilience and accelerating the community recovery process. Haigh and Amaratunga (2010: 15) affirm that 'the vital role of the built environment in serving human endeavours means that when elements of it are damaged or destroyed, the ability of society to function – economically and socially – is severely disrupted'. Zetter and Boano (2009: 206), in dealing with the post-disaster issue of providing dwellings, state that governments 'rarely focus on recuperating a sense of domestic and public space and place that is crucial for the long-term recovery of affected populations'. Vale and Campanella (2005: 347) also insist on the fact that 'resilience exploits the power of place' and that the physical infrastructure, which has been used by the community before the disastrous event, is a powerful instrument to repair the social networks of the community.

The argument about the connections between architecture and the social dimension of a community is certainly not a new topic in the theory of architecture. However, the interest shown by extraneous disciplines regarding the importance of providing and maintaining places where the community could perform and benefit from social networks reveals new perspectives and opens the way for an original and specific contribution of the architectural field to disaster studies. In accepting the efficacy of such a strategy, the substantive purpose of outlining design guidelines to enhance community resilience should be to delve into more complex solutions than the provision of the eleven cyclone shelters built by the Queensland Government after Cyclone Yasi (2011). Indeed, the speculation around the role of architecture in the aftermath of a natural disaster wants to be focussed on the catalytic value of community places and social networks as strategic means in fostering recovery. A distinctive character of this study is the fundamental aspiration to provide indications for ex-ante interventions which aspire to have urban breadth rather than being a punctual intervention.

The Foreshore: Three Case Studies

In this section, three Australian case studies will be presented. The cases of Tweed Head, Bowen and Yeppoon constitute a pool of good-practice examples. All the interventions are placed on the foreshore of an ocean, have an urban scale rather than an architectural dimension, and rely heavily on landscape to orchestrate and complete the projects with community and environmental resilience strategies. In fact, the projects provide public amenities for the local communities and attract visitors while equipping the coast with mitigation instruments to soften the impact of cyclonic events on the natural and built environment.

Even though cyclones are associated with highly destructive winds, the most devastating and life-threatening phenomena for the hit community are the storm surges and flooding events caused by heavy rains that accompany cyclones (Australian Government – Bureau of Meteorology 2018). Bearing this in mind, the foreshore acquires a strategic role. This liminal space which belongs to lands and water is very often the urban stage for activities, the place associated with recreation where social relationships are performed. In Queensland towns, the symbolic meaning of the foreshore has even deeper roots. As Walker (1981: 14) describes:

> towns in Queensland were founded to serve the development of the colony and the State's resources; namely, pastoral development, agricultural development and mining development, and to provide transport. Towns were not regarded by the Government as an end in themselves – for example, for manufacturing purposes – but rather, as a necessary adjunct to resource development.

Such utilitarian foundational reasons have greatly influenced the development of this territory and its communities. The coastal centres, equipped with harbours, played the role of hubs which collect the primary industry products and distribute them to national and foreign destinations. In this industrially driven scenario, the coastal town's foreshore was charged with high significance related to the very identity of the communities. Ultimately, the foreshore is the trembling line which separates the community from the destruction of cyclonic events.

After the Department of Climate Change (2009) *Climate Change Risks to Australia's Coast – A First Pass National Assessment* and Department of Climate Change and Energy Efficiency (2011) *Climate Change Risks to Coastal Buildings and Infrastructure* Australian federal government's reports, which highlighted the fragility of the Australian coast yet its centrality for social, cultural and economic vibrancy, large injections of government funds were made available to ameliorate and reduce risk to this national asset. Limiting the focus of the investigation to projects involving the architectural discipline and attempting to reinvent local foreshores in community social-pivots and instruments of mitigation, projects in Tweed Heads (2005–2011), Bowen (2006–2012) and Yeppoon (2001on) were selected. In these three cases, government funds helped in the progression or extension of already existing plans.

ASPECT Studios, Jack Evans Boat Harbour – Stage One, Tweed Heads New South Wales, 2005–2011

The Tweed Shire is a coastal community at the border between the states of New South Wales and Queensland. In 2005, the council decided to seek the advice of a landscape consultant to redevelop the foreshore of the Tweed Head community. Tweed Head was suffering from the fast-paced rising developments of the neighbouring city of Gold Coast, one of Queensland's preferred tourist destinations (Queensland Government – TEQ, 2017). The project aimed to establish a green civic core for the community. The objectives ranged from the provision of public facilities able to formalise and amplify local uses of the area to the reconnection of the community with the water. Ultimately, the project had to define a solution for a complex yet fragile hydrological environment. Maintaining the memory of the previous harbour; dealing with the proximity of the Tweed River mouth and related flooding issues; accounting for the ever-changing pressures from storm surges and tides; assuring water quality; and the diversity of local flora and fauna were among the primary factors to be orchestrated to reach a satisfying outcome (Figure 3.1). Georgina Wright (cited in Leach, 2012: 67), landscape architect for the Tweed Shire Council, stated 'many community members simply wanted a park with more grass and trees, but the council engineers needed a public asset that would be resilient to the threats of climate change and maintenance issues common in coastal environments'.

ASPECT Studios delivered a project able to provide a solution and incorporate the challenges of the site. In the few years since its completion,

Figure 3.1 ASPECT Studios. Jack Evans Boat Harbour – Stage One, master plan [Courtesy: ASPECT Studios]

the project has been able to realise its aspirations and it has become a remarkable example of the transformation of a forgotten part of the township into a prime civic space for the community. The park has become a major tourist attraction for Tweed Heads (Figure 3.2). This has been possible thanks to the richness of the experience provided – a new beach and beach deck, a new rocky headland, an 'urban pier', boardwalk, water amphitheatre, swimming areas, fishing points and boating opportunities. ASPECT Studios (2011) highlight how 'the entire water edge has been designed to withstand tidal inundation and potential storm surges to "future proof" the surrounding parklands against the effects of climate change and sea level rise'. It is important to underline how the project adopts architectural elements of socialisation for the implementation of environmental resilience strategies. The promenade that frames the intervention works with the changing water landscape rather than against it in a calculated acceptance of inundations mutating the park experience accordingly. The benefits of the intervention are evidently not limited to the social and environmental realms of the local community. In fact, Jack Evans Boat Harbour has supported economic revitalisation, and the success of the park has underpinned the request for additional funding of another coastal intervention in the northern side of the Shire.

Figure 3.2 ASPECT Studios. Jack Evans Boat Harbour intervention as a catalytic tool to reconnect the community with the ocean [Photo: Simon Wood]

Tract, Bowen Foreshore, Bowen Queensland, 2004–2012

The project for Bowen Foreshore aimed to revitalise Front Beach (Figure 3.3). Front Beach terminates the main commercial street of the town, and its harbour has held a focal role in Bowen history since its foundation as a supply centre for the pastoral industry in 1861. However, with the decline of the port's commercial activities in 1985, the area was subject to underutilisation and neglect. The Tract's project for Bowen Foreshore's master plan started in 2006. Completed in 2009, the project aimed to transform the foreshore into a 'major public domain providing a catalyst for development, consolidation of the local identity and meeting the growing recreational needs of the community and tourism industry' (Tract 2010). Tract's master plan condensed in an 800m land strip a promenade which accommodates a rich program of activities: a skate plaza; a play area; a memorial commemorating the settlement of Bowen (Sinclair Place); a plaza functioning as the lynchpin for the entire intervention providing an access point, and a civic hinge with the jetty and the port facilities; an urban stage for community congregations (Dalrymple Plaza); an open-air theatre combined with an information centre and a celebratory pavilion on the filming of the Hollywood production Australia in Bowen (Soundshell); and a Second World War interpretative centre named Catalina after the historic Flying Boats in operation on the site during WWII (Figure 3.4).

Figure 3.3 Front Beach, Bowen [Courtesy: Tract]

Figure 3.4 Tract. Bowen Foreshore, master plan [Courtesy: Tract]

The dense program of activities is completed by the pragmatic function of bridging the urban settlement with the beach and ultimately the ocean. The Tract's project is a stage for civic celebrations where the role of community identity plays a pivotal role. The intervention, in fact, is framed by the commemoration of the most significant historical moments of the town together with the homage to its past and current economic prosperity. The jetty and the architecture of the Dalrymple Plaza, named after Bowen's first European settlers, establish a continuous reminder of the four main Bowen industries: fishing, mining, agriculture and tourism. For instance, the adoption of striped pavement ribbons in Dalrymple Plaza mimics rail tracks and alludes to the past industrial coal loading use. Planter beds are shaped as mangos, one of the famous agricultural products of the area, and rows of Palms and Pandanus are planted to resemble the different patterns of the agricultural fields. In the Bowen intervention, community resilience is enhanced via the provision of a place for strengthening social connections and celebrating community identity. The jetty has an important symbolic role. Its physical permanence and adaptability, through the evolving economy and cyclonic events, become a symbol of the resilience of the Bowen community. Notwithstanding the fact that it has maintained an operational role as the base for the towing tugs for the nearby Abbot Point coal terminal, the jetty is a magnet for the local community and tourists who congregate for fishing, turtle watching or simply hanging out. In 2017, a photo competition was launched by the North Queensland Bulk Ports Corporation authority to celebrate the 150th anniversary of the jetty. The competition documents the different roles of the structure in the community's life.

TCL, Yeppoon Foreshore Revitalisation, Yeppoon Queensland, 2015–2018

Initial planning for the Yeppoon Foreshore started in 2001. However, it was only after 2015 when Cyclone Marcia hit Yeppoon that Taylor Cullity Lethlean (TCL) was engaged by the local council for the delivery of a master plan for the area. The project has seen the collaboration of TCL, who authored the strategy, executed the master plan and designed the lagoon, and Architectus and Brian Hooper Architect, who provided

Figure 3.5 TCL. Yeppoon Foreshore Revitalisation, master plan [Courtesy: TCL]

the architectural resolution of all the remaining components (new parks, gardens, boardwalks, shallows, water play elements, restaurants and a range of lagoon pavilions). The project proposal aimed to promote the idea of a public space which is at the same time a connector and a destination for the local community and tourists (Figure 3.5). It envisaged a connection with the natural landscape, between the built-up area of the town centre and the beach, and an urban stage for celebrating the reappropriation of the foreshore as a main public realm and asset for this small coastal community. The involvement of the community via direct consultation has been fundamental in shaping the project and prioritising key elements such as the lagoon. The consultation process was divided into two sessions. Firstly, a community Open Day was held in October 2015 with the aim to seek community views on the development of the Yeppoon Foreshore master plan. 136 community members participated (Figure 3.6). Secondly, in December 2015, TLC presented two concept proposals for the project in a consultation event with major community stakeholders, which encompassed representatives of the environment, business, community events, Livingstone Shire Council Internal Staff and Foreshore

Figure 3.6 Community consultation, Yeppoon [Courtesy: TCL]

Revitalisation Steering Committees. The consultation process highlighted the underutilisation of the area, lack of amenities, and the disconnection of the precinct from its urban and natural surroundings. Finally, a one-kilometre linear park, which connects the Yeppoon Surf Life Saving Club on the north side to Ross Creek on the south side, creates a green buffer zone between the built environment of the town and ocean. Ultimately, the project's success relies on the provision of a destination that provides a community hub for the locals while drawing in visitors.

Resilientscape: Five Design Strategies

The three projects presented have provided exemplar cases of foreshore revitalisation projects. The interventions' ultimate goal was not limited to the embellishment of underutilised areas but to become agents for transformation. The foreshores were turned into new revitalised assets with clear impacts on the communities' built and social environments. The foreshore revitalisations provide urban stages and forums for the celebration and strengthening of community identities and social ties. The revamped foreshore has played a positive role in attracting tourists to the three small coastal communities. Tweed Heads, Bowen and Yeppoon, in fact, can be considered satellites of more prestigious tourist destinations and benefit respectively from their proximity to the City of Gold Coast, Whitsunday Islands and Keppel Islands. The coupling of architectural artefacts and the valorisation of the landscape has also served the scope of supplying physical protection for the communities against catastrophic events. In the ASPECT Studio and TLC projects, the mitigation properties of the landscape are fully integrated and embedded in their compositional qualities as much as in their experiential propositions. Even though in the Tract's proposal the adoption of landscape as a mitigation tool appears not to be explicitly pursued by the designers, the planted green strip provides a buffer against the storm surge.

In the next section, five compelling design strategies for the foreshores of Far North Queensland tourist destinations able to promote community resilience are presented. The design strategies are drawn from the analysis of the previous three case studies. Those five design strategies aim to promote a *resilientscape*: the landscape for community resilience. The term resilientscape, formed by the union of resilience and landscape, aims to be an overarching term encompassing the different aspects involved in a more holistic approach for the architectural discipline in strengthening community resilience and sparking the process of recovery.

The five design strategies follow.

(1) Privileged location

The foreshore is a space of transition between the urban built-up area, the beach, and ultimately the ocean. In its indefiniteness resides its latent potential. Through analogue comparisons borrowed from ecology, Sennet (2006), the sociologist widely known for his studies of social ties in cities, presents a contrast between the concepts of borders and boundaries. 'The boundary is an edge where things end; the border is an edge where different groups interact. In natural ecologies, borders are the places where organisms become more interactive, due to the meeting of different species or physical conditions. ... The border is a liminal space' (Sennet, 2006). And again, Sennet (2006) provides a second analogy with 'the idea of a cellular wall, which is both resistant and porous'. While the engineering disciplines are led by a positivistic approach where the foreshore must be conceived as a boundary to protect the community from catastrophic events via, for instance, sea walls, this study aspires to cast light on the benefits of designing and programming the foreshore as a border. The foreshore can be envisioned not as a definitive line but as an active space able to supply social activation for the local community, attractiveness for the tourists thanks to the improvement of the natural experience and accessibility to the ocean, and finally, the creation of a buffer zone able to weaken the devastating effects of the storm surges during the cyclonic events.

(2) The landscape

The definition of the term 'landscape' by Wall (1999) is presented here to support a common understanding of the adopted acceptation and establish the strategic value of the concept behind its limited vision of a green space. 'The term landscape no longer refers to prospects of pastoral innocence but rather invokes the functioning matrix of connective tissue that organizes not only objects and spaces but also the dynamic processes and events that move through them. This is landscape as active surface, structuring the conditions for new relationships and interactions among the things it supports' (Wall, 1999: 233). The landscape, rather than being the connective tissue of the architectural interventions, becomes a strategic component of its success enhancing the quality of the space and functioning as a mitigation tool when the cyclonic events hit the communities.

(3) Functions

The adoption of multipurpose facilities with civic and socially driven functions provides a public forum in which to reinvigorate the social networks of the community. The selection of functions embodying symbolic meanings for the community and its identity is also proven to strengthen the community's social ties which, as previously argued, are a fundamental factor in enhancing community resilience.

(4) Compositional strategies

Symbols of community resilience and identity can be expressed through architectural language, compositional aspects and materials. As seen in the Bowen case, the orchestration of materials and compositional aspects support a sentiment of common identity via the representation of economic and historical related symbols.

(5) Community involvement

The centrality of community is evident in the core argument of the study. The community's role, therefore, has to be participative and active. As per the Yeppoon case, the participation of the local community was essential in shaping the priorities for the foreshore's master plan. Community participation can span from its involvement in the planning and decision-making phase to first-hand involvement during the actual construction process.

Conclusions

The three projects discussed in this chapter have focused on the strategic role of the foreshore in fostering community resilience in Far North Queensland coastal tourist destinations. The aim of this study was to cast light on the importance of facilitating and providing a place designed for the intensification and strengthening of social ties in the local communities. According to the presented literature, well-connected communities recover faster and are, therefore, deemed resilient. A gap in the existing literature, which explores the recovery of the tourist destination as a whole, has prompted the possibility of focusing on local communities to positively affect the tourist industry. Hence priority is accorded to the local community and recognises that concentrating on the resilience of the local community will consequently underpin and accelerate the resumption of tourist activities. In addition, the projects for the revitalisation of the foreshores ameliorate the attractiveness of the coastal towns for tourist visits. As a result, the cases represent the concept of resilientscape and illustrate the formalisation of the five design strategies able to summarise the criteria for intervention success on the cyclone affected foreshores of FNQ tourist destinations.

Note

(1) This chapter contains several extracts that are heavily based on my MPhil Thesis. Bischeri, Cecilia. 'A Cyclone-proof Community Centre for Atherton: Tropical Monumentality to Enable Resilience in Far North Queensland Communities.' 2015, https://doi.org/10.14264/uql.2015.839

References

ASPECT Studios (2011) Jack Evans Boat Harbour Stage 1 – Designed for Waterfront Leisure. [online] Available at: https://www.aspect-studios.com/au/project/jack-evans-boat-harbour-tweed-heads-stage-1

Australian Government – Bureau of Meteorology (2018) Storm Surge Preparedness and Safety. [online] Available at: http://www.bom.gov.au/cyclone/about/stormsurge.shtml

Berke, P.R. and Campanella, T.J. (2006) Planning for postdisaster resiliency. The ANNALS of the American Academy of Political and Social Science 604 (1), 192–207.

Campanella, T.J. (2006) Urban resilience and the recovery of New Orleans. Journal of American Planning Association 72 (2), 141–146.

Christopherson, S., Michie, J. and Tyler, P. (2010) Regional resilience: Theoretical and empirical perspectives. Cambridge Journal of Regions, Economy and Society 3 (1), 3–10.

Cutter, S.L., Barnes, L., Berry, M., Burton, C., Evans, E., Tate, E. and Webb, J. (2008) A place-based model for understanding community resilience to natural disaster. Global Environment Change 18 (4), 598–606.

Department of Climate Change (2009) Climate Change Risks to Australia's Coast: A First Pass National Assessment. Canberra: Department of Climate Change.

Department of Climate Change and Energy Efficiency (2011) Climate Change Risks to Coastal Buildings and Infrastructure: A Supplement to the First Pass National Assessment. Canberra: Department of Climate Change and Energy Efficiency.

Gordon, R. (2004a) The social system as site of disaster impact and resource for recovery. The Australian Journal of Emergency Management 19 (4), 16–22.

Gordon, R. (2004b) Community process and the recovery environment following emergency. Environmental Health 4 (1), 19–34.

Gupta, A. and Ferguson, J. (1997) Beyond "culture": Space, identity and the politics of difference. In A. Gupta and J. Ferguson (eds) *Culture, Power, Place: Explorations in Critical Anthropology* (pp. 374–386). Durham, NC: Duke University Press.

Haigh, R. and Amaratunga, D. (2010) An integrative review of the built environment discipline's role in the development of society's resilience to disasters. *International Journal of Disaster Resilience in the Built Environment* 1 (1), 11–24.

Holling, C.S. (1973) Resilience and stability of ecological systems. *Annual Review of Ecology and Systematics* 4 (1), 1–23.

Kapucu, N., Hawkins, C.V. and Rivera, F.I. (2013) Disaster resiliency: Interdisciplinary perspectives. In N. Kapucu, C.V. Hawkins and F.I. Rivera (eds) *Disaster Resiliency: Interdisciplinary Perspectives* (pp. 1–14). New York: Routledge.

Leach, A. (2012) Jack Evans Boat Harbour. *Landscape Architecture Australia* 133 (Feb), 62–67.

Norris, F.H., Stevens, S.P., Pfefferbaum, B., Wyche, K.F. and Pfefferbaum, R.L (2008) Community resilience as a metaphor, theory, set of capacities, and strategies for disaster readiness. *American Journal of Community Psychology* 41 (1–2), 127–150.

Paton, D. (2001) Responding to hazard effects: Promoting resilience and adjustment adoption. *The Australian Journal of Emergency Management* 16 (1), 47–52.

Queensland Government – Tourism and Events Queensland (2017) Gold Coast regional snapshot. [online] Available at: https://cdn2-teq.queensland.com/~/media/aa8ed-138ce5d444eba72d6f220f0ed8a.ashx?vs=1&d=20180130T102325

Queensland Government – Queensland Treasury (2017) Queensland economy: Queensland's tourism sector. [online] Available at: https://www.treasury.qld.gov.au/economy-and-budget/queensland-economy/

Sennet, R. (2006) The open city. *LSE Cities*. [online] Available at:. https://lsecities.net/media/objects/articles/the-open-city/en-gb/

Tobin, G.A. (1999) Sustainability and community resilience: The holy grail of hazards planning? *Global Environmental Change Part B: Environmental Hazards* 1 (1), 13–25.

Tourism Australia (2016) Consumer research – Consumer profile: Opportunity matrix. [online] Available at: http://www.tourism.australia.com/en/markets-and-research/consumer-research/consumer-research.html

Vale L.J. and Campanella T.J. (2005) Conclusion. Axioms of resilience. In L.J. Vale and T.J. Campanella (eds) *The Resilient City. How Modern Cities Recover from Disaster* (pp. 335–356). New York: Oxford University Press.

Vale, L.J. and Campanella, T.J. (2005) Introduction: The cities rise again. In L.J. Vale and T.J. Campanella (eds) *The Resilient City. How Modern Cities Recover from Disaster* (pp. 3–26). Oxford: Oxford University Press.

Walker, M. (1981) *Historic Towns in Queensland: An Introductory Study*. Brisbane: The National Trust of Queensland.

Wall, A. (1999) Programming the urban surface. In J. Corner (ed.) *Recovering Landscape: Essays in Contemporary Landscape Theory* (pp. 233–249). New York: Princeton Architectural Press.

Zetter, R. and Boano, C. (2009) Space and place after natural disasters and forced displacement. In G. Lizarralde, C. Johnson, and C. Davidson (eds) *Rebuilding After Disasters: From Emergency to Sustainability* (pp. 206–230). Abingdon: Routledge.

4 Understanding the Needs of Visitors During a Hurricane Advisory

Ignatius P. Cahyanto

Introduction

Hurricanes are one of the most disruptive natural disasters in the United States, not only because of the costs related to the impacts, but also due to the time-consuming nature of full recovery following a hurricane strike. The 2005 Atlantic hurricane season was considered the most active and harmful season in the recorded history of the United States, causing approximately 2300 deaths and over $130 billion in damages (National Hurricane Center (NHC), 2006). The economic losses linked to hurricanes from commerce and tourism are momentous, and it often takes several years to fully recover and return to normalcy (Lindell & Perry, 2004). In 2017, for example, there were 17 named Atlantic storms, 10 of which were hurricanes, and six of which become major hurricanes. Of these, hurricanes Harvey, Irma and Maria were the most destructive, causing an estimated $260 billion in economic damages for all three combined (Blake & Zalinsky, 2018). Mass evacuations were triggered as a result of these three hurricanes in Texas, Florida, Puerto Rico, and several Caribbean countries. These impacts are only expected to get worse in the future.

As evacuation is a leading mitigation strategy for reducing human losses along the US hurricane coast, the question of why some individuals choose to stay in the face of an imminent hurricane threat is of critical importance. An extensive body of research has identified many factors that influence individual responses to hurricanes (e.g. Lindell & Perry, 2004; Riad & Norris, 1998). Unfortunately, little attention has been focused on transient populations such as visitors (Bowser & Cutter, 2015; Cahyanto *et al.*, 2016; Phillips & Morrow, 2007). Consequently, while broad-spectrum findings in hurricane evacuation have facilitated emergency managers and policymakers in developing plans that make accurate assumptions about human behaviours pertaining to hurricanes, the limitations of the aforesaid studies are that they have not provided the necessary information that emergency management, policymakers and local Destination Management Organisations (DMO) need for specific predictions about visitor behaviour in their communities during a hurricane advisory in order to meet their critical needs.

Therefore, this chapter aims to provide a synthesis of the empirical research on hurricane evacuation behaviours, with a specific focus on visitor behaviours to better understand their needs and how such research is applied under hurricane advisory scenarios. Such understanding would assist local DMOs in meeting visitors' needs when a hurricane is probable. To that end, this chapter is structured as follows. In the second section, a review of empirical research on public evacuation behaviour and visitor evacuation behaviour is discussed. It highlights what we know about the factors influencing public evacuation behaviour specifically related to visitors. The third section provides key results of two focus groups of visitors pertaining to hurricane evacuations in 2017. The fourth section relates the key research findings to the state of Florida experience during Hurricane Irma in 2017 as lessons learned that other destinations can replicate to meet the needs of visitors during a hurricane advisory. The chapter concludes with a discussion of emergent issues related to visitor evacuation that warrant further research.

Factors that Influence Evacuation

Public evacuation

The evacuation response in general is multifaceted, involving numerous personal, social and experiential factors (Browser & Cutter, 2015). These factors influence all aspects of hurricane decision making, including whether to evacuate, when to leave, where to go, and when to return. For resident evacuation, there are seven significant predictors of evacuation intent and response based on the scientific consensus: personal risk perception (Dow & Cutter, 2002; Stein et al., 2013), official warnings (Hasan et al., 2011; Koshute, 2013), warning dissemination channels (Lindell et al., 2005; Siegrist & Cvetkovich, 2000; Taaffe et al., 2013), sheltering options (Mesa-Arango et al., 2013), transportation (Cheng et al., 2013), housing type (Horney et al., 2012), and storm characteristics (Petrolia et al., 2011).

A few other factors have been found to be conflicting in their effects on evacuation intention. The first is risk zone. Risk is a fundamentally spatial concept where location of the associated risk and individuals are critical. Despite this, little has been done to determine how spatial location affects an individual's appraisal of their own vulnerability related to hurricanes. While there is wide consensus among researchers that those in high-risk areas need to evacuate, less is known about how those in lower-risk areas influence evacuation intention. If the individuals do not assess their status in relation to various levels of storm surge on a map, they may plan inappropriately or inadequately in response to a hurricane advisory. Furthermore, research focused on knowledge of risk area accuracy is largely deficient in evacuation studies (Bowser & Cutter, 2015).

Demographic characteristics is the second area in which consensus among researchers is lacking. While there is a wide consensus that demographic characteristics influence individual evacuation intention and behaviour, these individual demographic variables are inconsistent and inadequate in helping to fully comprehend what prompts individuals to evacuate in the event of hurricanes. The most consistent finding is that females are more likely to evacuate than males. Many studies found inconsistent results on racial, ethnic and age differences. Age has often been found to significantly influence evacuation behaviours; nonetheless, multiple studies have yielded mixed results, with some finding age to have positive impacts, while others have found age to have a negative impact on the decision (Gladwin et al., 2001; Perry & Lindell, 1997). Experience is another perplexing factor in decision making and response in the role of past hurricane experience. Many studies recognise the salience of past hurricane experience; however, it remains unclear whether it influences evacuation decisions positively or negatively (Tinsley et al., 2012). Another grey area in evacuation studies is the role of individual social networks such as friends and family. Most studies to date have found the presence of a strong individual social network to be a decisive factor in the warning interpretation process. Despite this, hurricane evacuation studies often downplay the significance of individual social networks in an individual's response to natural disasters. Individual social networks not only affect the individual warning interpretation process but also influence evacuation probability and the ability to cope during a disaster (Beaudoin, 2007; Hilfinger Messias et al., 2012).

Visitor evacuation

While there are well established studies on resident evacuation, there are several areas where there is a paucity of evidence on how specific factors influence evacuation decision making and behaviour; this includes but is not limited to transient populations (rentals, visitors) and special needs populations (Bowser & Cutter, 2015). Visitors are a vulnerable group, and this is especially true of international visitors who are often not considered (Cahyanto et al., 2016). Due to their transient nature, it is challenging to investigate this population, hence their being ignored in many hurricane studies. Their variances in hurricane experience, along with discrepancies in logistical abilities compared to the resident population, make them a complex group for emergency managers to make predictions about.

Much of our contemporary understanding of visitor hurricane evacuation comes from a series of studies by Drabek (1991, 1993, 1994, 1995, 1996, 1999, 2000) which emphasised evacuation strategies and policies from a supply standpoint. More recent studies conducted by Cahyanto and Pennington-Gray (2015), Cahyanto *et al.* (2014), Cahyanto, Wiblishauser, Pennington-Gray and Schrouder (2016), Matyas *et al.* (2011) and Villegas *et al.* (2013) focused on visitor population behaviour during hurricanes. These studies examined the interplay between visitors' perceived risks and their likelihood to evacuate. These studies, however, were conducted in Florida, a state that is considered better prepared for mass evacuation compared to other states in the US. As such, while these studies have advanced our understanding of visitors' behaviours in the event of hurricanes, they are still a work in progress.

The aforesaid studies on visitor evacuation behaviour have yielded different sets of factors that affect evacuation decisions. Figure 4.1 outlines the model of visitors' evacuation decisions (Cahyanto & Pennington-Gray, 2015). The model specifies how visitors negotiate risk communication against individuals risk factors that lead to protective behavioural output; in this case, voluntary evacuation behaviour. Specifically, risk factors are factors that have been found to affect visitor evacuation.

It is critical to note that in the event of a hurricane advisory, the common procedure in the US pertaining to mass evacuation is that a mandatory evacuation for visitors is issued prior to a resident evacuation order. If a mandatory evacuation order is issued for visitors, visitors are required to leave the destination so that emergency personnel can focus on residents. Voluntary evacuation occurs when the aforesaid factors trigger evacuation by visitors following hurricane warnings without the issuance

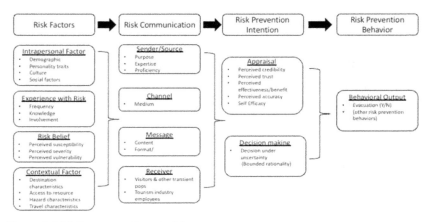

Figure 4.1 Visitor evacuation decision process

of a mandatory evacuation order. In many cases, hurricane warnings may not lead to mandatory evacuations for visitors, especially when the projected path of the hurricane changes.

Intrapersonal factors

Intrapersonal factors, such as demographic background, personality traits, culture and social interaction, have been found to influence how individuals appraise risks. Factors such as age, gender and family situations affect how people assess risks (Eisenman *et al.*, 2007; Becken, 2013). The basic assumption is that everyone is not equal in terms of risk and not all people view risk and threats in the same way. Elderly, females, and minority groups are deemed to be more vulnerable to major crises including hurricanes. They often lack support and frequently lack access to official information that might aid them in assessing threats, which in turn undermines their ability to respond to crisis events appropriately.

To date, evidence on how such factors affect evacuation decisions can be found in Matyas *et al.* (2011), Cahyanto and Pennington-Gray (2015) and Cahyanto *et al.* (2014). In their studies, they found that females were more likely to evacuate than males in the event of evacuation, which is consistent with general public evacuation studies. Likewise, age was also found to be a significant predictor, in which older visitors showed a higher propensity to evacuate than younger visitors. Visitor evacuation studies also found no significant effects related to the ethnicity of visitors; rather, the residence of origin of visitors was found to positively affect evacuation likelihood, with international visitors demonstrating a higher propensity to evacuate than out-of-state domestic visitors or in-state visitors. However, little information has been found regarding the mobility of visitors during evacuations. The aforesaid studies also found that individuals with higher risk aversion were more likely to leave than those who exhibit lower risk aversion.

Experience with risk

An individual's experience with one risk can be transferred to their responses to other risks (Johnson & Tversky, 1983). This includes engaging in the same information strategies as the ones the individual employed in the past. Despite these findings, previous studies in hurricane evacuation have yielded inconclusive results regarding the effects of past hurricane experience on information search behaviours, with some studies finding that past experiences positively affect the modes of information seeking that individuals employ in the decision-making process (Johnson & Meischke, 1993). Individuals with more experience are more likely to obtain information regarding how to get accurate hurricane information compared to those who have never experienced hurricanes before (Gladwin & Peacock, 1997). On the contrary, Whitehead (2003) argued that those who have experienced hurricanes in the past tend to use their own past experience to guide their evacuation decisions and hence demonstrate lower levels of information search behaviour.

The evidence from visitors' hurricane behaviour studies shows the complexity of knowledge and past experience of hurricanes in relation to hurricane evacuation likelihood. While Matyas *et al.* (2011), Cahyanto *et al.* (2014) and Cahyanto *et al.* (2016) found that those with lower hurricane knowledge and lack of hurricane experience were more likely to leave, they also warned of potential reverse impacts of these two variables. Conversely, higher hurricane knowledge and experience could potentially result in visitors remaining in a destination even after mandatory evacuations are issued due to an overconfidence in their ability to respond to hurricane threats. This is understandable as studies on public behaviour regarding risk show that an overreliance on individual risk experience is a common reason why people defy public evacuation orders.

Risk belief

While individual beliefs about hazards have been found to influence individual responses and coping mechanisms during threats, and have been supported by several studies related to visitors and hazards such as Ebola (Cahyanto *et al.*, 2016), stronger evidence on how this variable affects visitor evacuation behaviour in the event of hurricanes is still needed. Cahyanto *et al.* (2014) found that visitors with higher risk belief showed a higher propensity to evacuate than those with lower risk belief. The effect of perceived susceptibility, perceived severity of the hurricane, and perceived vulnerability regarding hurricane evacuations needs further exploration.

Contextual factors

Contextual factors reflect multiple variables that might affect visitors' evacuation likelihood. This includes but is not limited to destination characteristics, access to resources, hazard characteristics, and travel characteristics. What we know to date related to the influence of these factors is very limited. One consistent finding is that access to resources indeed influences evacuation likelihood, most notably access to transportation, with those who travel by personal car being more likely to evacuate than those with a rental car or without a car. Those who fly are likely to rush to an airport to get a flight to leave the area (Cahyanto *et al.*, 2016). This access to resources also ties to financial resources, with those with higher financial resources being better able to access multiple modes of transportation, allowing for greater options for leaving a destination. We also know that the characteristics of hurricanes affect the decision-making process, with projected hurricane category at landfall being the greatest predictor of evacuation (Matyas *et al.*, 2011).

Risk communication and evacuation

Phillips and Morrow (2007) argued that people go through seven steps between the time that a risk message is issued and action is taken: (1) warning receipt; (2) affirming its credibility; (3) confirmation; (4) determination of relevance; (5) deciding if action is required; (6) deciding if the action is feasible; and (7) deciding specific actions to be taken. This progression can be misinterpreted if the warning is not fully understood, or something inhibits the processing of the seven steps. The relevance of the warning to the recipient cannot be established and action cannot be taken if the recipient does not understand the content of the message. This is especially relevant in the context of visitor evacuation.

Past studies have focused on reviewing various characteristics of warnings such as the type of message, language used, timeliness and so forth (Wolshon *et al.*, 2005). However, Dash and Gladwin (2007) argued that a warning by itself has no value since it's considered based on its perceived credibility, interpretation and an individual's aversion to risk. Researchers have expressed source credibility as the extent to which a message receiver perceives the message source to have the required expertise and intention to be truthful (Spencer *et al.*, 1992). Aspects of high source credibility include higher persuasion levels demonstrated by changes in attitudes toward the message or the advocated behaviour, less counterargument generation, and a higher likelihood to behave in a positive direction (Eagly & Chaiken, 1993). In the context of visitors, little exploration has been done in this area. In their study on Cyclone Larry, Prideaux, Coghland and Falco-Mammone (2007) found that domestic tourists have a higher perception of the credibility of television than international tourists.

Risk factors and messages have been used to appraise the associated risk and, depending on this appraisal, different risk protective behaviours were performed. In the context of hurricane advisories, this was whether the individual left the destination voluntarily and, if so, when the individual left. It is also important to note that under threats such as a hurricane advisory, individuals often do not seek a wide range of information sources to guide their decisions, and instead often maximise the utility of options that are available for them at a given time. This is commonly known as 'bounded rationality' (Viscusi, 1995), which emphasises the psychological constraints that bind human decision making.

Visitor Focus Groups

To expand our understanding of visitor needs during a hurricane advisory, two focus groups were conducted in May 2017 with visitors in South Florida. This section presents key results of the aforesaid focus groups. Focus group was selected as the method of data collection as it has been found to result in better revelation of deeper perceptions, attitudes and experiences compared to a quantitative survey. In focus groups, participants can 'feed off each other' as they respond to each other's comments and can support or disagree with one another, producing more energy and therefore richer data (Krueger, 1988). Nonetheless, the use of a focus group was also challenging as group dynamics can inhibit insightful discussion. With multiple individuals, data is often more arduous to analyse, and the environment can easily impact the responses. As such, multiple steps were put in place to minimise any potential drawbacks of using focus groups. For instance, a casual and friendly ambiance was created, and refreshments and incentives were also utilised.

The objective of the focus group was to examine the linkage between visitors' needs and potential evacuation behaviours. Guiding questions

Table 4.1 Key demographics of focus group participants

Variable	N (16)
Gender	
• Female	9
• Male	7
Ethnicity	
• White Caucasians	8
• African American	4
• Hispanic	3
• Asian	1
Visit to Florida	
• First visit (Y)	5
• First visit (N)	11
State of Residence	
• Maryland	2
• Georgia	2
• New York	2
• California	1
• Connecticut	1
• Minnesota	1
• Massachusetts	1
• Nevada	1
• South Dakota	1
• Illinois	1
• Colorado	1
• Maine	1
• Ohio	1

used in the focus group were related to participants' needs in the event of a hurricane advisory as well as their decision-making process. Hypothetical hurricane scenarios were also used to help visualise the decision-making process.

Due to the inherent challenge in recruiting visitors for participating in the focus group, a convenience sample method was selected with one person from each travel party. Sixteen visitors were recruited for two separate focus groups. Table 4.1 presents the key demographics of the participants. Only one person from the same travel party was invited. Potential participants were given the option to join the first or the second focus group. None of the participants knew each other prior to the focus group being formed. Each focus group lasted 2.5 hours. As an incentive, each participant received an Amazon gift card. The focus groups were video recorded after receiving participants' approval. Prior to participating, completed consent forms with participants' signatures were gathered. Participants were free to leave anytime. Following the focus group, a debriefing was conducted by the moderator. A field notes summary included descriptions of non-verbal behaviours and group interactions. The data analysis comprised three stages: transcription, coding, and validating. Thematic analysis was used to extract emerging dominant themes with respect to the likelihood to evacuate from the current destination as well as visitors' needs in the event of hurricane evacuations.

Key results

The focus groups provided rich data regarding visitor behaviour in the event of a hurricane landfall and the subsequent protective behaviours. The following are eight major themes extracted from two focus groups.

(1) Distance and time from hurricanes

One of the prominent issues discussed by the focus group was the time the participants would have in the event of a hurricane warning and the potential evacuation. The discussion centred on the issue of when a warning is heard for the first time by those who just arrived at the destination and learned that they need to leave. The consensus was that these individuals would remain in the destination as long as they could, while those who has been in the area longer or near the end of their visit showed a greater likelihood to leave the destination: 'If I just arrive and I hear that a hurricane is coming, I would stay and at least take some precaution, but if I have been here for a while, then I would just leave'. One explanation is that visitors have invested resources (money and time) for the trip, and the greater the investment for the trip, the less likely they would be to leave right after arriving when they hear a warning. This also ties to how long they have before a mandatory evacuation is issued: 'If we have to leave, we'll drive back sooner than planned, but today, we hit the beach'. Because most participants viewed the trip as an investment, it makes sense that they would maximise their shortened time in the destination prior to a mandatory evacuation.

(2) Likelihood of getting hit by a hurricane

The second issue that was raised during the focus groups was the likelihood of getting hit by a hurricane. This sentiment was common among participants, especially those from neighbouring states or those who experienced hurricane impacts in the past. Interestingly, participants also noted that their location when they hear the first warning mattered, for example whether they were on the road, in a hotel, etc. If they heard the warning while driving to a destination, they might not continue to the destination, and instead move to another destination depending on the projected path of the hurricane. Checking multiple media outlets was prominent among their strategies to deal with the uncertainty presented by hurricane projection maps: 'I will check the news regularly, but I would wait until we have to leave, sometimes it moves around'. For those already in the destination, they indicated that they would ask the hotel regarding what their options were. This is prominent among those who feel they have little prior knowledge or experience with hurricanes.

(3) Mode of transportation

Participants pointed out that the availability of modes of transportation is critical, with those traveling in their own car indicating greater freedom regarding when to leave: 'We're lucky, we have the mobility,' one participant said. 'I'm terrified for the people that no one cares about, those that don't have the ability to make the decisions that we do'. Another participant echoed this sentiment by saying, 'It depends, I have a rental car, so I can't just leave. I have to return the car and then find the way out'. This echoes past studies on visitor evacuation behaviours and public evacuation that showed that access to transportation is key to evacuation decisions. What makes the finding interesting is that it sheds light on carless visitor behaviour during a hurricane advisory.

(4) Possibilities to leave

Another issue that was raised was the possibility of leaving the destination. This was prevalent among those who flew and did not have personal cars: 'Will my flight be cancelled, and if so, are there any other options to leave? Otherwise, I might just take Uber and move to another hotel. Speaking of Uber, will they increase the rate?' The most common issue raised regarding a hurricane warning situation is that most visitors indicated that they would pack their belongings and go to airports without checking the status of their flights or changing their flight plans. Most airlines have different policies regarding changing flight tickets during evacuations. Most of them cap their rate for one way out. A few days prior to Hurricane Irma's projected landfall in Florida, airlines cancelled over

4000 flights to and from airports in Irma's path (Reuters, 2017). These cancellations caused a surge in ticket prices due to high demand. While many people argued that the airline engaged in price gouging, such price surges occur frequently despite the implementation of a price cap (Reuters, 2017). Later, JetBlue, American Airlines, United Airlines and Delta Air Lines all capped their one-way ticket prices out of Florida ahead of Irma's arrival, although there were still reports of price fluctuations despite the caps. Dealing with last minute airfares, pet-friendly accommodation, and overwhelming lines for gas were also major concerns raised during the discussion.

(5) Travel party composition

Travel party composition was another issue that was discussed by participants. For those who travel solo, it provides greater freedom in choosing to leave or to wait until a mandatory evacuation is issued. For those travelling with others, the presence of children in their party increased the likelihood to leave once the hurricane warning was issued: 'I have my kids with me, so I would leave once I hear the hurricane is coming; I do not care about the traffic'. Several participants also highlighted the presence of individuals whom they deemed knowledgeable about the area or who had experience with hurricanes. They indicated that they would consider the individual's evaluation of the severity of the event before deciding whether to leave. This highlights the role of the negotiation process in decision making during evacuations.

(6) Infrastructure (highway accessibility)

Another interesting issue that emerged from the focus group was potential traffic issues related to highways and other access points to leave the destination, including airports: 'Interstates will be jam packed, the airport will be busy, so I would expect to know what my options are if I need to leave'. This highlighted the need to inform visitors about how they can get a real-time update on highway accessibility. Traffic information, therefore, is critical information that is being sought by visitors who drive. In addition to traffic, another issue is gas availability. To meet this need, the state of Florida recommends that the public follow their 511 information system for highway traffic information. The 511 site also has a Twitter account and app that allow the public to monitor traffic in real time. In addition, apps such as Gasbuddy, which help to locate the nearest gas station, have become popular during crises such as hurricanes.

(7) Sheltering options

Another contended issue raised by participants was related to sheltering options. One participant said, 'I need to know where I can go if they ask us to leave. Can I take my dog?' The pet issue was echoed by a few other participants. Visitors are more likely to find hotel rooms in a safer destination, assuming they could leave their current destination. For those who were unable to leave the destination because of flight cancellations and were unable to find another flight to depart on, most would first check with their hotel to see if they could extend their stay, and if the hotel could not accommodate them, they would seek another sheltering option. As such, information on sheltering options such as available shelters and hotel rooms is information that was needed to help them make a well-informed decision.

(8) Source of information

In the event of hurricanes, visitors received information from multiple sources and through multiple media. While information from law enforcement and elected officials was deemed credible, often the message was not created with visitor needs in mind aside from asking visitors to leave. As one participant said, 'If a law official said it is serious, I would follow it'. Another participant said that often law enforcement simply asked them to leave without providing necessary information, leaving visitors to figure out the details on their own. As such, after receiving the hurricane warning or evacuation order, visitors often contact their hotel front desk to seek other information to help them make decisions regarding cancellation policies, transportation and so forth. They also noted that they would use multiple media sources (social media, radio) to help them gather information regarding the severity of the event and the recommended protective behaviours.

To sum up, findings from the focus groups confirmed past quantitative studies on visitor behaviour during hurricanes. However, they provided much richer data in understanding the meaning of the experience that was needed to fully understand the complex nature of hurricane evacuations. The biggest issue surrounding the visitor evacuation decision was related to the costs associated with changing travel plans. This includes but is not limited to changing flight tickets, extra cost for gas, and accommodation. The second issue was related to the uncertain nature of hurricanes. While hurricane projection path modelling has advanced significantly and has become more precise, there remains uncertainty involved with the projected path since it might change closer to landfall. This uncertainty can potentially create visitor confusion and a reluctance to follow the recommended protective behaviour, which in this case is leaving the destination. As such, visitors need real-time and credible information during a hurricane advisory, including where to evacuate, how to evacuate, when to evacuate, and other information in between.

Lessons Learned from Hurricane Irma 2017

A few months following the focus groups, six major hurricanes were formed, with Harvey, Irma and Maria being the most damaging ones. This situation provided a unique opportunity to tie in the key results of the focus groups, as well as past findings on visitors needs and behaviours, with the strategies implemented by the state, Visit Florida (the official state tourism marketing organisation), and local Convention and Visitor Bureaus (CVBs) to meet the needs of visitors. This section is not intended to exhaustively discuss the applied strategies, but rather to illustrate key lessons learned from Florida's experience that other destinations can replicate in meeting the needs of their visitors in the event of a hurricane advisory.

Context

Hurricane Irma was a long-lived hurricane that reached Category 5 intensity on the Saffir-Simpson Hurricane Wind Scale. The hurricane made seven landfalls, four of which occurred as a Category 5 hurricane across the northern Caribbean Islands. According to the National Hurricane Center report, Irma remained a Category 5 hurricane for 3.25 days, which tied it with the Cuba hurricane of 1932 for the longest-lived Atlantic Category 5 hurricane on record. It was the strongest storm (180 mph max winds) on record, and the strongest Atlantic storm on record outside of the Gulf of Mexico and the Caribbean. Irma made landfall as a Category 4 hurricane in the Florida Keys and struck south-western Florida as Category 3. Irma caused widespread devastation across the affected areas and was one of the strongest and costliest hurricanes on record in the Atlantic Basin. It was the first time two Category 4 hurricanes (along with Harvey) made mainland US landfall in the same year (Cangialosi et al., 2018).

The NOAA National Centers for Environmental Information (NCEI) estimates that damage in the United States caused by Irma totalled approximately $50 billion, which makes Irma the fifth-costliest hurricane to affect the United States, behind Katrina (2005), Harvey (2017), Maria (2017) and Sandy (2012) (Cangialosi et al., 2018). After making landfall in the Caribbean on 8 September 2017, Irma made its final landfall near Marco Island, Florida, on 10 September 2017. The hurricane continued northward across central Florida with hurricane conditions decreasing in aerial coverage when Irma's centre approached the Orlando and Tampa areas. Tropical storm conditions were experienced on both the west and east coasts of the state on 10 and 11 September 2017.

Irma prompted mass evacuation in every part of the state of Florida from the southern-most county, Monroe County in the Florida Keys, to the state capital Tallahassee in the northern part of the state. Despite the massive evacuation, the direct casualty number due to Irma was low, with only seven direct deaths in the United States; a breakdown of these deaths by state is as follows: Florida (four), Georgia (two), South Carolina (one) (Cangialosi et al., 2018).

The high propensity to evacuate was also triggered by the so-called 'Harvey effect'. Irma was preceded by Hurricane Harvey that created havoc in southern parts of Texas and Louisiana on 26 August 2017. Harvey was the most significant tropical cyclone rainfall event in US history both in scope and peak rainfall amounts since reliable rainfall records began around the 1880s. The damage caused by Harvey's flooding was catastrophic over a large area of south-eastern Texas, with an estimated 40,000 flood victims being evacuated or taking refuge in shelters across Texas or Louisiana. The latest estimated economic damage for Harvey reached $125 billion (Blake & Zalinsky, 2018). During Harvey, the media in the US was constantly broadcasting live coverage of the hurricane and its impacts. Because Irma immediately followed Harvey, the memory of its destruction was still vivid in the public consciousness, which in turn triggered higher evacuation numbers in Florida when Hurricane Irma was projected to make landfall.

Lessons learned

The role of DMOs is heightened in the event of disasters, as they assume a leadership role in communicating risks to visitors and function as a 'caretaker' of visitors in the destinations, assisting them with travel plan changes and other logistics. Pennington-Gray and Schroeder (2018) coined the term 'crisis concierge' to describe this role based on the Lee County Visitor and Convention Bureau's Visitor Assistance Program. Assisting visitors during hurricanes is complex and requires planning prior to hurricane season. The following are three lessons that other destinations can adopt to meet the needs of visitors in the event of hurricanes.

(1) Partnership and collaboration among agencies across state lines for evacuation

The tourism industry in Florida collaborated with government agencies to provide detailed information regarding emergency hurricane situations and where visitors can seek information in assessing the severity of the situation. For example, the Visit Florida front page promoted the hurricane watch for Irma issued for the southern part of Florida. The partnership and collaboration with neighbouring states (e.g. Georgia and Alabama) was in place prior to hurricane season, allowing for sufficient time to execute the agreed upon plan.

Additionally, the Florida Division of Emergency Management website provides links to hotels in Florida, Alabama and Georgia, shelter location information, alternative evacuation routes, congestion and incident information, and services such as gas stations and rest area locations. One example of the result of such partnerships was the evacuation assistance across Interstate 75 and 95 North and Interstate 10 West, including adding restrooms to rest stops. Also, before the hurricane hit, employees from the Florida Welcome Center assisted the Alabama Welcome Center with travellers heading west and north of Interstate 10, Interstate 75, and Interstate 95. When the traffic shifted in the following direction after the hurricane passed, Alabama returned the favour, including providing information on road conditions and gas availability. Volunteers provided meals and dog walking for evacuees at rest stops and welcome centres.

(2) Strategic use of social media

The use of social media such as Twitter in communicating hurricane advisories received significant attention following Hurricane Irene in 2011, which hit New York City, Washington, DC, and other cities on the east coast of the US. It provided a good example of how social media (Twitter) became an alternative way to disseminate evacuation orders. When Irma was probable, people began to tweet helpful information about traffic, shelter availability, and responded to their fellow tweeps in need. Consequently, connecting with friends and family is tweets away, and the ability to help someone is also far more personal.

Nonetheless, it should be acknowledged that just as social media can magnify the good in humanity, it can also intensify the bad. Individuals can easily become overwhelmed by information overload, which can lead to confusion stemming from false rumours and outdated data or misinformation regarding evacuation routes, where to seek assistance and other data that can make information filtering a challenge. To date, most emergency agencies and local authorities have aggressively used their social media profiles to communicate quickly about hurricane advisories. In this sense, DMOs can also encourage tourists to subscribe or pay attention to authorities, DMOs and news agency social posts during their stay in the destinations.

Visit Florida promoted #FloridaNow as their tourism marketing campaign prior to Irma. As part of the marketing campaign, the Visit Florida website provided a map of the state with Twitter account handles of local Convention and Visitor Bureaus (CVB), allowing visitors to follow the local CVBs to keep updated on current news in the local destination. During Irma, this strategy was deemed useful as the same local CVBs were able to update their current local conditions in relation to Irma using the same hashtag, thus allowing visitors to know the changing situation in real time.

(3) Room availability monitoring

One important need for visitors during hurricane evacuation is information on hotel room availability, as most visitors that leave the destination need a hotel room in another safer destination. In Florida, most local CVBs first inform hotels in their areas regarding price gouging laws in effect upon the issuance of a hurricane warning. This is typically done at the beginning of the hurricane season. Then, local CVBs ask hotels in their area to inform them of their room availability periodically. This information is then used by CVBs to inform the public of room availability on their website. For example, Miami-Dade collected data from hotels in terms of name, location, local telephone number, toll free number, pet-friendliness, room rates, and room availability. The inventory relies on receiving information on a voluntary basis, and as such it might not reflect the actual availability in the area. Nonetheless, the procedure allows CVBs to provide the public, including visitors, with some indication of room availability.

Conclusion and Recommendations for Future Research

Hurricane behavioural research related to visitors has offered insight into critical elements such as how visitors perceive hurricane risks and act upon them. Nonetheless, to date, this area is still in its infancy. Climate change is leading to increased hurricane intensity and frequency, and a higher probability that hurricanes will penetrate further inland. Therefore, it is essential that researchers advance our knowledge of factors that influence the behaviours of visitors and other transient populations in the event of a hurricane advisory. An improved understanding of visitor hurricane behaviour applied in destinations that have never experienced the full impacts of hurricanes is one understudied area, as are the differences between various types of visitors such as domestic and international, particularly among carless visitors. Another future area of research could be to examine the evacuation behaviour of those staying at short-term rentals or Airbnbs, as well as information channels used by non-English speaking visitors.

With recent technological developments such as social media, geo-tagging, artificial intelligence, and augmented reality, it is time to rethink, reconceptualise and re-evaluate warning systems and their impact on visitors' individual preparedness and responses. Furthermore, there are a variety of issues that have emerged with the creation and development of the aforesaid technology:

- How can we leverage such technology, especially as it relates to communicating extreme weather forecasts, warnings, and evacuation information to visitors?
- How effective, accurate, and reliable is that technology to circulate hurricane advisories to visitors?
- How can we leverage social media such as Twitter with its geo-tagging ability to track the evacuation route and distance, as well as visitor behaviour in real time?
- How has this technology augmented our resilience as well as our vulnerability to natural or human-induced hazards?

As the goal of visitor evacuation communication is to assist visitors in taking preventive risk reduction actions that mitigate their hurricane risk, it is a complex issue. The cost of evacuation, both from the visitor's perspective (e.g. changing travel plans) and the destination's perspective (e.g. shelters, logistics), all leads to complexity in meeting visitors' needs in the event of a hurricane advisory. Future studies need to consider the aforesaid questions in order to broaden our understanding regarding visitors' behaviour in the event of a hurricane.

References

Beaudoin, C.E. (2007) News, social capital and health in the context of Katrina. *Journal of Health Care for the Poor and Underserved* 8 (2), 418–430.

Becken, S. (2013) Measuring the effect of weather on tourism: A destination- and activity-based analysis. *Journal of Travel Research* 52 (2), 156–167.

Blake, E.S. and Zelinsky, D.A. (2018) *Hurricane Harvey (AL092017)* National Hurricane Center Tropical Cyclone Report. National Oceanic and Atmospheric Administration.

Bowser, G.C. and Cutter, S.I. (2015) Stay or Go examining decision making and behavior in hurricane evacuations. *Environment* 57 (6), 28–41.

Cahyanto, I. and Pennington-Gray, L. (2015) Communicating hurricane evacuation to tourists: Gender, past experience with hurricanes and place of residence. *Journal of Travel Research* 54 (3), 329–343.

Cahyanto, I., Wiblishauser, M., Pennington-Gray, L. and Schrouder, A. (2016) The dynamics of travel avoidance: The case of Ebola in the U.S. *Tourism Management Perspective* 20, 195–203.

Cahyanto, I., Pennington-Gray, L., Thapa, B., Srinivasan, S., Villegas, J., Matyas, C. and Kiousis, S. (2014) An empirical evaluation of the determinants of tourist's hurricane evacuation decision making. *Journal of Destination Marketing & Management* 2 (4), 253–265.

Cahyanto, I., Pennington-Gray, L., Thapa, B., Srinivasan, S., Villegas, J., Matyas, C. and Kiousis, S. (2016) Predicting information seeking regarding hurricane evacuation in the destination. *Tourism Management* 52, 264–275.

Cangialosi, J.P., Latto, A.S. and Berg, R. (2018) *Hurricane Irma (AL112017)* National Hurricane Center Tropical Cyclone Report. National Oceanic and Atmospheric Administration.

Cheng, G., Wilmot, C. and Baker, E.J. (2013) Development of a time-dependent disaggregate hurricane evacuation destination choice model. *Natural Hazards Review* 14 (3), 163–74.

Dash, N. and Gladwin, H. (2007) Evacuation decision making and behavioral responses: Individual and household. *Natural Hazards Review* 8 (3), 69–77.

Dow, K. and Cutter, S.L. (2002) Emerging hurricane evacuation issues: Hurricane Floyd and South Carolina. *Natural Hazards Review* 3 (1), 12–18.

Drabek, T.E. (1991) Anticipating organizational evacuations: Disaster planning by managers of tourist-oriented private firms. *International Journal of Mass Emergencies and Disasters* 9 (2), 219–245.

Drabek, T.E. (1993) Variations in disaster evacuation behavior: Public responses versus private sector executive decision-making processes. *Disasters* 16 (2), 104–118.

Drabek, T.E. (1994) *Disaster Evacuation and the Tourist Industry (Program on Environment and Behavior Monograph Series, 57)*. Boulder, CO: Natural Hazards Research and Application Information Center.

Drabek, T.E. (1995) Disaster responses within the tourist industry. *International Journal of Mass Emergencies and Disasters* 13 (1), 7–23.

Drabek, T.E. (1996) *Disaster Evacuation Behavior: Tourist and Other Transients. (Program on Environment and Behavior Monograph, 58)*. Boulder, CO: Natural Hazards Research and Application Information Center.

Drabek, T.E. (1999) *Disaster-Induced Employee Evacuation. (Program on Environment and Behavior Monograph, 60)*. Boulder, CO: Institute of Behavioral Science, University of Colorado.

Drabek, T.E. (2000) Disaster evacuation behavior: Tourist-business managers rarely act as customers expect. *Cornell Hotel and Restaurant Administration Quarterly*, August, 48–57.

Eagly, A.H. and Chaiken, S. (1993) *The Psychology of Attitudes*. San Diego, CA: Harcourt Brace.

Eisenman, D., Cordasco, K., Asch, S., Golden, J. and Glik, D. (2007) Disaster planning and risk communication with vulnerable communities: Lessons from hurricane Katrina. *American Journal of Public Health* 97, S109-S115.

Gladwin, C., Gladwin, H. and Peacock, W. (2001) Modeling hurricane evacuation decisions with ethnographic methods. *International Journal of Mass Emergencies and Disasters* 19 (2), 117–143.

Gladwin, H. and W.G. Peacock (1997) Warning and evacuation: A night for hard houses. In W.G. Peacock, B.H. Morrow and H. Gladwin (eds) *Hurricane Andrew: Ethnicity, Gender, and Sociology of Disaster* (pp. 52–74). London: Routledge.

Hasan, S., Ukkusuri, S., Gladwin, H. and Murray-Tuite, P. (2011) Behavioral model to understand household-level hurricane evacuation decision making. *Journal of Transportation Engineering* 137 (5), 341–48.

Hilfinger Messias, D., Barrington, C. and Lacy, E. (2012) Latino social network dynamics and the hurricane Katrina disaster. *Disasters* 36 (1), 101–121.

Horney, J., MacDonald, P., Van Willigen, M. and Kaufman, J. (2012) The importance of effect measure modification when using demographic variables to predict evacuation. *Risk, Hazards & Crisis in Public Policy* 3 (1), 1–19.

Johnson, E.J. and Tversky, A. (1983) Affect, generalization, and the perception of risk. *Journal of Personality and Social Psychology* 45 (1), 20–31.

Johnson, J.D. and Meischke, H. (1993) A comprehensive model of cancer-related information seeking applied to magazines. *Human Communication Research* 19 (3), 343–367.

Koshute, P. (2013) Evaluation of existing models for prediction of hurricane evacuation response curves. *Natural Hazards Review* 14 (3), 175–181.

Krueger, R.A. (1988) *Focus Groups: A Practical Guide for Applied Research*. Thousand Oaks, CA: Sage Publications.

Lindell, M.K. and Perry, R.W. (2004) *Communicating Environmental Risk in Multiethnic Communities*. Thousand Oaks, CA: Sage Publications.

Lindell, M., Lu, J. and Prater, C. (2005) Household decision making and evacuation in response to hurricane Lili. *Natural Hazards Review* 6 (4), 171–179.

Matyas, C., Srinivasan, S., Cahyanto, I., Thapa, B., Pennington-Gray, L. and Villegas, J. (2011) Risk perception and evacuation decisions of Florida tourists under hurricane threats: A stated preference analysis. *Natural Hazards* 59 (2), 871–90.

Mesa-Arango, R., Hasan, S., Ukkusuri, S. and Murray-Tuite, P. (2013) A household-level model for hurricane evacuation destination type choice using hurricane Ivan data. *Natural Hazards Review* 14 (1), 11–20.

National Hurricane Center (NHC) (2006) *Tropical Cyclone Report: 2005 Atlantic Hurricane Season*. Washington DC: NOAA.

Pennington-Gray, L. and Schroeder, A. (2018) Crisis concierge: The role of the DMO in visitor incident assistance. *Journal of Destination Marketing & Management* 9, 381–383.

Perry, R.W. and Lindell, M.K. (1997) Aged citizens in the warning phase of disasters: Re-examining the evidence. *International Journal of Aging and Human Development* 44 (4), 257–67.

Petrolia, D., Bhattacharjee, C. and Hanson, T. (2011) Heterogeneous evacuation responses to storm forecast attributes. *Natural Hazards Review* 12 (3), 117–24.

Phillips, B. and Morrow, B. (2007) Social science research needs: Focus on vulnerable populations, forecasting, and warnings. *Natural Hazards Review* 8 (3), 61–68.

Prideaux, B., Coghlan, A. and Falco-Mammone, F. (2007) Post crisis recovery: The case of after cyclone Larry. *Journal of Travel and Tourism Marketing* 23 (2–4), 163–174.

Reuters (2017) U.S. Airlines are struggling to evacuate residents as hurricane Irma nears. *Fortune*, 7 September. [online] Available at http://fortune.com/2017/09/07/u-s-airlines-evacuate-hurricane-irma/ (accessed 1 January 2018).

Riad, J.K. and Norris, F.H. (1998) *Hurricane Threat and Evacuation Intentions: An Analysis of Risk Perception, Preparedness, Social Influence and Resources, Preliminary Paper 271*. University of Delaware Disaster Research Center.

Siegrist, M. and Cvetkovich, G. (2000) Perception of hazards: The role of social trust and knowledge. *Risk Analysis* 20 (5), 713–719.

Spencer, J.W., Seydliz, R., Laska, S. and Triche, E. (1992) The difference influences of newspaper and television news reports of a natural hazard on response behavior. *Communication Research* 19 (3), 299–325.

Stein, R., Buzcu-Guven, B., Dueñas-Osorio, L., Subramanian, D. and Kahle, D. (2013) How risk perceptions influence evacuations from hurricanes and compliance with government directives. *Policy Studies Journal* 41 (2), 319–42.

Taaffe, K., Garrett, S., Huang, Y.-H. and Nkwocha, I. (2013) Communication's role and technology preferences during hurricane evacuations. *Natural Hazards Review* 14 (3), 182–90.

Tinsley, C.H., Dillon, R.L. and Cronin, M.A. (2012) How near-miss events amplify or attenuate risky decision making. *Management Science* 58 (9), 1596–613.

Villegas, J., Matyas, C., Srinivasan, S., Cahyanto, I., Thapa, B. and Pennington-Gray, L. (2013) Cognitive and affective responses of Florida tourists after exposure to hurricane warning messages. *Natural Hazards* 66 (1), 97–116.

Viscusi, W. (1995) *Fatal Tradeoffs: Public and Private Responsibilities for Risk*. Oxford: Oxford University Press.

Whitehead, J.C. (2003) One million dollars a mile? The opportunity costs of Hurricane evacuation. *Ocean and Coastal Management* 46 (11–12), 1069–1089.

Wolshon, B., Urbina, E., Wilmot, C. and Levitan, M. (2005) Review of policies and practices for hurricane evacuation. *Natural Hazards Review* 6 (3), 129–142.

5 Taiwanese Hazard Management of Typhoons and their Impact on Tourism

Robert Kiss and Heidi Chang

Introduction: Taiwan and Typhoons

Natural catastrophes significantly disrupt everyday life. Beyond the increasing influence of people on their environment, Taiwan, a small Western Pacific Asian country, has suffered frequent natural disasters throughout the centuries coupled with a recent history of inbound tourism. This geographically sensitive area is prone to significant earthquakes, landslides, floods, and typhoons. This chapter focuses on the latter phenomenon.

According to a World Bank (2005) survey, Taiwan had the highest exposure to multiple hazards, and the potential risk of the highest mortality of countries exposed to the threat of more than three types of natural disaster risk (Table 5.1). All the countries are located within the tropical or subtropical belt where typhoons (also known as hurricanes or cyclones) are active. The World Bank survey indicated that 95.1% of Taiwan's total population is exposed to more than three types of disasters, and 90.2% of the area remains at risk.

The North-West Pacific Ocean region is one of the most frequently hit areas by tropical cyclones in the world, with an average 26.28 typhoons per annum (The Central Weather Bureau (CWB), 2018). Taiwan has an average of 3.43 typhoons annually; its season usually starts in June and lasts until the end of October, which directly coincides with the country's peak tourism season (CWB, 2018). Taiwan's exposure to typhoons is such that inevitable landfall on the island has a huge impact, as no less than 360 of them hit the country or passed close offshore from 1911 to 2015 (Table 5.2).

Taiwan, as the fourth highest island in the world, has more than 165 peaks which exceed 3000 meters. The highest of all is called Jade Mountain, also known as Yu Shan, and stands at 3952 meters high. As characterised by its high mountain chains and its relative location, Taiwan

Table 5.1 Top 10 countries exposed to the threat of more than three types of natural disaster risk

Ranking	Country	Percentage of Total Area at Risk	Percentage of Population in Area at Risk
1	Taiwan	90.2	95.1
2	El Salvador	51.7	77.7
3	Costa Rica	38.2	77.1
4	Philippines	45.6	72.6
5	Dominica	70.8	71.1
6	Antigua and Barbuda	46.2	69.5
7	Guatemala	28.8	69.4
8	Japan	40.5	69.4
9	Dominican Republic	33.7	66.0
10	Jamaica	23.2	58.8

Source: The World Bank (2005).

Table 5.2 Monthly occurrences of typhoons in Taiwan (1991–2015)

Month	Apr	May	Jun	Jul	Aug	Sep	Oct	Nov	Dec
Frequency	1	9	26	93	106	84	30	10	1
Average	0.01	0.09	0.25	0.89	1.01	0.80	0.29	0.10	0.01

Source: CWB (2018).

acts as a kind of natural barrier for the Chinese mainland in the sense that the mountain ranges weaken incoming typhoons and protect hinterland areas from loss. The forest-covered mountain ranges that occupy the eastern two-thirds of the island create a natural obstacle for typhoons arriving from the Pacific Ocean, although this also means that one side of the island is the most exposed with the eastern counties of Hualien, Taitung and Yilan being the most vulnerable and high-risk.

The eastern coast from New Taipei in the north of the country to Hengchun in the south faced almost 87% of the 182 typhoons ever to cross the island in the last century (1911–2015). On the other side of the country, some of the north-western corner counties, such as Taoyuan, Hsinchu and Miaoli, benefit from their leeward location as they have never experienced typhoon landfalls (CWB, 2018), although they have still endured huge losses as a result of other disasters.

Conceptual Framework

Because typhoons are the most predictable of the major disasters regularly hitting Taiwan, they have been the focus of government attention for the longest time. This provides an opportunity to observe a large set of emergency plans developed with the tourism industry in mind. The first theoretical framework of a tourism-related disaster management strategy to reduce the impact of unpredictable catastrophic changes on enterprises (Faulkner, 2001) was the basis for much further literature in the Taiwanese and other contexts. Research has related to the different forms of hazard risk management (Tsai, 2013) and general crisis management planning (Huang *et al.*, 2008). Other studies have focused on destination-level impacts of natural disasters on the tourism industry (Becken & Hughey, 2013; Hall *et al.*, 2016), as well as emphasising the importance of disaster risk reduction approaches (Hughey & Becken, 2016). More recently, Jiang and Ritchie (2017; this volume) concentrated on stakeholder collaboration among tourism entities. The exposed position of the Taiwanese tourism and hospitality industry generated emergency plans and management procedures (Tsai, 2013; Tsai & Chen, 2010; Chen & Lin, 2014), as well as an assessment model for the tourism industry (Tsai & Chen, 2011). Similar research has been conducted in other parts of the world (Ritchie, 2004; Tompkins, 2005; Becken & Hughey, 2013; Hughey & Becken, 2016; Jiang & Ritchie, 2017). Beyond the theories applied to management issues, arguably much less frequent observation has been concentrated on natural disasters' human and psychological impacts (Regehr *et al.*, 2008).

This chapter provides another investigation by observing all the major participants' best practice efforts in the Taiwanese travel, tourism and hospitality industry, including hotels, restaurants, theme parks, travel agencies, cruise companies and local authorities. The examination of such a wide range of sector representatives was undertaken in order to gain a general overview of the representative hazard management policies of the different industry actors.

Forecasting the mostly westbound route of tropical storms is a crucial tool in typhoon preparation and response. Modelling helps decision makers (i.e. governments, authorities, management) and venue operators to trigger their emergency procedures when needed. Some responders are able to act according to their standard hazard management policy; others respond by either allowing customers to cancel or to postpone their journey, or help accommodate existing guests who are unable to return home in time to avoid the typhoon.

Huang *et al.* (2008) summarised Faulkner's (2001) integrated crisis management framework, which has also been adopted in this chapter. Therefore, the current chapter focuses on the relative approaches and the determined actions that industry representatives follow during the course of natural disasters. The two approaches are regarded as the pro-active (before the disaster) and the reactive (during or after the disaster) steps. Four essential crisis management actions were considered: reduction, readiness, response and recovery (Falkner, 2001). Reduction and readiness actions happen before the disaster, response during, and recovery after (Becken & Hughey, 2013).

Method

In order to explore how the effects of and reactions towards the crisis management affect the Taiwanese hospitality and tourism industry, this study uses typhoon-related case studies to examine the interplay of variables that will provide a more complete understanding of situational disasters. Yin (1984) defined the case study research method as an empirical inquiry that investigates a contemporary phenomenon within its real-life context. It is used when the boundaries between phenomenon and context are not clearly evident and in which multiple sources of evidence are used. This study began with a basic literature review taken from governmental data and documents, newspapers, contemporary weather announcements and reports, and relevant secondary data. Based on the literature review and secondary data, structured interview questions were then developed. The open-ended interview questionnaire contained four main categories: organisation policies for natural disasters, crisis management plans, crisis management strategies, and government policies.

The entire island of Taiwan has been under the influence of typhoons at some time or another (CWB, 2018). Therefore, the data was collected by means of in-depth interviews directed towards hospitality and tourism organisations throughout Taiwan. Interviews helped to explore the boundaries of a problem, obtained evidence of the natural disaster, probed for latent attitudes and feelings about the crisis management of typhoons, and identified potential typhoon-related crisis management solutions. Sixteen organisations were initially contacted, with eight agreeing to participate in interviews (Table 5.3). The participating hotel and tourism companies are located throughout Taiwan. Participants were managers from resort hotels, a luxury hotel, bed and breakfast, travel agent, cruise company, food and beverage corporation, and theme park.

Results and Findings

Some of the chain hotels refused to participate in interviews due to crisis management plans being regarded as sensitive information not to be shared with others or to be shared on a need-to-know basis only. In some hotels, public relations departments are in charge of the crisis management plan, while in others the security department or functional management team are responsible for implementing crisis management strategies. The qualitative data from the interviews were analysed in terms of time, approach and action (Mitroff, 1988; Mitroff & Pearson, 1993; Burnett, 1998; Faulkner, 2001; Wilks & Moore, 2004; Moe & Pathranakul, 2006). Crisis management plans before, during and after typhoons were explored

Table 5.3 Information on participating organisations

	Category	Industry	Ownership	Location in Taiwan	Participant	Note
A	Resort Hotel and Theme Park	Lodging and Tourism	Individual	South (Ping-tung)	Front-desk Managers	52 rooms
B	Resort Hotel	Lodging	Individual	South (Kaohsiung)	General Manager	24 rooms
C	Bed and Breakfast	Lodging	Individual	East (Hua-lien)	General Manager	14 rooms
D	Travel Agent	Tourism	Individual	South (Kaohsiung)	General Manager	
E	Cruise	Cruise	Individual	West (several locations)	Marketing Manager	
F	Luxury Hotel	Lodging	Chained	South (Kaohsiung)	Marketing Manager	436 rooms
G	Food and Beverage Corporation	Food and Beverage	Chained	North, East and South (Taipei, Tai-chung, Tainan, Kaohsiung)	Marketing Manager	
H	Theme Park	Tourism	Individual	South (Kaohsiung)	Director of President' office	

through proactive and reactive approaches, and four actions: reduction, readiness, response and recovery (Table 5.4).

Reduction

Hospitality and tourism companies need to prepare for the arrival of a typhoon. Unlike sudden and unpredictable natural disasters like earthquakes, most of the entities would have sufficient information and time before a typhoon impacts their business activities. Therefore, the existence of a regular crisis management plan and an appropriate training regimen is the most common method companies use in crisis management. The wind and rain from typhoons often cause damage to water or electrical systems, thereby affecting guests. Therefore, organisations often have their own immediate emergency water and electrical supply rather than just relying on municipal supplies. However, typhoons can still cause some unpredictable harm, even with the presence of a detailed crisis management plan. Hotel and tourism properties in Taiwan also frequently take out typhoon-related insurance to reduce the financial impacts of damage.

Readiness

Damage occurring in conjunction with a typhoon includes the effects of strong wind, heavy rain, and floods. Therefore, organisations need to

Table 5.4 Crisis management before, during and after a typhoon

Time	Before		During	After
Approaches	Proactive		Reactive	
Actions	Reduction	Readiness	Response	Recovery
A	• Have crisis management standardised operation process (SOP) ready and apply training twice a year • Have the evacuation signs on the entrance door of each room • Have the evacuation route posted in the hallway and stairways • Have emergency water supply and electricity system	• Follow the announcements and warnings provided by the CWB • Tape all the windows to prevent breakage • Tie and stabilise the trees in the garden and theme park • Deal with cancellations	• Check the hotel property • Ensure the safety of customers and employees	• Repair damage • Apply for insurance coverage if applicable • Deal with cancellations, refunds and rebooking
B	• Have crisis management SOP ready and apply fire and evacuation training twice a year • Have emergency water supply and electricity system • Have lightning rod on the roof	• Follow the announcements and warnings provided by the CWB • Tape all the windows to prevent breakage • Prepare sandbags and place around every entrance and exit • Deal with cancellations	• Regularly check the hotel property every 30 minutes • Ensure the safety of customers and employees • Deal with any emergency accordingly	• Repair damage • Clean the mess on the beach • Deal with cancellations, refunds and rebooking
C	• When building the hotel, make sure the foundation of the building can survive the heavy rain and strong winds of typhoons	• Follow the Disaster Prevention and Emergency Plan proposed by the Taiwan Ministry of Tourism Bureau • Follow the announcements and warnings provided by the CWB for cancellation and refund	• Ensure the safety of customers and employees	• Repair damage and undertake cleaning • Ask for government help with recovery if necessary; when the damage is substantial, the military will help with the cleaning • Deal with cancellations, refunds and rebooking

(Continued)

Table 5.4 (Continued)

Time	Before		During	After
Approaches	Proactive		Reactive	
Actions	Reduction	Readiness	Response	Recovery
D	• Prepare crisis management plans toward natural disaster but focus on cancellation and refund policies	• Deal with cancellation and rescheduling • If the typhoon leads to a delay in return of tourists, deal with the additional expenses of the extension of the stay	• Follow up the announcements of local government with typhoon holiday decisions; if the typhoon is severe, each local government area can determine typhoon holidays	• Deal with refunds and rescheduling of time, trip and destination
E	• Prepare crisis management plans focusing on cancellation and refund policies • Have insurance plans covering typhoon loss due to cancellation, rescheduling and refund	• Deal with cruise rescheduling, travel times and refunds • Follow the travel warning given by the Bureau of Consular Affairs, Ministry of Foreign Affairs in Taiwan	• Follow the announcements and warnings provided by the CWB	• Deal with refunds and rescheduling
F	• Have crisis management SOP ready and undertake annual training hosted by the security department • Purchase the 'water insurance plan' for any damage caused by water	• Follow the announcements and warnings provide by the CWB • Tape all the windows to prevent breakage • Prepare sandbags and place around every entrance and exit • Deal with cancellations	• Ensure the safety of customers and employees • Regularly check if there is any typhoon damage • Higher level of managers required for hotel supervision until the weather warning is clear	• Repair damage and undertake cleaning • Deal with cancellations, refunds and rebooking

G	• Follow the training and guidelines of department stores where the restaurants are located	• Follow the announcements and warnings provide by the CWB and local government • Deal with cancellations	• Comply with the commands of local government on the decision of typhoon holiday • For restaurants located in the department store, employees shall follow the store's decisions regarding holidays • If the typhoon is not severe and people have typhoon holidays, restaurants that are open need to prepare for an increase in customers	• Deal with rebooking
H	• Follow the company training and guidelines of the theme park where the restaurants are located • Construction provides special attention to the hazardous environment • Have emergency plan, according to which the venue is open or closed	• Prepare for the total closure of the venue • Tape all windows to prevent from winds breakage • Prepare enough sandbags and place around every entrance and exit • Ensure large mobile outdoor equipment is fixed in place, with smaller equipment moved to cover	• Follow the announcements and warnings provided by the CWB • Make sure employees are safe	• Repair damage and do cleaning • Statistically observe attractions (e.g. roller coasters) • In special cases, offer promotional packages

follow the announcements and warnings from the CWB, Ministry of Tourism Bureau in Taiwan, local government, and even the Bureau of Consular Affairs, Ministry of Foreign Affairs. The CWB constantly updates the typhoon's route and intensity so the hospitality and tourism companies can make pertinent decisions and react accordingly during the crisis. Before a typhoon makes landfall in Taiwan, the local government plays a very important role to determine if employees can take time off due to a typhoon or not. In this case, companies need to comply with governmental decisions to arrange their labour supply given that hotel businesses operate 24/7 even during a typhoon. Thus, when the government announces a typhoon holiday, hotel companies need to ensure employees' safety while working during inclement weather as well as increase the wages for working during the holiday. A major task the hospitality and tourism industry faces before and during typhoons is handling the cancelation, reschedule or refund of customer bookings. It also means preparing for guests who are affected by the typhoon. In order to prepare the tourism destination or property against typhoon-related damage, it is also essential to secure windows and trees, store breakable items, obtain sandbags for possible flooding, and check the water and electrical back-up system.

Response

During typhoons, the focus of crisis management action switches to following the announcements and warnings provided by the CWB in order to have sufficient information to make correct judgements regarding employee and customer safety.

Recovery

Many hospitality companies and tourism destinations put great efforts into handling damage, losses, and expenses at the recovery stage. The goal of recovery is to put the organisational functions back to normal. There is some focus on handling cancelations, refunds, and rebooking, along with some focus on repair, replacement, and cleaning. When damage is substantial, the Taiwanese military volunteers for the necessary recovery processes of the affected area.

Conclusions

There appear to be no significant differences among the responses from the venues in terms of how they apply the relevant risk management policies. This is probably due to the cultural homogeneity of the participants, which results in everyone following the central government's decisions for the most part. The Taiwanese government has a well-developed hazard management system, established after the most devastating typhoon ever, *Morakot*, hit the country in 1999 (Tsai *et al.*, 2012). Interestingly, the super-trio of typhoons that made landfall in Taiwan in September 2016 within the space of a fortnight was not regarded as particularly significant according to the interviewees. None of them emphasised it as an outstanding event regarding negative impact and losses.

Although the observations provided only focused on typhoons and the preparedness of individual stakeholders within the tourism and hospitality industry, there are indirect consequences as well. Most of which is handled post-event. In a negative sense, they bring a huge quantity of rainfall in a relatively short period of time that could cause landslides (Venue C). In addition, cyclonic winds may cause severe damage to exposed glass surfaces and unsecured roofing if inadequate preparation has taken place (all venues, A–H).

Another consequence of any typhoon is flooding, with debris sweeping through to other areas due to the heavy rainfall (all venues, A–H). The consequences are twofold: on the one hand, temporarily accumulated high water can break into the lower parts of venues; on the other hand – a much worse scenario – the strong torrential rapids may cause serious damage to structures.

The timing of the typhoon is also important, especially in the littoral areas where tourism venues are located (Venue B), as it can lead to tidal surges. Therefore, businesses need to know the ebb and tide zones and areas affected by typhoon related storm surges. Some coastal resorts (e.g. Venue B) must also face the corrosive salt-wind's negative effects, which result in biannual refurbishment of outdoor facilities and extra costs arising from the additional regular maintenance.

Every business, large or small, public or private, should have a crisis management plan (Fink, 1986). Although most of the participating hospitality and tourism organisations have a crisis management plan, their crisis SOP are not developed specifically for typhoons. Even though typhoons are the most frequent natural disaster in Taiwan, there is no specific crisis management training focusing on typhoons in the hospitality and tourism industry. Accordingly, this chapter suggests a number of findings that should be considered by the Taiwanese hospitality and tourism industry as well as the government.

Relative impact of disasters on tourists, destinations, tourism organisations and the tourism system

Taiwan's high mountain ranges effectively divide the island into two separate and unequal zones regarding the level of risk accorded to hazard management practices. The east coast is considered to be a high-risk zone due to the frequency of typhoons, while the west coast is the lower-risk zone. However, the crisis management plans and strategies from tourism-based enterprises and governments treat these two zones similarly. It is therefore suggested that there should be different crisis plans in place for high-risk and low-risk zones.

Mitigation strategies used by tourism organisations and destinations

Since typhoons are natural disasters, free cancellations and refunds are often applied due to circumstances beyond the control of either party. However, cancellations and rescheduling involve concomitant expenses and losses. It is hence important to have sufficient and reliable insurance plans to cover the expected damages and frequent losses caused by typhoons. Nevertheless, typhoon insurance is not available in the Taiwanese insurance market on a stand-alone basis and comes with fire insurance or earthquake insurance. Hotels should purchase insurance for nature disasters as a prevention against eventual financial losses.

Responses of tourists, tourism organisations and tourism systems to disaster

Every stakeholder follows government guidance regarding working days and adapts this to their particular context. Regardless of standard emergency hazard management procedures, the consistent communication and trust which exists between the tourism-related businesses and their clientele means that there is a need for effective and coordinated collaboration after any disaster (Carlsen & Liburd, 2008; Jiang & Ritchie, 2017). Crisis communication is considered by experts to be a constructive method to recover from a crisis (Fink, 1986). Likewise, the emergency policy could benefit from quick decision-making and fast leadership needed in critical times (Heath, 1995).

Recovery of tourism organisations, destinations and tourism systems from disaster

Sometimes all the preparation in the world cannot prevent human folly, or at least misjudgement. As a result, high-level implementation of hazard management is necessary for maintaining the positive image and reputation of Taiwan as a desired tourist destination. After the crisis, as part of long-term recovery efforts, it is suggested to review problems and evaluate how organisations have managed the immediate crisis. The gains and losses in handling any crisis should be reviewed, the details of how the crisis was managed recorded, and the experience transferred into guidelines for future potential crisis situations. Although this chapter has focused on the negative and reactive side of typhoons, one has to admit that their positive outcome is bringing much-needed water to the island of Taiwan, which ends the drought in spring (March–May).

Existence of inevitable phenomena

There are inevitabilities of natural phenomena, such as typhoons, where the question is not, 'Should it happen at all?' but rather, 'When it is going to happen?' Therefore, hazard management is also an inevitable and crucial tool for effective defence and proactive preparation in mitigating the impact of such a natural disaster.

References

Becken, S. and Hughey, K.F.D. (2013) Linking to tourism into emergency management structures to enhance disaster risk reduction. *Tourism Management* 36, 77–85.

Burnett, J.J. (1998) A strategic approach to managing crisis. *Public Relations Review* 24 (4), 457–488.

Carlsen, J.C. and Liburd, J.J. (2008) Developing a research agenda for tourism crisis management, market recovery and communications. *Journal of Travel and Tourism Marketing* 23 (2–4), 265–276.

Central Weather Bureau (CWB) (2018) [online] Available at: www.cwb.gov.tw

Chen, C.-M. and Lin, Y.-C. (2014) The effect of weather on the demand for rooms in the Taiwanese hotel industry: An examination. *Tourism Management Perspectives* 12, 81–87.

Faulkner, B. (2001) Toward a framework for tourism disaster management. *Tourism Management* 22 (2), 135–147.

Fink, S. (1986) *Crisis Management: Planning for the Inevitable*. New York: American Management Association.

Hall, C.M., Malinen, S., Vosslamber, R. and Wordsworth, R. (eds) (2016) *Business and Post-disaster Management: Business, Organisational and Consumer resilience and the Christchurch Earthquakes*. Abingdon: Routledge.

Heath, R. (1995) The Kobe earthquake: Some realities of strategic management of crises and disasters. *Disaster Prevention and Management* 4 (5), 11–24.

Huang, Y.-C., Tseng, Y.-P. and Petrick, J.F. (2008) Crisis management planning to restore tourism after disasters. *Journal of Travel & Tourism Marketing* 23 (2–4), 203–221.

Hughey, K.F.D. and Becken, S. (2016) Value-engaged evaluation of a tourism-specific disaster. *Tourism Management Perspectives* 19, 69–73.

Jiang, Y.-W. and Ritchie, B.W. (2017) Disaster collaboration in tourism: Motives, impediments and success factors. *Journal of Hospitality and Tourism Management* 31, 70–82.

Moe, T.L. and Pathranarakul, P. (2006) An integrated approach to natural disaster management: Public project management and its critical success factors. *Disaster Prevention and Management* 15 (3), 396–413.

Mitroff, I.I. (1988) Crises management: Cutting through the confusion. *Sloan Management Review* 29 (2), 15–20.

Mitroff, I.I. and Pearson, C.M. (1993) From crises prone to crises prepared: A framework for crises management. *Academy of Management Executive* 7 (1), 48–59.

Regehr, C., Roberts, A.R. and Bober, T. (2008) On the brink of disaster: A model for reducing the social and psychological impact. *Journal of Social Service Research* 34 (3), 5–13.

Ritchie, B.W. (2004) Chaos, crises and disasters: A strategic approach to crises management in the tourism industry. *Tourism Management* 25 (6), 669–683.

Tompkins, E.L. (2005) Planning for climate change in small islands: Insights from national hurricane preparedness in the Cayman Islands. *Global Environmental Change* 15 (2), 139–149.

Tsai, C.-H. (2013) Multi-hazard risk assessment and management in tourism industry – A case study from the island of Taiwan. *International of Economics and Management Engineering* 7 (8), 2205–2207.

Tsai, C.-H. and Chen, C.W. (2010) An earthquake disaster management mechanism based on risk assessment information for the tourism industry – A case study from the island of Taiwan. *Tourism Management* 31 (4), 470–481.

Tsai, C.-H. and Chen, C.W. (2011) The establishment of a rapid natural disaster risk assessment model for the tourism industry. *Tourism Management* 32 (1), 158–171.

Tsai, C.-H., Tseng, C.J., Tzeng, S.Y., Wu, T.J. and Day, J.D (2012) The impacts of natural hazards on Taiwan's tourism industry. *Natural Hazards* 62 (1), 83–91.

The World Bank (2005) *Natural Disaster Hotspots – A Global Risk Analysis.* Washington, DC: Hazard Management Unit, The World Bank.

Wilks, J. and Moore, S. (2004) Tourism risk management for the Asia-Pacific region: An authoritative guide for managing crises and disasters. *APEC International Centre for Sustainable Tourism (AICST)* [pdf] Available at: https://www.apec.org › 2004/12 › 04_twg_risk__management_report

Yin, R.K. (1984) *Case Study Research: Design and Methods.* Newbury Park, CA: Sage.

6 Tropical Cyclones and Tourism: The Case of the South-West Indian Ocean

Jennifer M. Fitchett, Gijsbert Hoogendoorn and Su-Marie van Tonder

Introduction

Research on tropical cyclones in the Southern Indian Ocean (SIO) has largely been restricted to the south-western corner of the basin (SWIO), with a particular focus on the landfall of these storms in Madagascar and Mozambique (Malherbe *et al.*, 2012; Malherbe *et al.*, 2013; Fitchett & Grab, 2014; Astier *et al.*, 2015; Matyas, 2015; Burns *et al.*, 2016). The majority of these studies have relied on storm track data to determine spatial and temporal patterns in tropical cyclone genesis and landfall (Ho *et al.*, 2006; Malherbe *et al.*, 2012; Fitchett & Grab, 2014). On average, nine tropical cyclones develop in the South-West Indian Ocean each year (11 if tropical storms are included), of which only 5% make landfall over the African continent; a net mean of 0.45 landfalls per annum (Reason, 2007; Mavume *et al.*, 2009; Figure 6.1). By contrast, an average 2.3 and 3.7 extreme tropical cyclones make landfall over the south-east USA and Guangdong Province (China) each year, respectively (Goldenberg *et al.*, 2001; Elsner & Liu, 2003).

Clearly, coastal countries of south-east Africa are not as regularly affected by tropical cyclones as those in the Gulf of Mexico, the south-eastern United States, China, Japan and Australia. However, the consequences of recent southern African tropical cyclones have been devastating. As an economically developing region with relatively poor disaster warning, preparedness and coping strategies, countries such as Madagascar and Mozambique are in some respects more vulnerable to tropical cyclone disasters than regions with robust disaster risk reduction mitigation initiatives (Ash & Matyas, 2012). The landfall of an occasional severe tropical cyclone may have substantial consequences, including loss of human life and devastation to agriculture and infrastructure (Jury *et al.*, 1993; Shanko & Camberlin, 1998; Vitart *et al.*, 2003; Fitchett & Grab, 2014). Of concern, given the heightened vulnerability of the region to tropical

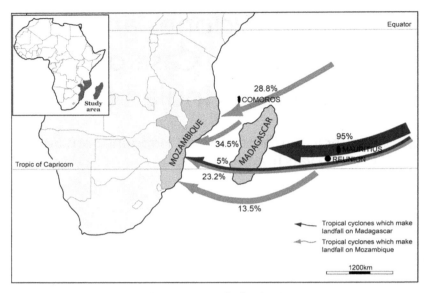

Figure 6.1 Mean tropical cyclone storm tracks for the SIO

cyclone landfall, is the rapidly changing nature of these storms as a result of global-scale warming. The first South Indian Ocean Category 5 tropical cyclone occurred in 1994 (Fitchett, 2018). This is significantly later than the first Category 5 storms for the Atlantic Ocean (1924) and the North Pacific Ocean (1951). There has been a net southward shift in the latitudinal position of landfall of tropical cyclones in the SWIO, coupled with a proportional increase both in storms tracking south of Madagascar and forming within the Mozambique Channel, heightening the threat of landfall on South Africa (Fitchett & Grab, 2014; Chikoore *et al.*, 2015). Compounding these effects is a growing population density in the SWIO islands and within the east and north of South Africa, and a heightened popularity of tourism establishments in these regions (Durbarry, 2004).

The Small Island Developing States (SIDS) of the South-West Indian Ocean, including Mauritius, Comoros and Reunion, are predominantly coastal and beach resort destinations. Tourism operators on the islands offer a variety of outdoor beach and adventure activities that rely heavily on good weather and are marketed aesthetically for their 'pristine' environments (Shabaan *et al.*, 2013; Nunkoo & Ramkissoon, 2010a). These resort destinations are often run by large hotel chains with substantial capital backing (Nunkoo & Ramkisoon, 2010b), which often does not include local community involvement or support for small, medium and micro enterprises that characterise accommodation establishments in the southern African subcontinent (Booyens & Visser, 2010). This results in a contribution of tourism to the Gross Domestic Product (GDP) that is significantly higher than the regional averages and above the global average of 10.2%; in 2016, tourism comprised 10.5% of Comoros's GDP, 10.9% of Mauritius; and 25.6% of Reunion's (World Travel and Tourism Council (WTTC), 2017a, 2017b, 2017c). These figures reflect the extreme importance of tourism to the economies of small island states in the SWIO. The predominance of large, multi-national hotel chains does, however, heighten the adaptive capacity of tourism in these island nations.

The Limpopo Province of South Africa receives about 13% of the country's foreign tourists, and dominates domestic tourist numbers, which is largely fuelled by visiting friends and relatives (VFR) travel (Rogerson & Hoogendoorn, 2014). Tourism contributes 5% of the economy of Limpopo Province, while Limpopo Province represents 7.1% of the national South African economy (Karuaihe *et al.*, 2015). Therefore, although Limpopo Province hosts a large number of tourists, the economic benefits are not filtering through. In response to this, policy development with the intention of supporting Small, Medium and Micro Enterprises (SMMEs) has become widespread with special focus on tourism SMMEs (Booyens & Visser, 2010). Tourism SMMEs now outnumber other types of tourism business (Nemasatoni & Rogerson, 2005). However, they are particularly vulnerable to climate change because of low adaptive capacity related to limited capital and a lack of policy support regarding climate change preparedness (Rogerson, 2016). Tropical cyclones, in particular, represent a key threat to tourism SMMEs in Limpopo Province, with few top-down adaptationary plans in place (Fitchett *et al.*, 2016).

Tropical cyclones represent one of the most severe climatic threats to tourism in the SIO, and one of the greatest challenges under climate change (Fitchett *et al.*, 2016). Although short-lived, the large volumes of rainfall, extreme wind speed, and associated storm surges along the coastline result in severe damage to infrastructure in almost all instances (Fitchett & Grab, 2014; Nash *et al.*, 2015; Resio & Irish, 2015). This is in part due to the poor adaptive capacity of the countries of the SWIO (Resio & Irish, 2015), yet the devastation that followed Hurricane Katrina in 2005 demonstrates the severity of destruction globally (Kates *et al.*, 2006). In countries in the Global South, where the primary needs of the majority of the population necessarily trump long-term adaptation, such storm events result in significant damage at the scale of individual properties through to the infrastructure of entire municipalities (Fitchett *et al.*, 2016). This is of particular concern to the tourism sectors of these countries due to the prevalence of beach tourism within regions marketed as sunny destinations for 'sun, surf and sea' (Hoogendoorn & Fitchett, 2018).

Despite the severity of tropical cyclone induced damage, the literature on the impacts of tropical cyclones on tourism in the SWIO is sparse. This chapter presents three exploratory case studies interrogating the impacts of tropical cyclones on tourism in the region. The first reflects on a published case study of the impact of Tropical Cyclone Dando on the tourism accommodation establishments of the Mopani District Municipality, Limpopo Province, South Africa. The second case study follows on from the first, investigating the impacts of the 2017 Tropical Cyclone Dineo on tourism accommodation establishments across Limpopo Province, reflecting on the degree of adaptation following Tropical Cyclone Dando. The third explores tourists' reflections on tropical cyclones through TripAdvisor reviews of accommodation establishments in the SWIO islands, with a comparison to storm-track derived counts of tropical cyclones for those islands.

Tropical Cyclone Impacts on Southern African Tourism Accommodation Establishments

Case Study 1: Tropical Cyclone Dando 2012

Tropical Cyclone Dando made landfall over southern Madagascar on 17 January 2012, resulting in a severe flood event in the Lowveld region of the Limpopo Province in South Africa from 17 to 19 January 2012. Over 500 mm of rainfall was recorded over the first 24 hours following landfall, coupled with maximum wind speeds of 85km/h (Chikoore *et al.*, 2015). The Mopani District Municipality of Limpopo Province declared a local state of disaster following these floods. This is notable given that this storm was one of the lowest-intensity tropical cyclones in the SIO during the 2011/2012 season (Chikoore *et al.*, 2015). This emphasised the severity of the impact of even low-intensity tropical cyclones due to the low adaptive capacity of the region and an absence of disaster preparedness and risk management strategies (Fitchett *et al.*, 2016). Including the town of Hoedspruit, this region represents an important tourism hub within the northern region of South Africa, with nature and adventure tourism centred around private game farms representing the primary tourist attractions (Rogerson, 2007; Nelwamondo, 2010).

Interviews were conducted with 24 lodges and conservation establishments, which were selected through purposive and later snowball sampling in the year following the flood. Results indicate a total direct cost of R58.92 million [US$4.93 million, April 2018], 'costs' from loss of business of R4.230 million [US$0.35 million, April 2018], and an increase in long-term expenses, including insurance, adaptation and mitigation, of R458 600 [US$38,335, April 2018] (Fitchett *et al.*, 2016). Due to the small sample size, the economic damage to the local tourism sector undoubtedly exceeds that of the farms and local businesses interviewed. Damage ranged from the loss of household contents to the complete destruction of all buildings on the property. The capacity for the tourism establishments interviewed to recover from the floods depended primarily on the type and value of their insurance. This, in turn, revealed considerable differences in the ability to survive the storm event on the basis of the size and strength of the business. Those that were forced to close down or were unable to replace damaged infrastructure and possessions were predominantly small and micro-sized enterprises. Additional strain was placed on tourism establishments through the damage to roads, poor water supply during the floods, the removal of trees, and a loss of the aesthetic attractiveness of the region.

The vulnerability of individual accommodation establishments to this tropical cyclone was accentuated by the inaccurate forecasting, which underestimated the rainfall associated with the storm and projected a northward rather than westward track within the Mozambique Channel (Chikoore *et al.*, 2015). Moreover, the flooding in the region was intensified by the deep easterly flow that continued in the aftermath of the storm (Chikoore *et al.*, 2015). This case study represents the first documentation of tropical cyclone impacts on tourism in southern Africa. It provides insights into the nature and severity of the impacts of floods induced by even low-intensity tropical cyclones on the South African tourism sector. This case study provides important local evidence from which the impacts of global climate change on tourism in countries of the Global South can be more accurately projected and in turn managed.

Case Study 2: Tropical Cyclone Dineo 2017

A natural point of comparison to the 2012 floods associated with Tropical Cyclone Dando is the aftermath of the subsequent Category 1 Tropical Cyclone Dineo that made landfall in southern Mozambique on 15 February 2017 (Enenkel *et al.*, 2017). With maximum wind speeds of 150km/h (Enenkel *et al.*, 2017) and 100mm of rainfall within 24 hours (Maunganidze & Mawere, 2017), Tropical Cyclone Dineo was higher in intensity than Tropical Cyclone Dando, yet as both were Category 1 storms they represent low magnitude events by global standards. The higher intensity and more southerly landfall position heightened the severity of the damage, which in turn resulted in this storm receiving a significantly greater level of media attention. Estimates of the total number of people affected range considerably, but at least nine deaths, 55 injuries and 100,000 displacements across southern African states represent the lower boundary of the extent of human impacts as a direct result of the storm.

Given the greater climatological severity and human impact of this storm, it is notable that unlike during Tropical Cyclone Dando, states of disaster were not declared in the affected countries of Mozambique, Botswana or South Africa (Enekel *et al.*, 2017). The greatest damage following Tropical Cyclone Dineo was centred in remote rural communities, distributed across southern Zimbabwe, southern Mozambique and western Botswana (Maunganidze & Mawere, 2017). The storm intensity was lower in the affected northern regions of South Africa, at least equivalent if not more severe than that of Tropical Cyclone Dando. The key factor relating to the reduced damage was the more accurate local forecasting of Tropical Cyclone Dineo in terms of both the anticipated storm track and the severity of winds and rain (Enekel *et al.*, 2017). This, coupled with the experience of Tropical Cyclone Dando's aftermath in 2012, likely increased preparedness among accommodation owners and municipalities. However, it could equally be hypothesised that the damage incurred during 2012, both economically and in terms of infrastructure, further reduced the adaptive capacity of SMME tourism operations, and consequently heightened their vulnerability to future high-intensity storms associated with regional tropical cyclone landfall.

To assess the comparative damage experienced in the wake of Tropical Cyclone Dineo, online questionnaires following the same format as the survey of Tropical Cyclone Dando were distributed electronically to 341 accommodation establishments in Limpopo Province. A notably poor response rate was reflected in the 15 questionnaires completed. This alone is of interest, as the previous storm yielded significantly higher levels of interest among accommodation establishment proprietors. Of the 15 respondents, only one indicated that they had experienced damage to their property as a result of Tropical Cyclone Dineo. The damage in this instance resulted from the uprooting of large trees, one of which fell onto a guest cottage, and another of which caused damage to their orchards. Additional, more minor damage to this property included water damage to the roof and flooding of the buildings comprising the establishment. Notably, a second respondent indicated that while they did not incur any damage directly from the 2017 storm, they were still struggling with poor access to their establishment at the time of the storm due to infrastructural damage following Tropical Cyclone Dando in 2012. Four respondents indicated that the town or municipality where their accommodation establishment is located experienced damage to infrastructure resulting from the storm, which in turn compromised their ability to operate. These impacts included damage to bridges, roads becoming inaccessible due to flooding, trees falling down and blocking roads and electricity lines, and resultant electricity blackouts for up to 10 days following the storm. Three accommodation establishments indicated that they were forced to close during and after the storm, with time periods ranging from a day post-storm to a couple of months. Four accommodation establishments were required to operate with reduced bed availability for durations spanning a few days to a few months, with a related loss of occupancy of up to 25%.

Financial costs and losses reported by the respondents were significantly lower than for Tropical Cyclone Dando, and with a considerably greater success rate in claiming from insurance. The maximum opportunity cost of loss of business incurred by any one accommodation establishment following Tropical Cyclone Dineo was R50,000, while the maximum cost to repair damaged infrastructure was R70,000. Insurance claims were paid out to the extent of 78–100% of the total claimed value. By contrast, one of the respondents indicated that they had benefitted financially from the storm as the repair team who were working on the municipal damage required a place to stay, and hence increased their occupancy rates for the months directly following the storm.

Despite the reduced impact relative to Tropical Cyclone Dineo, there does not appear to be a conscientious commitment to individual-level adaptation to prevent damage from tropical cyclones. One respondent argued that nothing could be done, as one cannot control the weather, while five respondents indicated that they had not put in place any adaptation measures. A few respondents reflected an active commitment to proactive adaptation in order to continue to prevent flood damage to their establishments, and to reduce consequential losses due to inadequate town infrastructure. Notably, two respondents were involved in upgrading water outflow canals and runoff systems to encourage more efficient water runoff during severe rain events and prevent the retention of water on their property.

Further research is required to more comprehensively assess the damage incurred by tourism operations in South Africa as a result of Tropical Cyclone Dineo and the long-term adaptation measures spanning national, municipal and individual business levels. However, these preliminary results confirm the regional experience of greater preparedness for the storm, and in turn a reduced vulnerability to the intense rainfall and wind speeds associated with a tropical cyclone. This highlights the importance of high-resolution storm forecasting and effective communication of climatic warnings, particularly to the more vulnerable isolated rural communities.

Case Study 3: Indian Ocean Islands

The Comoros, Mauritius and Reunion are small island nations located in the South-West Indian Ocean. As mentioned previously, all three countries rely substantially on tourism to support their economy, and benefit from the tropical climate, pristine beaches and an array of adventure activities to attract tourists (Durbarry, 2004). Positioned to the west of Madagascar, Reunion and Mauritius are situated within the dominant storm track of tropical cyclones that go on to make landfall on Madagascar, while Comoros is situated in the northern region of the Mozambique Channel, which increasingly represents a dominant zone of cyclogenesis (Fitchett & Grab, 2014; Chikoore *et al.*, 2015; Matyas, 2015). Tropical cyclones are thus a common feature on these islands during the summer months and have a tangible impact on travel prices during the peak storm season.

TripAdvisor reviews were consulted for a minimum of five hotels on each island, spanning the period 2012–2016. All reviews were manually transcribed and coded according to the climatic mentions. From this database, tourist mentions of flooding, severe and prolonged rainfall, high wind speeds, rough waves and storm surge conditions were extracted and cross checked against storm track records. Comments reporting on tropical cyclones represented a very small proportion of all reviews, and of reviews mentioning climatic conditions. A total of 22 of the 5277 reviews (3.95%) consulted from Mauritius made mention of tropical cyclone related weather phenomena, 14 of which specifically mentioned the passage of tropical cyclones. This outweighed the four reviews from Reunion (1.19%, $n = 336$ reviews) and one review from the Comoros (0.45%, $n = 224$ reviews) which indicated weather related to tropical cyclones, but which did not mention the storm itself. The heightened number of reviews on tropical cyclone associated weather in Mauritius is notable for two reasons. First, Mauritius is no more susceptible to tropical cyclone landfall than Reunion located adjacent to it, or the Comoros in the northern Mozambique Channel (Matyas, 2015). Second, with a mean storm diameter of 500 km, it is likely that any storm influencing the weather of Mauritius would simultaneously affect the conditions in Reunion. The variation in sensitivity to tropical cyclone associated weather may therefore relate more closely to the anticipated conditions, the level of comfort required by the tourists, and the popularity of the destination.

For the three islands, the small proportion of reviews reflecting on tropical cyclone conditions is notable given the high wind speeds (>120 km/h), heavy rainfall, and infrastructural damage associated with these storms. This may reflect a greater degree of preparedness among the local governmental structures and accommodation establishments mitigating tropical cyclone related damage, and caution among tourists. The low number of reviews for each of the islands reflecting on tropical cyclone conditions could be explained by the lower proportion of reviews during the tropical cyclone season of December through April (Figure 6.2). Arguably, however, this reduction in reviews during the months spanning the tropical cyclone season may be proportional to the reduction in visitor numbers, which would reflect the adaptation among tourists to avoid the poor climatic conditions.

Comments from Mauritius were largely matter of fact and did not reveal the degree of preparedness of the tourists or their level of anticipation of adverse weather conditions. One tourist reflected that they did not know that the month in which they travelled fell within tropical cyclone season for the region: 'The only thing that spoiled out holiday was the rain, and rain and rain, but then it was the cyclone season (which we didn't realise when we booked), so don't go in January', while three further reviewers reflected that they had visited during tropical cyclone season, yet did not indicate whether they had been aware of this prior to booking or travelling to the destination. Many of the reviews stated the storm event; for example, a review on 05/02/2014 reads: 'cyclone Edison hit the area'. Some mention the storm only in passing, with little detail on

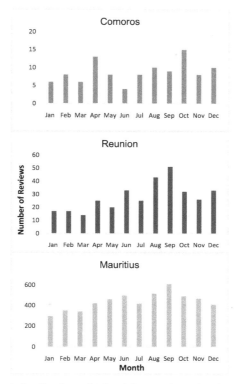

Figure 6.2 Seasonal distribution of Tripadvisor reviews for the Comoros, Reunion and Mauritius

the associated weather, any local damage, or difficulties that they had in changing their itineraries or activities. For example, a review from 30/12/2013 included only: 'there was a cyclone', and a review on 11/03/2014 only mentioned: 'there was cyclone on second day'. By contrast, others include a wealth of information, such as a review on 11/01/2015: 'we did experience cyclone Bansi knocking at the door for a week, wet and very windy but still warm', and a review on 19/04/2014: 'We did end up being under a category 2 cyclone warning whilst there and the weather was windy and very very wet for a couple of days'. The majority of the tourists reflecting on tropical cyclone conditions in Mauritius report to be resident in the United Kingdom, and so no clear reviewer bias in terms of preparedness for storms can be detected.

Discussion and Concluding Remarks

These three case studies demonstrate that despite tropical cyclones occurring far less frequently than in the North Atlantic and East Pacific Oceans, the impact on the tourism sectors of these island nations and countries of the southern African subcontinent is significant (Durbarry, 2004). This in turn poses a considerable threat to the sustained GDP of these countries, as they each rely significantly on tourism in bolstering both economic stability and long-term growth (Durbarry, 2004; Rogerson, 2016). The relatively low frequency of storm landfall could arguably be a factor in accentuating the losses incurred through storm damage. The small composite dataset of storm landfall compiled through a combination of port records, ship logs and satellite imagery reduces the capacity for high-resolution modelling of storm trajectory, intensification and landfall location (Fitchett & Grab, 2014; Nash *et al.*, 2015). Second, their infrequent occurrence reduces the governmental urgency in building mitigatory infrastructure, or in developing disaster risk management plans that span forecasting, evacuation and rebuilding activities (Silva *et al.*, 2015; Fitchett *et al.*, 2016). Moreover, despite the significant and ever-growing contribution of tourism to the local economies, tourism sectors are perceived to be a luxury, and hence their restoration is not prioritised relative to more 'essential' sectors such as agriculture (Hänke & Barkmann, 2017).

The shortfalls in terms of forward planning and adaptation to long-term threats cannot be attributed to the governments of each country, or even the municipal management, alone. A sense of denialism regarding climate threats plagues the management of tourism accommodation establishments and tourism operators across southern Africa (Hoogendoorn *et al.*, 2016; Giddy *et al.*, 2017). Although much of the literature discusses future threats of climate change, which are perceived to occur beyond the lifespan of the tourism operation (Fitchett *et al.*, 2016), tropical cyclones represent more tangible immediate threats. However, disasters related to these storms are often seen as one-off events, so little adaptation follows. This is in part due to a lack of capital to do so, particularly when basic repairs from the storms are costly and inadequately covered by insurance (Fitchett *et al.*, 2015). However, as the responses from the survey following Tropical Cyclone Dineo indicate, there remains a persistent sentiment that the weather cannot be managed, and that freak events cannot be planned or controlled for. On a more positive note, the adaptation responses which have been initiated around stormwater management do appear to be well considered and will likely minimise at least the flood damage to the accommodation establishments in future storms.

Secondary effects of tropical cyclones resulting from damage to municipal road infrastructure and electricity networks result in damage to tourism sectors that is often longer in duration and incurs greater monetary costs than the damage incurred by individual establishments (Fitchett *et al.*, 2016). The monetary costs are both direct and indirect in nature, including the closure of accommodation establishments until roads and bridges are repaired, as was the case following Tropical Cyclone

Dando, and the overall reduction in tourist visits to a region due to the loss of aesthetic quality of the destination, difficulties in traversing the damaged roads, and concerns surrounding further flood events. Although respondents of the questionnaires concerning both Tropical Cyclones Dando and Dineo reflect on these challenges, there is no clear indication that the accommodation establishments themselves are mobilising to engage with the government to improve long-term adaptation measures. Instead, as with their own accommodation establishments, they are more concerned with immediate repairs to the damaged infrastructure, which, due to the rapid response required, often prohibits longer-term planning and mitigatory changes to the systems (Silva *et al.*, 2015).

The case study from the SWIO islands indicates tourist awareness of tropical cyclones, particularly in the wealthier and more prominent tourist destination of Mauritius. The textual content of these mentions of tropical cyclone conditions within the Tripadvisor reviews is of interest. Many are brief and factual, capturing the occurrence of a tropical cyclone but with no details of the associated weather conditions. Those which do mention the weather predominantly reflect on the heavy rainfall and high wind speeds, often coupled with commentary on the seasonality of the storms, indicating a reasonably high level of climatological awareness. Notably, none of the reviews comment on damage caused by these storms to either the accommodation that they are staying in or to the local or regional infrastructure. A few of the respondents comment on being unable to take part in outdoor activities. As these represent an important component of the tourism sector in these island nations, such impacts likely carry a financial burden.

The contemporary impact of SWIO tropical cyclones on the tourism sectors of southern African countries is of heightened concern under climate change. Global projections suggest an increase in both the frequency and severity of tropical cyclones, with a heightened variability in storm occurrence (Webster *et al.*, 2005). Analysis for the SWIO indicates a negligible change in the mean annual storm numbers, but significant changes to the location of landfall and the severity of these storms (Malherbe *et al.*, 2013; Fitchett & Grab, 2014; Nash *et al.*, 2015). The first Category 5 tropical cyclone was recorded for the region within the last 30 years, some 80 years after the first Category 5 storms for the North Atlantic and North Pacific Oceans. Over this three-decade period, the number of Category 5 storms has increased, and their genesis and landfall positions have migrated southwards. These shifts in storm occurrence have been recorded across all storm intensity classes, heightening the storm risk for southern Mozambique, South Africa and Mauritius. Meanwhile, an intensification in the mean sea surface temperature of the Mozambique Channel has resulted in a heightened number of storms forming within this region, which in turn increases the storm risk to the Comoros (Chikoore *et al.*, 2015). Concurrent to these changes in tropical cyclone formation has been an increase in the coastal populations of each of these countries, and the number and size of accommodation establishments. Thus, not only is there a greater threat of high-intensity tropical cyclones, but also a greater potential for damage, particularly to the tourism sector (Silva *et al.*, 2015).

Adequate adaptation to the heightened threats of tropical cyclones to the SWIO and the southern African subcontinent requires an accurate knowledge of contemporary storm intensity and return rate, high-resolution projections for changes in storm intensity and landfall probability under climate change, real-time forecasting, and suitable adaptation responses (Fitchett & Grab, 2014; Silva *et al.*, 2015). The case studies from Tropical Cyclone Dineo in southern Africa and the analysis of Tripadvisor reviews for the SWIO indicate the importance of preparedness for tropical cyclone associated wind and rainfall in mitigating the detriments to the tourism sector. Efforts to model tropical cyclone intensity, landfall location and timing for the region are improving considerably (Malherbe *et al.*, 2013; Maoyi *et al.*, 2018). However, until such model outputs are coupled with a high-resolution risk map of tourism operations and real-time communication about both storm threat and impending cyclone landfall, these scientific outputs are unlikely to drive a shift in mitigatory response among tourism operators (Fitchett *et al.*, 2016). Key challenges for the region therefore involve accurate storm forecasting, an understanding of climate change impacts on tropical cyclones, and effective communication of these climatic dynamics to the tourism sector.

References

Ash, K.D. and Matyas, C.J. (2012) The influences of ENSO and the subtropical Indian Ocean dipole on tropical cyclone trajectories in the Southwestern Indian Ocean. *International Journal of Climatology* 32 (1), 41–56.

Astier, N., Plu, M. and Claud, C. (2015) Associations between tropical cyclone activity in the Southwest Indian Ocean and El Niño Southern Oscillation. *Atmospheric Science Letters* 16 (4), 506–511.

Booyens, I. and Visser, G. (2010) Tourism SMME development on the urban fringe: The case of Parys, South Africa. *Urban Forum* 21 (4), 367–385.

Burns, J.M., Subrahmanyam, B., Nyadjro, E.S. and Murty, V.S.N. (2016) Tropical cyclone activity over the Southwest Tropical Indian Ocean. *Journal of Geophysical Research: Oceans* 121 (8), 6389–640.

Chikoore, H., Vermeulen, J.H. and Jury, M.R. (2015) Tropical cyclones in the Mozambique Channel: January – March 2012. *Natural Hazards* 77 (3), 2081–2095.

Durbarry, R. (2004) Tourism and economic growth: The case of Mauritius. *Tourism Economics* 10 (4), 389–401.

Elsner, J.B. and Liu, K.B. (2003) Examining the ENSO-typhoon hypothesis. *Climate Research* 25 (1), 43–54.

Enenkel, M., Papp, A., Veit, E. and Voigt, S. (2017) Top-down and bottom-up: A global approach to strengthen local disaster resilience. In *Proceedings of the IEEE Global Humanitarian Technology Conference,* San Jose, CA, USA, 537–543.

Fitchett, J.M. (2018) Recent emergence of CAT5 Tropical Cyclones in the South Indian Ocean. *South African Journal of Science* 114 (11–12), 1–6.

Fitchett, J.M. and Grab, S.W. (2014) A 66-year tropical cyclone record for south-east Africa: Temporal trends in a global context. *International Journal of Climatology* 34 (13), 3604–3615.

Fitchett, J.M., Grant, B. and Hoogendoorn, G. (2016) Climate change threats to two low-lying South African coastal towns: Risks and perceptions. *South African Journal of Science* 112 (5–6), 1–9.

Fitchett, J.M., Hoogendoorn, G. and Swemmer, A.M. (2016) Economic costs of the 2012 floods on tourism in the Mopani District Municipality, South Africa. *Transactions of the Royal Society of South Africa* 71 (2), 187–194.

Giddy, J.K., Fitchett, J.M. and Hoogendoorn, G. (2017) A case study into the preparedness of white-water tourism to severe climatic events in Southern Africa. *Tourism Review International* 21 (2), 213–220.

Goldenberg, S.B., Landsea, C.W., Mestas-Nunez, A.M. and Gray, W.M. (2001) The recent increase in Atlantic hurricane activity: Causes and implications. *Science* 293 (5529), 474–479.

Hänke, H. and Barkmann, J. (2017) Insurance function of livestock, farmers coping capacity with crop failure in southwestern Madagascar. *World Development* 96, 264–275.

Ho, C.H., Kim, J.H., Jeong, J.H., Kim, H.S. and Chen, D. (2006) Variation of tropical cyclone activity in the South Indian Ocean: El Niño–Southern Oscillation and Madden-Julian Oscillation effects. *Journal of Geophysical Research: Atmospheres* 111 (D22), https://doi.org/10.1029/2006JD007289.

Hoogendoorn, G. and Fitchett, J.M. (2018) Tourism and climate change in Africa: A review of threats and adaptation. *Current Issues in Tourism* 21 (7), 752–759.

Hoogendoorn, G., Grant, B. and Fitchett, J.M. (2016) Disjunct perceptions? Climate change threats in two-low lying South African coastal towns. *Bulletin of Geography. Socio-economic Series* 31 (31), 59–71.

Jury, M.R., Pathack, B., Wang, B., Powell, M. and Raholijao N. (1993) A destructive Tropical cyclone season in the SW Indian Ocean: January–February 1984. *South African Geographical Journal* 75 (2), 53–59.

Karuaihe, S., Tsoanamatsie, N., Mashile, L., Molokomme, M. and Nhemachena, C. (2015) The contribution of the tourism industry to the local economy. In M. Kozak and N. Kozak (eds) *Tourism Economics: A Practical Perspective* (pp. 39–54). Newcastle upon Tyne: Cambridge Scholar Publishing.

Kates, R.W., Colten, C.E., Laska, S. and Leatherman, S.P. (2006) Reconstruction of New Orleans after Hurricane Katrina: A research perspective. *PNAS* 103 (40), 14653–14660.

Malherbe, J., Engelbrecht, F.A. and Landman, W.A. (2013) Projected changes in tropical cyclone climatology in the Southwest Indian Ocean region under enhanced anthropogenic forcing. *Climate Dynamics* 40, 2967–2886.

Malherbe, J., Engelbrecht, F.A., Landman, W.A. and Engelbrecht, C.J. (2012) Tropical systems from the southwest Indian Ocean making landfall over the Limpopo River Basin, Southern Africa: A historical perspective. *International Journal of Climatology* 32 (7), 1018–1032.

Maoyi, M.L., Abiodun, B.J., Prusa, J.M. and Veitch, J.J. (2018) Simulating the characteristics of tropical cyclones over the South West Indian Ocean using a Stretched-Grid Global Climate Model. *Climate Dynamics* 50 (5–6), 1581–1596.

Matyas, C.J. (2015) Tropical cyclone formation and motion in the Mozambique Channel. *International Journal of Climatology* 35 (3), 375–390.

Maunganidze, G. and Mawere, M. (2017) Disasters, the marginalised and media preparedness in Zimbabwe: Reflections on the Masvingo-based community media organizations' coverage of the 2017 Cyclone Dineo victims. In M. Mawere (ed.) *The Political Economy of Poverty, Vulnerability and Disaster Risk Management:*

Building Bridges of Resilience, Entrepreneurship and Development in Africa's 21st Century (pp. 361–386). Bamenda: Langaa Research & Publishing CIG.

Mavume, A.F., Rydberg, L., Rouault, M. and Lutjeharms, J.R.E. (2009) Climatology and landfall of tropical cyclones in the South-West Indian Ocean. *West Indian Journal of Marine Science* 8 (1), 15–36.

Nash, D.J., Pribyl, K., Klein, J., Endfield, G.H., Kniveton, D.R. and Adamson, G.C. (2015) Tropical cyclone activity over Madagascar during the late nineteenth century. *International Journal of Climatology* 35 (11), 3249–3261.

Nelwamondo, T. (2010) Tourism Development Through Strategic Planning for Non-metropolitan Small to Medium size Accommodation Facilities in Limpopo Province, South Africa. PhD, University of Pretoria.

Nunkoo, R. and Ramkissoon, H. (2010a) Small island urban tourism: A residents' perspective. *Current Issues in Tourism* 13 (1), 37–60.

Nunkoo, R. and Ramkissoon, H. (2010b) Modelling community support for a proposed integrated resort project. *Journal of Sustainable Tourism* 18 (2), 257–277.

Reason, C.J.C. (2007) Tropical cyclone Dera, the unusual 2000/01 tropical cyclone season in the Southwest Indian Ocean and associated rainfall anomalies over Southern Africa. *Meteorological and Atmospheric Physics* 97 (1–4), 181–188.

Resio, D.T. and Irish, J.L. (2015) Tropical cyclone storm surge risk. *Current Climate Change Reports* 1 (2), 74–84.

Rogerson, C.M. (2007) The challenges of developing adventure tourism in South Africa. *Africa Insight* 37 (2), 228–244.

Rogerson, C.M. (2016) Climate change, tourism and local economic development in South Africa. *Local Economy* 31 (1–2), 322–331.

Rogerson, C.M. and Hoogendoorn, G. (2014) VFR travel and second home tourism: The missing link? The case of South Africa. *Tourism Review International* 18 (3), 167–178.

Shabaan, I.A., Ramzy, Y.H. and Sharabassy, A.A. (2013) Tourism as a tool for economic development in poor countries: The case of the Comoros Islands. *African Journal of Business and Economic Research* 8 (1), 127–145.

Shanko, D. and Camberlin, P. (1998) The effects of the Southwest Indian Ocean tropical cyclones on Ethiopian drought. *International Journal of Climatology* 18 (12), 1373–1388.

Silva, J.A., Matyas, C.J. and Cunguara, B. (2015) Regional inequality and polarization in the context of concurrent extreme weather and economic shocks. *Applied Geography* 61, 105–116.

Vitart, F., Anderson, D. and Stockdale, T. (2003) Seasonal forecasting of tropical cyclone landfall over Mozambique. *Journal of Climate* 16 (23), 3932–3945.

Webster, P.J., Holland, G.J., Curry, J.A. and Chang, H.R. (2005) Changes in tropical cyclone number, duration, and intensity in a warming environment. *Science* 309 (5742), 1844–1846.

World Travel and Tourism Council (WTTC) (2017a) *Travel & Tourism Economic Impact 2017 Comoros*. [pdf] Available at https://www.wttc.org/-/media/files/reports/economic-impact-research/countries-2017/comoros2017.pdf

World Travel and Tourism Council (WTTC) (2017b) *Travel & Tourism Economic Impact 2017 Reunion*. [pdf] Available at https://www.wttc.org/-/media/files/reports/economic-impact-research/countries-2017/reunion2017.pdf

World Travel and Tourism Council (WTTC) (2017c) *Travel & Tourism Economic Impact 2017 Mauritius*. [pdf] Available at https://www.wttc.org/-/media/files/reports/economic-impact-research/countries-2017/mauritius2017.pdf

7 The Impact of Cyclones on Tourist Behaviour and Demand: Pam and Vanuatu

Minghui Sun and Simon Milne

Introduction

Most Pacific island tourism depends on nature-based resources, such as sun, sea, and sand alongside the allure of local culture (Harrison & Pratt, 2015). Natural disasters, such as cyclones, in these nations can cause huge economic losses. Apart from community and environmental damage associated with such events, tourists' travel desire may decrease because of concerns about safety, and uncertainty about the availability of accommodation and tourist activities.

The aim of this study is to provide a deeper understanding of the influence of a cyclone on tourist demand. Most severe natural disasters are sudden and unpredictable. Little empirical study has been done to compare the difference before and after disasters in terms of the nature of the impacts on tourism and visitor experiences (Pearlman & Melnik, 2008). Drawing on data from the Vanuatu International Visitor Survey, this chapter provides new academic insights into the impacts of cyclones on Pacific Island Countries (PICs) tourism and presents information that can also assist the local tourism industry and relevant government agencies in learning about the impacts of such a disaster and how to develop strategies for the future.

SIDS, Cyclone and Tourism

Small Island Developing States (SIDS) represent a distinct group of developing countries recognised by the United Nations Conference on Environment and Development (UNCED) in 1992. The common obstacles to economic growth in SIDS can be categorised as: small size; insularity or remoteness; environmental vulnerability; and socioeconomic factors

(Harrison & Pratt, 2015). Although South Pacific countries differ in population and land area, they all suffer from small internal markets, remoteness, high shipping costs, limited commodity exports, unemployment, and a limited skills-based labour market (Milne, 1992, 2013). Based on a sustainable economic base (aid and remittances), tourism is considered as an economic bonus that provides great opportunities for economic growth and employment (Milne, 1992, 2013).

Tourism is a key driver in the economies of South Pacific SIDS and it is becoming increasingly important to the local economies (Harrison & Pratt, 2015; Milne, 1992). In the South Pacific region, tourism is the largest export sector and offers great opportunities for economic growth, employment, and sustainable development (Jiang *et al.*, 2009; Milne, 1992). According to the latest data from the South Pacific Tourism Organisation (SPTO) (2017), the 12 following Pacific island nations – Cook Islands, Fiji, French Polynesia, New Caledonia, Niue, Palau, Papua New Guinea, Samoa, Solomon Islands, Tonga, Tuvalu and Vanuatu – welcomed 2,030,529 tourists in 2016, representing a 4% increase compared with 2015. Although the visitor arrivals to this region are small on a world scale, the small populations of the South Pacific countries mean that even small increases in visitor numbers can increase the ratios of visitors to local residents to high levels (Harrison & Pratt, 2015).

According to Bettencourt *et al.* (2006), the South Pacific is one of the most natural disaster prone regions on Earth. Bettencourt *et al.* (2006) reported 207 major natural disasters occurring in the Pacific region during 1995 to 2004, which affected 3.5 million people with an economic damage cost of US$6.5 billion. Natural disasters, including tsunamis, earthquakes and cyclones, affected island tourist destinations severely, and the ongoing challenge of climate change only exacerbates these issues (Becken, 2005; Becken *et al.*, 2014; Cioccio & Michael, 2007; Huebner & Milne, 2012). In addition to infrastructure damage, these above-mentioned natural disasters affect tourism demand hugely in terms of the tangible aspect of visitor arrivals, as well as the intangible aspect of destination image (Meheux & Parker, 2006). To date, only limited research has been done on the impact of natural disasters on South Pacific SIDS tourism from the perspective of visitor behaviour and characteristics exhibited before and after the event.

The Vanuatu Case

Vanuatu is an island nation consisting of 83 small islands. Vanuatu was a condominium administered by France and the United Kingdom jointly since 1906; the country gained political independence in 1980 (de Burlo, 1996). The economy of Vanuatu is heavily dependent on external donor assistance (Milne, 1992, 2008, 2013).

Tourism accounts for about 20% of Vanuatu's GDP (Walters & Mair, 2015). Since the establishment of the National Tourism Office in 1982, tourism in Vanuatu increased steadily in the last two decades (de Burlo, 1996). With 42.4% of total employment provided by the tourism sector, the sector was identified as one of the key areas for National Focus in the Priorities and Action Agenda of Vanuatu 2006–2015 (Jiang *et al.*, 2009). Economic leakage in Vanuatu's tourism industry is significant; the main accommodation and restaurants are entirely owned and operated by for-eigners, so they cannot generate much local income and employment (Milne, 1992). Tourism in Vanuatu offers typical South Pacific experi-ences based around sun, sand and sea (Milne *et al.*, 2017; Wilkinson, 1989). Apart from that, Vanuatu offers a strong French culture, war relics, and land-based physical attractions including a live volcano in Tanna (Milne, 1992, 2013). The main tourist source countries are Australia, New Zealand, New Caledonia and Japan (de Burlo, 1996). However, tourism arrivals to Vanuatu are not stable because of cyclone damage, unstable political systems, and disruptions in air services (de Burlo, 1996; Milne, 1992, 2013).

Vanuatu is vulnerable to a range of natural disasters, most notably cyclones. According to the Vanuatu Meteorology and Geo-hazard Department, Australian Bureau of Meteorology, and Commonwealth Scientific and Industrial Research Organisation (CSIRO) (2011), 94 tropi-cal cyclones passed within 400 km of Port Vila from 1969 to 2010, which is an average of two to three cyclones per season. Cyclone damage has been significant for this country. According to the International Monetary Fund (IMF) (2015), 16 major tropical cyclones occurred in Vanuatu from 1980 to 2014, causing a total damage of US$205 million. In the Vanuatu region, the frequency of tropical cyclones showed a decrease by the late 21st century but there was an increase in the proportion of the more intense storms (Vanuatu Meteorology and Geo-hazard Department, Australian Bureau of Meteorology & CSIRO, 2011). The National Disaster Management Office (NDMO), established in 2013, is the govern-ment agency tasked with coordinating disaster preparedness, response and recovery operations. The NDMO works with local and international NGOs to coordinate disaster risk reduction and disaster risk management programs. However, the remote location and limited institutional capacity of the country hinders the efficiency of disaster recovery programmes (Meheux & Parker, 2006).

Cyclone Pam, a devastating category-five storm, hit Vanuatu on 13 March 2015. With wind speeds of up to 250 kilometres per hour, 90% of the housing stock was severely damaged or destroyed, and about half of Vanuatu's population of roughly 270,000 people was affected (IMF, 2015). As one of the most important economic sectors in Vanuatu, the impact of Cyclone Pam on tourism development is apparent (Dornan, 2015). By June 2015, tourism arrivals by air were down by 24% and arrivals by cruise ship were down by 56% from a year earlier (Asian Development Bank (ADB), 2015). The ADB (2015) estimated that the economy's output in 2015 would be US$4 million lower than in the previous year. With the majority of hotels and resorts experiencing severe damage to their facilities, the government struggled to provide assistance and the support of donor agencies was required (Neef & Wasi, 2017).

Method

This study draws on survey data collected by the Vanuatu International Visitor Survey (IVS) which was funded by the International Finance Corporation (IFC) of the World Bank (2015–2017) and implemented by the New Zealand Tourism Research Institute (NZTRI). This project provides a detailed understanding of tourists visiting Vanuatu and the impacts associated with them. The survey also includes a section that focuses on visitor satisfaction with individual accommodation operators and provides detailed satisfaction data on a broad range of experiences. The IVS continues to run until at least 2020 with current funding from New Zealand's Ministry of Foreign Affairs and Trade through PACER PLUS regional funds and the Vanuatu Strategic Tourism Action Plan.

An online IVS is used to gather vital data on the visitor profile, satisfaction levels and economic impacts. The questionnaire is available in three languages: English, French and Chinese (Mandarin). Visitors to Vanuatu are contacted via email and asked to complete the survey within a few weeks of the completion of their visit. The IVS uses a 'crowd sourcing' approach to maximise awareness of, and response to, the survey. This approach involves industry and a range of government stakeholders working together to achieve maximum visitor awareness of the survey and to capture a high number of email addresses. Development of industry awareness of (and buy-in to) the project is an integral part of the work. Not only is this approach cost effective, but it also increases industry and government awareness of the importance of tourism research and uses research as a tool to strengthen and develop networks.

By early 2018, the survey had generated over 15,000 individual responses. This chapter, however, only focuses on visitors for the period directly before and after the cyclone. The survey was originally scheduled to run continuously from January to December 2015 and then beyond. Due to the impact of Cyclone Pam, the work was halted in the period of mid-March to May and recommenced from 25 June 2015. Thus, data collection actually consisted of two stages over eight months. The first stage (pre-cyclone) survey commenced in January 2015. Until mid-March 2015, 4917 visitors were contacted by email to take part in the survey and 877 responses were received with a conversion rate of 18%. The second survey period (post-cyclone) covered visitors who visited Vanuatu during May to

July 2015. Over this three-month period, of the 8273 visitors approached, 1060 responses were received, resulting in a response rate of 13%.

These two datasets are used to make comparisons between visitor characteristics and behaviour prior to and post Cyclone Pam. The post-cyclone data reflects an industry very much in the process of rebuilding from the natural disaster. The pre-cyclone data is considered as a point of reference to monitor the recovery of the Vanuatu tourism industry. Independent samples t-tests were conducted to examine whether there were significant differences between pre-cyclone and post-cyclone visitors in terms of their visitor experiences.

Findings and Discussion

More females than males completed the survey (Table 7.1). This gender imbalance with online survey respondents has been seen in

Table 7.1 Demographics

Demographics	Pre-cyclone		Post-cyclone	
	n	%	*n*	%
Gender:				
Female	444	59	560	58
Male	312	41	404	42
Age group:				
18–29	159	21	156	16
30–39	153	20	174	18
40–49	165	22	221	23
50–59	178	23	236	24
60–69	79	10	146	15
70–79	19	3	37	4
80+	5	1	3	0
Annual household income (US$):				
<$50,000	185	30	293	38
$50,001–100,000	216	35	268	35
$100,001–150,000	120	19	132	17
$150,001–200,000	58	9	46	6
$200,001–250,000	31	5	14	2
$250,001–300,000	4	1	6	1
>$300,001	12	2	5	1
Mean annual household income (US$):	$94,239		$76,242	
From:				
Australia	463	62	515	53
New Zealand	156	21	297	31
Pacific	58	8	76	8
Europe	33	4	33	3
Asia	20	3	14	1
US/Canada	16	2	24	2

*Source: Vanuatu international visitor survey 2015.

previous studies (Smith, 2008). This is also in line with broader experiences in online IVS research in the South Pacific conducted by NZTRI, for instance, the Cook Islands international visitor survey 2012–2017. There is a significant difference for age groups (p < 0.000) between the pre- and post-cyclone periods. More elderly people (60 plus age bracket) and fewer young people (18–39 years old) visited Vanuatu after the cyclone. There are statistically significant differences between two groups in relation to their income and nationalities (p < 0.001 and p < 0.000). The average household income for pre-cyclone visitors is higher than post-cyclone visitors. The majority of the visitors surveyed in both stages come from Australia, while fewer Australian visitors and more New Zealanders visited Vanuatu after the cyclone.

There is a statistically significant association between pre-cyclone and post-cyclone visitors in terms of the main reason for visiting (P < 0.000) (Table 7.2). The impact of Cyclone Pam can be seen with 13% fewer holidaymakers and a higher percentage of business and conference travellers. It is also clear that more volunteers arrived in Vanuatu to help with the recovery effort. Further analysis shows that visitors from Pacific countries were more likely to travel to Vanuatu after the cyclone for volunteer work, or business and conference activities, than those from Australia, New Zealand, and long-haul markets. While there is a slight decrease in the percentage of those who are first time visitors after the cyclone, it is not statistically significant. Further analysis shows that more first-time visitors come from other Pacific countries after the cyclone, but fewer first-time visitors come from Australia, New Zealand and long-haul markets. This finding is consistent with the purpose of the visit – more people from

Table 7.2 Visitor characteristics

Visitor Characteristics	Pre-cyclone		Post-cyclone	
	n	%	n	%
Main reason for visit:				
Holiday	648	74	650	61
Visiting friends or relatives	77	9	76	7
Business	51	6	109	10
Honeymoon	35	4	19	2
Volunteering	20	2	96	9
Conference	20	2	38	4
Education	17	2	25	2
Wedding party	8	1	46	4
Times visited Vanuatu:				
First time	456	60	565	58
1 or 2 times	158	21	217	22
3 or 4 times	55	7	64	7
5+ times	85	11	122	13

Source: Vanuatu international visitor survey 2015.

other Pacific countries come to Vanuatu for business and conferences, and also more volunteering activities happened after the cyclone.

There is a statistically significant association between pre- and post-cyclone visitors in terms of the sources of information used to find out about Vanuatu as a tourist destination ($P < 0.000$) (Table 7.3). After the cyclone, visitors are more likely to rely on their family members and own experience to find out information about Vanuatu, and rely less on general websites. Similar trends can be seen with respect to the information sources used for planning trips. Visitors were using more information obtained from their own experience and 'other' information sources for post-cyclone travelling, such as conferences, business partners, and local people. This indicates that people tend to seek more first-hand information when they decide to travel to a place where a disaster has occurred rather than rely on potentially outdated information from secondary sources.

Visitors were asked to think about 'why you chose to visit Vanuatu' using a 5-point Likert scale. The quiet and relaxing atmosphere is ranked as the most influential factor, followed by beaches, accessibility, water-based activities, and natural beauty. Post-cyclone, these factors still dominate the decision-making process, but with a notable drop on almost all factors (Table 7.4). Instead, business and conference opportunities

Table 7.3 Source of information

Source of Travel Information	Pre-cyclone		Post-cyclone	
	n	%	*n*	%
How find out about Vanuatu:				
Friends/family	293	34	398	38
Previous experience	249	29	332	32
General travel websites	147	17	120	12
Travel agent/brochures	98	11	113	11
Vanuatu Travel website	28	3	23	2
Magazines and newspaper articles	20	2	22	2
Television or radio programmes	16	2	24	2
Social media	11	1	15	1
Main information sources used for planning the trip*:				
General travel websites	418	48	447	42
Friends/family	371	43	454	43
Previous Vanuatu visits	258	30	345	33
Vanuatu Tourism website	261	30	302	28
Travel agent/travel brochures	231	27	284	27
Other sources	56	6	119	11
Social media	60	7	90	8
Magazine and newspaper articles	47	5	48	5
Travel books	18	2	17	2
Television or radio programmes	19	2	13	1

*Source: Vanuatu international visitor survey 2015.
*Multiple response.

Table 7.4 Decision-making factors

Why you chose to visit Vanuatu	Pre-cyclone		Post-cyclone	
	Mean	SD	Mean	SD
Quiet and relaxing atmosphere**	3.9	1.1	3.5	1.3
Beaches and swimming**	3.6	1.1	3.2	1.2
Accessible**	3.5	1.2	3.3	1.3
Snorkelling and diving**	3.4	1.3	3.0	1.4
Nature attractions/volcano/ecotourism/photography*	3.4	1.2	3.2	1.2
Affordable*	3.3	1.2	3.2	1.3
Culture and history	3.2	1.0	3.2	1.1
Food*	2.5	1.2	2.4	1.2
Friends and family in Vanuatu	2.1	1.6	2.2	1.6
Fishing	1.6	1.0	1.5	0.9
Business or conference**	1.5	1.2	1.8	1.5

*Source: Vanuatu international visitor survey 2015.
*Statistically significant difference from pre-cyclone: ** $P < 0.000$; * $P < 0.05$.

become more influential than in pre-cyclone trips. There are statistically significant differences between pre-cyclone and post-cyclone visitors in nearly all aspects listed ($P < 0.05$ or $P < 0.000$) except 'culture and history', 'friends and family in Vanuatu' and 'fishing'. It is evident that the disaster affected the visitors' decision-making factors dramatically. The changes in the factors that influence the choice of choosing Vanuatu is evident. Destination image is a critical factor during the decision making process when tourists think of their potential trips (Pearlman & Melnik, 2008).

There is a statistically significant association between pre- and post-cyclone visitors in terms of expenditure ($P < 0.000$) (Table 7.5). The post-cyclone period shows a considerable decline in tourist spend in Vanuatu. Before the cyclone, visitors to Vanuatu spent US$92 per person per day in the country. Post cyclone, visitors to Vanuatu spent US$75 per person per day. Reconstruction and recovery activities were already underway; however, some tourist activities were still not available during this period, and this was one reason for the lower expenditure.

In contrast, prepaid visitor spend increased after the cyclone. This reflects a number of factors ranging from decreased room capacity, the focus on business and aid travellers who often have many costs paid for by their organisations before arrival, and the fact that discounted packages at many resorts were unavailable in the short term.

Visitors were asked to rate their level of satisfaction with nine different statements and the overall satisfaction relating to their most recent visit to Vanuatu using a 5-point Likert scale (Table 7.6). There is a statistically significant association between pre- and post-cyclone visitors in terms of the overall satisfaction ($P < 0.05$), and 'General quality of service', 'Taxis/car/bus/car rental/ground transport', 'Local handicrafts/artwork', 'Value

Table 7.5 Expenditure

Expenditure	Pre-cyclone		Post-cyclone	
	n	%	*n*	%
Prepaid expenditure (US$):				
$1–499	66	9	131	14
$500–999	215	29	315	34
$1000–1499	215	29	212	23
$1500–1999	118	16	138	15
$2000–2499	79	11	64	7
$2500–2999	13	2	22	2
$3000–3499	13	2	14	2
$3500 or more	16	2	29	3
Prepaid expenditure (US$):	n = 736		n = 925	
Covering people	1820		2131	
Mean expenditure (per person)	Mean: $1330		Mean: $1284	
Local expenditure (US$):	n = 631		n = 825	
Covering people	1558		1793	
Food and beverage (restaurant, café)**	28		23	
Accommodation*	24		20	
Domestic travel within Vanuatu**	8		4	
Tours/tour operator services*	7		7	
Taxis/bus/car hire*	6		5	
Supermarket/general store items*	6		6	
Entertainment activities/casinos*	2		2	
Handicraft, souvenirs, artwork	3		3	
Services (e.g. massage, hairdressing, spa)**	2		1	
Purchases of clothing (incl. T shirt)*	2		2	
Duty free shop (alcohol, tobacco, cosmetics)	2		2	
Internet and telecommunication	1		1	
Purchases of watches & jewellery	1		1	
Local food from the market	1		2	
Total per person per day (average)	92		77	

*Source: Vanuatu international visitor survey 2015.
*Statistically significant difference from pre-cyclone: ** $P < 0.000$; * $P < 0.05$.

for money' and 'General shopping opportunities' ($P < 0.05$, or $P < 0.000$). The data reveals that visitors expressed a higher level of satisfaction when visiting Vanuatu after the cyclone. This could well be because the tourists showed a higher level of tolerance during post-cyclone times due to a clear understanding that there were bigger issues at play and that staff and management in the industry were facing significant challenges both outside and inside the workplace.

The Vanuatu IVS contains open-ended questions that ask visitors to discuss aspects of their visit that were most/least appealing and to also provide thoughts on how their experience could have been improved (Table 7.7). The open-ended responses were analysed using NVivo and categorised according to key words and phrases. The key themes were then presented as a percentage of the total number of responses provided.

Table 7.6 Satisfaction

Satisfaction	Pre-cyclone		Post-cyclone	
	Mean	SD	Mean	SD
Satisfaction with the following:				
Variety of things to see and do	4.0	0.8	4.0	0.9
General quality of service**	3.9	0.9	4.0	0.9
Taxis/car/bus/car rental/ground transport**	3.7	1.0	3.9	1.0
Restaurants, cafes, bars, evening entertainment	3.6	1.0	3.7	1.0
Visitor information in Vanuatu (incl. signage)	3.5	1.0	3.5	0.9
Local handicrafts/artwork*	3.4	1.0	3.5	1.0
Value for money*	3.4	1.1	3.5	1.0
Internet/phone availability, cost and coverage	3.1	1.1	3.2	1.1
General shopping opportunities*	3.0	1.0	3.2	1.0
Rubbish collection and general cleanliness	3.0	1.2	3.0	1.1
Overall satisfaction with Vanuatu	4.2	0.9	4.4	0.8

*Source: Vanuatu international visitor survey 2015.
*Statistically significant difference from pre-cyclone: ** $P < 0.000$; * $P < 0.05$.

Table 7.7 Most appealing aspects of Vanuatu

Most Appealing Aspects	Pre-cyclone		Post-cyclone	
	n	%	n	%
Local people	375	46	591	59
Activities/attractions/entertainment	316	39	300	30
Environment	299	37	279	28
Atmosphere	95	12	118	12
Accommodation	71	9	57	6
Food and beverage	70	9	62	6
Level of service	66	8	43	4
Culture and history	46	6	49	5
Convenience of Vanuatu as a destination	39	5	33	3
Un-commercial	31	4	19	2
Overall good experience	29	4	11	1
Value for money	18	2	6	1
Safety	16	2	17	2

*Source: Vanuatu international visitor survey 2015.
* Share of respondents who made a comment that falls into each theme. Respondents could give more than one answer, so total does not add up to 100%.

For both datasets, the most appealing elements of the Vanuatu experience are considered to be the friendly local people, attractions and activities, entertainment and events, the beautiful natural environment, and quiet and relaxing atmosphere. While rankings remain similar for post periods, it is clear that the focus on local people increases significantly post-cyclone while the percentage of responses emphasising activities and environmental features as being the most appealing aspects decreases significantly.

For some visitors (7%), the most appealing part of their trip was to see for themselves how the locals had recovered from Cyclone Pam. Some of these visitors were surprised by how normal the scenery looked, or how happy and friendly the local people were, even though the cyclone had happened only a few months earlier. The comments included:

'Despite the extensive damage incurred, it was surprising to see the place appearing relatively unscathed by the cyclone'.
'Given the cyclone only two months previously, the people were all so friendly, as had been the case in previous visits'.
'We travelled three months after Cyclone Pam. We were very surprised that the people still had a wonderful smile on their faces even though they were still dealing with the clean-up and loss of their homes'.
'We were some of the first visitors following the cyclone and were very impressed with the work completed on this outing. The resort still had damaged buildings but we were accommodated in the best they had'.

Visitors were also asked, 'What did you find least appealing about Vanuatu on your most recent visit?' (Table 7.8). The least appealing elements of the Vanuatu experience relate to public services, facilities and infrastructure, rubbish, cleanliness and natural environment care, and the price of goods and services. It is notable that fewer post-cyclone comments focused on the price of goods and services, attractions and activities, local people and standard of service, transportation, and accommodation. Tourists are less likely in general to mention negative elements when there

Table 7.8 Least appealing aspects of Vanuatu

Least Appealing Aspects	Pre-cyclone		Post-cyclone	
	n	%	n	%
Public services and facilities	174	23	260	28
Rubbish, cleanliness, natural environment care	165	21	199	21
Price of goods and services	141	18	140	15
Attractions and activities	83	11	30	3
Food and beverages	88	11	93	10
Local people and standard of service	77	10	42	4
Rental cars or scooters, transport	78	10	59	6
Accommodation	51	7	39	4
Shopping experience	40	5	25	4
Cruise ships	30	4	7	1
Stray animals, mosquitoes/flies and diseases	31	4	14	1
Social divide and other social issues	25	3	36	4
Weather	23	3	35	4
Flight-related issues	16	2	19	2
Safety-related issues	10	1	16	2

*Source: Vanuatu international visitor survey 2015.
* Share of respondents who made a comment that falls into each theme. Respondents could give more than one answer, so total does not add up to 100%.

are clearly broader constraints and issues at play. In particular, visitors are less likely to comment on service-related issues. Because so few activities were available, there was a clear drop in mentions in this category.

A total of 11% of responses mentioned specifically that the direct effects of Cyclone Pam were the least appealing aspect of their stay. Respondents commented on the rubbish and damage left over from the cyclone, the fact that many shops or accommodation providers were still closed, the lack of fresh produce, and the devastating impact of the cyclone for local people. Comments included:

'Due to Pam there was very little variety and a lot of resorts were closed'.
'Availability of fresh produce had been effected by cyclone'.
'This time, possibly due to cyclone Pam there was a lot of rubbish everywhere which is such a shame and the roads were terrible. The road to Island Magic had been completely washed away in parts and where there are roads most were very rough'.
'The leftover stranded boats from Cyclone Pam in the Harbour. It dropped my spirits/made me feel sad during my holiday'.

When asked if there was anything that could have improved their visit to Vanuatu (Table 7.9), most suggestions mentioned by respondents, pre- and post-cyclone, focused on public services and infrastructure, entrance fees/value for money, food quality and price, entertainment and activities. Post-cyclone visitors are, however, less likely to suggest areas for improvement than their pre-cyclone counterparts, especially around areas such as value for money and service standards.

A number of respondents provided suggestions specifically relating to recovery management related to Cyclone Pam and several also expressed an understanding of the challenges presented by the situation:

Table 7.9 Suggestions to improve the visit

Suggestions to Improve the Visit	Pre-cyclone		Post-cyclone	
	n	%	n	%
Public services and infrastructure	130	32	133	30
Charges, entrance fee, value for money	63	16	39	9
Local people, standards of service	46	11	35	8
Entertainment, activities, transport	37	9	41	9
Food quality and price	38	9	38	9
Stayed longer and see more	33	8	38	9
Environment	29	7	40	9
Accommodation	23	6	24	5
Flights	22	5	25	6
Shopping experience	22	5	11	3

*Source: Vanuatu international visitor survey 2015.
* Share of respondents who made a comment that falls into each theme. Respondents could give more than one answer, so total does not add up to 100%.

'More aid for repairs/clean up after cyclone...Evidence of where aid is spent'.

'A lot of things were not open but we did understand after the cyclone'.

'More budget accommodation/options. Completely understand if prices have gone up since Pam'.

'I understand that cyclone Pam caused devastated some areas and therefore some attractions were not there but please tell tourists. Don't take their money and try to cover up with something else'.

A higher percentage of tourists visiting post-cyclone say they would like to pay a visit again in the future. In addition, more visitors from this group said that they would like to visit the outer islands when they revisit Vanuatu when compared to the pre-cyclone counterparts. Qualitative data from the IVS also showed a number of tourists who were motivated to help local people to recover from the disaster and who plan to take actions in the future – such as donating to local schools.

Conclusions and a Way Forward

This case of Cyclone Pam and its impact on Vanuatu visitor behaviour provides empirical findings about the impact of such events on tourist behaviour by comparing and contrasting pre-cyclone and post-cyclone datasets. It is hard to predict the path and strength of a cyclone in advance. Thus, it is important to learn from previous disasters to plan emergency procedures and recovery strategies. When a natural disaster occurs, the destination can react more efficiently and effectively with a proper tourism recovery plan.

The IVS data shows that people tend to seek information from personal contacts and connections after a cyclone. It is also important for local government and media to provide timely and accurate information to the public and to provide 'on-site' updates and information.

The IVS responses reveal that the image of Vanuatu as a tourism destination was affected by Cyclone Pam. Post-cyclone tourists note the main factors influencing their decision to visit are the quiet and relaxing atmosphere, beautiful natural environment, beaches and swimming, snorkelling and diving. While these factors dominate pre-cyclone, their role in shaping the decision-making process is less important. Pearlman and Melnik (2008) have confirmed the important effect of mass media on destination image information. Also, as Walters and Mair (2015) indicated recently, media plays an important role in drawing awareness to the natural disaster, and it also shapes tourist perceptions about the destination. Thus, it is critical for media to maintain a balance between positive and negative news. Although the Vanuatu Tourism Office started a social media campaign using the hashtag #VanuatuStillSmiles to deliver a positive image (Neef & Wasi, 2017), the majority of images of Vanuatu at the international level showed houses and food crops completely destroyed and a devastated waterfront in Port Vila. Further research is required to better understand perceptions of destination image, and to see how long the negative image can be reduced or mitigated.

Visitor spend in-country reduced significantly in the wake of the cyclone. Tourist expenditure for post-cyclone trips is lower than pre-cyclone trips due to the lack of things to do and because supplies may not always be available and sufficient.

It is also important to note the specific attraction of nature as an appealing aspect for visitors to Vanuatu. This reinforces the fact that careful environmental planning is needed to preserve and restore the natural beauty of the destination. Marketing messages should clearly contain information that can convince tourists that these natural features, while diminished in the short term, will 'bounce back'.

The IVS data also indicates that post-cyclone visitors show a higher level of satisfaction than pre-cyclone visitors. We believe this is in large part because any problems experienced are tempered by an awareness of the greater challenges facing the destination and its people. A similar trend can be seen in some of the qualitative analysis conducted with the IVS data: tourists showed great compassion for the suffering of the local people. The results show a higher level of tolerance on infrastructure, price, and level of service than before the cyclone. Some tourists also express interest (and occasional concern) about the ways international aid is being used to help local people. It is important that destinations think carefully about how to leverage word of mouth from emotionally engaged visitors in the aftermath of events like Cyclone Pam. While visitors face reduced levels of activities post-cyclone, they tend to be less dissatisfied and to show a lower tendency to raise the least appealing aspects of their visit.

In the wake of the cyclone and related industry rebuilding, the areas that will require greatest future attention will be managing environmental quality, strengthening cultural experiences, and ensuring that food and accommodation services really represent good value for money. It is critical that service levels meet visitor expectations and it is clear that there are opportunities for improvement in this area.

One limitation of this study is that the research was not designed specifically to focus on disaster recovery investigation; rather, the data is drawn from an ongoing international visitor survey. Nevertheless, two similar data samples make it possible to compare visitor characteristics, expenditure, and satisfaction. It is notable that the level of satisfaction during post-cyclone trips is higher in some items relating to the recovery process. The bias might be generated because more business/conference visitors and volunteers came to Vanuatu after the cyclone. In order to explore factors that may influence the decision not to travel, further research should be done on those tourists who have not visited Vanuatu because of the cyclone, or cancelled their plans, to explore the influential factors of not visiting.

References

Asian Development Bank (ADB) (2015) Vanuatu: Economy. [online] Available at: http://www.adb.org/countries/vanuatu/economy

Becken, S. (2005) Harmonising climate change adaptation and mitigation: The case of tourist resorts in Fiji. *Global Environmental Change* 15 (4), 381–393.

Becken, S., Mahon, R., Rennie, H.G. and Shakeela, A. (2014) The tourism disaster vulnerability framework: An application to tourism in small island destinations. *Natural Hazards* 71 (1), 955–972.

Bettencourt, S., Croad, R., Freeman, P., Hay, J., Jones, R., King, P., Lal, P., Mearns, A. Miller, G., Pswarayi-Riddihough, I., Simpson, A., Teuatabo N., Trotz, U. and Van Aalst, M. (2006) *Not If But When: Adapting to Natural Hazards in the Pacific Islands Region – A Policy Note. 2006.* Washington DC: The World Bank, East Asia and Pacific Region, Pacific Islands Country Management Unit.

Cioccio, L. and Michael, E.J. (2007) Hazard or disaster: Tourism management for the inevitable in Northeast Victoria. *Tourism Management* 28 (1), 1–11.

de Burlo, C. (1996) Vanuatu. In C.M. Hall and S.J. Page (eds) *Tourism in the Pacific: Issues and Cases* (pp. 235–255). Boston MA: International Thomson Business Press.

Dornan, M. (2015) *Vanuatu After Cyclone Pam: The Economic Impact.* [Blog] DevPolicy Blog. Available at: http://devpolicy.org/vanuatu-after-cyclone-pam-the-economic-impact-20150410/

Harrison, D. and Pratt, S. (2015) Tourism in Pacific Island countries. In S. Pratt and D. Harrison (eds) *Tourism in Pacific Islands: Current Issues and Future Challenges* (pp. 3–21). Abingdon: Routledge.

Huebner, A. and Milne, S. (2012) Donor funding and climate change: Tourism adaptation in Kiribati and Tuvalu. In E. Fayos-Sola (ed.) *Knowledge Management in Tourism: Policy and Governance Applications* (pp. 193–208). Bingley: Emerald Group Publishing.

International Monetary Fund (IMF) (2015) *Regional Economic Outlook: Asia and Pacific.* Washington, DC: IMF.

Jiang, M., DeLacy, T. and Noakes, S. (2009) Tourism, the millennium development goals and climate change in the South Pacific Islands, paper presented at the meeting of the Millennium Development Goals: Old Problems, New Challenges, Melbourne, Australia, 30 November – 1 December 2009.

Meheux, K. and Parker, E. (2006) Tourist sector perceptions of natural hazards in Vanuatu and the implications for a small island developing state. *Tourism Management* 27 (1), 69–85.

Milne, S. (1992) Tourism and development in South Pacific microstates. *Annals of Tourism Research* 19 (2), 191–212.

Milne, S. (2008) Tourism. In D. Gay (ed.) *Vanuatu: Diagnostic Trade Integration Study 2008 Report.* Port Vila, Vanuatu: Integrated Framework Partnership 2008, 117–129.

Milne, S. (2013) Tourism. In M. Rappaport (ed.) *The Pacific Islands: Environment & Society* (2nd edn). Honolulu, HI: University of Hawaii Press, 392–400.

Milne, S., Deuchar, C., Berno, T., Taumnoepeau, S., Pusinelli, M. and Raymond, J. (2017) *Private Sector Investment in the Pacific: Final Report – September 2017.* Auckland, New Zealand: New Zealand Institute for Pacific Research.

Neef, A. and Wasi, S.A. (2017) *Disaster Response and Recovery of the Tourism Sector: The Case of Vanuatu in the Aftermath of 2015 Cyclone Pam.* Auckland, New Zealand: Development Studies.

Pearlman, D. and Melnik, O. (2008) Hurricane Katrina's effect on the perception of New Orleans leisure tourists. *Journal of Travel & Tourism Marketing* 25 (1), 58–67.

Smith, G. (2008) Does Gender Influence Online Survey Participation?: A Record-Linkage Analysis of University Faculty Online Survey Response Behavior. PhD, San José State University

South Pacific Tourism Organisation (SPTO) (2017) *Annual Review of Visitor Arrivals in Pacific Island Countries 2016*. [pdf] Suva, Fiji: SPTO. Available at: http://spto.org/resources/rtrc

Vanuatu Meteorology and Geo-hazard Department, Australian Bureau of Meteorology and Commonwealth Scientific and Industrial Research Organisation (CSIRO) (2011) *Current and Future Climate of Vanuatu*. [pdf] Available at: http://www.pacificclimatechangescience.org/wp-content/uploads/2013/06/15_PCCSP_Vanuatu_8pp.pdf

Walters, G. and Mair, J. (2015) *How Vanuatu's Tourism Industry Can Recover After Cyclone Pam*. The Conversation. [online] Available at: http://theconversation.com/how-vanuatus-tourism-industry-can-recover-after-cyclone-pam-38975

Wilkinson, P.F. (1989) Strategies for tourism in island microstates. *Annals of Tourism Research* 16 (2), 153–177.

8 Collaborative Structure and Actions in Tourism Disaster Management: The Case of Cyclone Marcia in Central Queensland, Australia

Yawei Jiang and Brent W. Ritchie

Introduction

In recent decades, a significant number of natural disasters have severely affected the physical world and damaged the tourism industry. A stable management environment is unrealistic for the tourism industry as very few destinations are immune from external threats (Carlsen & Hughes, 2008). The unique characteristics of the tourism industry make it difficult to recover after a disaster. The tourism industry comprises different sub-sectors that are interrelated and jointly contribute to visitors' travel experience, such as restaurants, transportation entities, accommodation, and attractions (Evans *et al.*, 2003). Negative impacts on one part of the tourism system can easily spread to other parts within the system due to their interconnectedness and interdependency (Laws & Prideaux, 2005). From an external perspective, tourism is highly susceptible to the wider operating environments because its current global scale makes it exposed to external impacts. Even small-scale crises in one part of the world can have negative impacts on tourism in other parts of the world (Ritchie, 2004) due to their 'ripple effects' (Heath, 1998).

Given the vulnerability of the tourism industry and ripple effects, many scholars have noted the importance of proactive planning and management in dealing with tourism disasters (Henderson, 1999; Faulkner, 2001; Ritchie, 2004). It is widely recognised that a comprehensive crisis/disaster management approach is critical to reduce ripple effects (Santana,

2004) and can lead to successful recovery (Mansfeld, 1999; Niininen &
Gatsou, 2008). Effective cooperation with other important stakeholders
can also help achieve a faster recovery from disasters (Campiranon &
Scott, 2014; Pennington-Gray *et al.*, 2014). Collaboration is described as
a process of joint decision-making among key stakeholders of a problem
domain (Gray, 1989) that incorporates the diverse views of multiple and
interdependent stakeholders (Jamal & Getz, 1995). The main goals of
stakeholder collaboration are to achieve common interests and benefits as
well as to solve problems and issues. Collaboration can embrace and solve
a wide range of issues and problems in the context of tourism management, such as economic development, poverty alleviation and heritage
management (Jamal & Stronza, 2009). It can also be employed in disaster
management to achieve effective recovery.

The subject of collaborative tourism disaster management has
attracted limited attention of tourism scholars in the field. Past research
on tourism disaster management only discussed stakeholder collaboration
on community collaboration (Williams & Ferguson, 2005; Cioccio &
Michael, 2007), human resource development in risk reduction and preparation (Pforr & Hosie, 2008), stakeholder framework (Hystad & Keller,
2008), and collaboration between tourism and emergency agencies
(Becken & Hughey, 2013). Other studies only acknowledge stakeholder
collaboration as an important principle and strategy for disaster management, without detailed research and discussion (Prideaux, 1999;
Armstrong & Ritchie, 2008; Tew *et al.*, 2008; Campiranon & Scott, 2014;
Orchiston & Higham, 2016). Despite this weakness, no studies have
examined collaborative structures among stakeholders and suitable collaborative management actions for tourism disaster recovery. Key research
questions, such as what types of collaborative structures can be used for
effective coordination, and what collaborative actions are important for
successful recovery, largely remain unanswered. The questions also highlight broader issues concerning suitable governance for disaster
management.

This chapter seeks to better understand stakeholder collaboration by
examining both collaborative structures and key collaborative actions in
the context of tourism disaster management. Two main components were
studied: (1) the multi-level structure of stakeholder collaboration in tourism disaster management, and (2) key actions taken within the collaborative management system at different stages of a disaster. Australia, and
Queensland in particular, were chosen as a case study because their disaster management structures and systems are relatively well developed
(Abrahams, 2001) and they are popular tourist destinations. Further,
Queensland has experience in disaster management and it received worldwide acclaim for its handling of natural disasters in 2010–2011 (Arklay,
2012). Hence Queensland, Australia may act as an exemplary case study
for this exploratory research on tourism disaster management. In-depth

information was collected from key stakeholders who were directly involved in the disaster management of Cyclone Marcia in Central Queensland. Findings reported in this chapter extend our current understanding of stakeholder collaboration (structure and actions) in tourism disaster management and provide suggestions for effective operation of collaborative disaster management for tourism destinations.

Stakeholder Collaboration and Tourism Disaster Management

Disaster management is defined as *'a progress that seeks to prevent or lessen the negative outcomes and therefore protects the organisation, stakeholders and industry from damage'* (Coombs, 2007: 5). It is closely associated with the concept of sustainable development in terms of economics, social-culture and environment (Ritchie, 2004). Without effective disaster management, there might be a 'ripple effect' causing crises in other systems through the interdependence (Heath, 1998), or secondary impacts on tourism destination images after a disaster (Huang *et al.*, 2008).

Stakeholder collaboration is described as a process of joint decision-making among key stakeholders of a problem domain (Gray, 1989; Jamal & Getz, 1995). Any individual, business or organisation with an interest in the success of tourism and the potential to become involved in tourism disaster planning can be considered as a stakeholder (Hystad & Keller, 2008). The main goals of stakeholder collaboration are to achieve common interests and benefits as well as to solve problems and issues. Waugh and Streib (2006) indicated that cross-sector stakeholder collaboration is important for managing extreme events, especially when dealing with natural disasters that affect the tourism industry (Faulkner, 2001; Ritchie, 2004; Xu & Grunewald, 2009). This is because (1) the tourism environment is complex and dynamic with linkages and interdependencies among multiple stakeholders who may have divergent views and values (Jamal & Stronza, 2009); (2) tourism destinations often cross various geographical boundaries which have different management systems in emergency setting, policymaking, and leaderships during the disaster response and recovery period (Granot, 1997; Huque, 1998). Although stakeholder collaboration has been widely recognised as one of the important elements in tourism disaster management (Faulkner, 2001; Pennington-Gray *et al.*, 2014), understanding of the nature of collaboration and management structures is lacking.

Ritchie (2004) argued an integrated approach is required for tourism disaster management because the tourism industry comprises many individual businesses from a wide range of sectors, and public sector organisations at the international, national, regional and local level. In times of disasters, destinations demonstrating shorter recovery periods and better post-disaster growth are grounded in the establishment of a formal recovery stakeholder alliance (Armstrong & Ritchie, 2008; Pennington-Gray *et al.*, 2014; Xu & Grunewald, 2009). Stakeholder collaboration should be included in the long-term recovery strategies for destination resilience (Carlsen, 2006). This chapter provides a brief review of studies on stakeholder collaboration structures, collaboration stages and relevant actions. The literature was then used to design the fieldwork to explore collaborative structures and key actions in tourism disaster management.

Stakeholder collaboration structure

Collaboration itself does not solve all the problems and cannot guarantee positive outcomes (Bryson *et al.*, 2006), because collaborative activities commence formally or informally depending on the structure (Jamal & Stronza, 2009). Collaboration outcomes and effective network governance are strongly dependent on the distribution of power among all stakeholders who can influence decision-making (Gray, 1989) and the structures developed for responding to both internal and external legitimacy needs (Provan & Kenis, 2008). Thus, it is important to develop appropriate organisational structures to support effective management outcomes (Atkinson *et al.*, 2000). Furthermore, because of the highly interconnected nature of tourism (Laws & Prideaux, 2005), tourism collaborations usually span across different organisational levels and planning scales (Jamal & Stronza, 2009). A well-developed collaborative structure is needed to improve the effectiveness of tourism disaster management.

Literature on collaborative structures originates from the Public Administrative perspective to manage social problems and effectively deal with public challenges (Bryson *et al.*, 2006). Structure includes several elements such as goals, tasks specialisation, division of labour, operating procedures, and authority relationships (Bryson *et al.*, 2006), as shown in Figure 8.1. A formal operating procedure is important in maintaining stability of the structure (i.e. co-management agreements). Informal agreements based on flexible authority relationships can also be considered as collaborative arrangements (Jamal & Stronza, 2009) and can be helpful in dealing with unexpected changes (Bryson *et al.*, 2006).

Developing a governance structure that is both stable and flexible in light of new developments and a willingness to make needed changes are important (Provan & Kenis, 2008). Disasters or crises can have different impacts on tourism (Zeng *et al.*, 2005), and therefore require for an alterable and adaptive tourism disaster management plan and structure (Campiranon & Scott, 2014). Furthermore, effective coordination through clear role division is challenging but essential to achieve positive outcomes (Jamal & Getz, 1995).

Tourism disaster management closely links with, and operates under, a general disaster management structure. However, limited research has been published on understanding collaborative structures for tourism disaster management and how tourism stakeholders collaborate within the tourism system and their integration with the broader disaster management system. Different collaboration models should be evaluated on their suitability and effectiveness. In order to investigate the application of collaborative structure in tourism disaster management, the case of Cyclone Marcia was used to provide initial insights.

Collaborative stages and corresponding actions

In the process of collaborative disaster management, it is important to clarify responsibilities of stakeholders during all stages of a disaster (Hystad & Keller, 2008). This can be the assigned tasks in a collaborative structure mentioned in Figure 8.1 (Bryson *et al.*, 2006). Faulkner (2001) put forward a tourism disaster management framework (six management phases) based on the disaster management stages discussed by Fink (1986) and Roberts (1994). Different stages can have different management foci and plans. Some researchers have identified four main elements of the general strategic planning and management (Johnson & Scholes, 1993; Viljoen, 1994) and these elements can be integrated with disaster management stages as shown in the left two columns in Table 8.1. For tourism disaster management, Pennington-Gray *et al.* (2014) argued that collaboration fits in all stages of a disaster: reduction, readiness, response, and recovery (right column in Table 8.1). Hystad and Keller (2008: 159) also highlighted stakeholder roles, indicating that '*understanding the roles of various stakeholders throughout the stages of a disaster is a significant step to improving tourism disaster management*'.

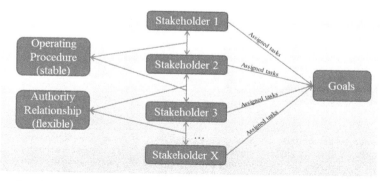

Figure 8.1 Structure concept (developed by the authors based on Bryson *et al.*'s (2006) elements)

It is argued that although stakeholder collaboration is involved throughout all disaster management phases, the priorities and responsibilities of different stakeholders will change in different phases and geographic scales. For the tourism industry, information- and resource-sharing among various levels of stakeholders would be particularly important in the response phase (Pennington-Gray *et al.*, 2014). Ritchie (2004) identified that 'stakeholder understanding and collaboration' act as an important element of strategic implementation in the post-disaster management stage (immediate and long-term). Hystad and Keller (2008) supported this view and indicated that tourism organisations and businesses play a primary role in post-disaster management. Major tasks for this stage are to maintain consistent communication and establish marketing recovery strategies, while emergency organisations have a more important leading role before and during the disasters. This research investigated the key collaborative actions in tourism disaster management at different stages, with a particular focus on the post-disaster stages as highlighted in Table 8.1.

Table 8.1 Disaster management stages, strategies and stakeholder collaboration

Faulkner's Framework of Disaster Management Stages (2001)	Key Elements of Strategic Management (Johnson & Scholes, 1993; Viljoen, 1994)	Stakeholder Collaboration (Pennington-Gray *et al.*, 2014)
Pre-event: when action can be taken to prevent or mitigate the effects of potential disasters	*Strategic analysis* - examining the macro and micro-operating environment	Collaboration in terms of prevention, preparedness and mitigation
Prodromal: when it is apparent that a disaster is imminent		
Emergency: The effect of the disaster is felt and action is necessary to protect people and property	*Strategic direction and choice* - develop and select strategic directions and specific generic strategies to achieve the goals	Collaboration in terms of emergency response (e.g. evacuation, rescue, healthcare)
Intermediate: short-term needs of people/tourists have to be addressed and media communication is critical	*Strategy implementation and control* - develop suitable structure, human and financial resource strategies, providing leadership to control - Stakeholder Understanding and Collaboration (Ritchie, 2004)	
Long-term (recovery): rebuilding of infrastructure, marketing of destination		Collaboration in terms of communication, re-development, recovery marketing of tourism destinations
Resolution: evaluation and feedback	*Strategic evaluation and feedback* - continuous improvements, learn how to improve the effectiveness of strategies through evaluation and monitoring	Collaboration in terms of experience sharing and revision of disaster management plans

Method

Case selection and sampling

A Category Five Tropical Cyclone Marcia hit the Capricorn region in Central Queensland, Australia on 20 February 2015. It crossed the coast north of Yeppoon and tracked south towards Yeppoon and Rockhampton with sustained winds in excess of 200km per hour and gusts of up to 285km. This severe Cyclone Marcia brought great physical, reputational and psychological damage to the regional tourism industry (Harmon, 2015; Rockhampton Regional Council, 2015). An estimated 4000 to 5000 tourism jobs were lost in the Central Queensland region (Moore, 2015). The cyclone has caused devastating damage to the local rainforest resources and the local community were left with no power and internet connection. Many local businesses were closed and lost their customers for nearly six weeks. Although the local operators and governments tried to reopen businesses and repair the natural environment, the misinterpretations of the local damage and sensationalist media coverage further affected destination reputation and impeded its recovery. For local business people, psychological impacts were caused by either the shock of the cyclone and isolation, lack of information, or the pain of losing a home and business. The implications of these effects posed a serious challenge for Central Queensland's recovery after Cyclone Marcia.

This research adopted Eden and Ackermann's (1998) two indicators of 'interest and power' to identify key stakeholders for the research. An initial list of key stakeholders was obtained from an internet search of the state *Disaster Management Act*, government reports, state/local disaster management websites and media reports. The degree of relevance relied on their level of power and interest with tourism disaster management. In order to select the most appropriate respondents, an exponential discriminative snowball sampling technique was embraced by setting additional criteria to validate recommendations provided by participants. Potential stakeholders recommended by participants were only selected if they: (1) were mentioned or recommended by more than one participant before or during the interview; (2) had a close relationship with the research topic (power and interest grids for assessment).

Data collection and analysis

From 20 July to 1 September 2015, semi-structured interviews were undertaken and recorded with 15 key stakeholders who were involved in the disaster management of Cyclone Marcia. Interviews were conducted in Brisbane, Rockhampton and Yeppoon. Detailed information of participants is shown in Table 8.2. Apart from primary interview data, secondary data (such as government and organisation reports from both state and local level, and official webpages related to Cyclone Marcia

Table 8.2 Number of participants in different categories

Management Level	Number	Organisation Types	Number
State	5	Government	6
Regional	4	Industry association/organisation	5
Local	6	Business	4
Total Participants	15	Total Participants	15

Collaborative Management) were also collected to help investigate the collaborative management structure and key actions during and after the disaster. Descriptive results were built from the key statements identified from transcripts as well as the collaboration information from government reports and official webpages.

Data analysis was conducted in two stages. First, all interview transcripts were coded according to the research questions using NVivo 10. This enables the researcher to index and coordinate the analysis of text (Veal, 2011) and assists in organising and understanding the data. All statements reflecting collaborative structures and key actions in different stages were identified and categorised into themes. Second, secondary data (government and organisation reports, official webpage information) were also coded and analysed to provide supplementary information to the findings. Six coding names were used for displaying the results: *State Government (SG), State Organisation (SO), Regional Government (RG), Regional Organisation (RO), Local Government (LG) and Local Business (LB)*. Qualitative validity and reliability strategies/procedures following Creswell (2014) and Gibbs (2007) were used in this research. For further details please see Jiang and Ritchie's (2017) study.

Findings and Discussion

Collaboration structure across multiple management levels and sectors

Standard disaster management structure

Past literature on collaborative structures discusses different governance structures or cross-sector collaboration based on the leading organisation (Provan & Kenis, 2005), or collaboration patterns/intensity (Proulx *et al.*, 2014). This study first investigates the formal management framework to provide an overview of a mature disaster management structure in Australia. The results show that Queensland has a well-arranged tiered disaster management structure supported by the state *Disaster Management Act*.

Queensland has a series of disaster management documents established for state, district and local level management based on the *Disaster Management Act 2003*. The disaster management structure and

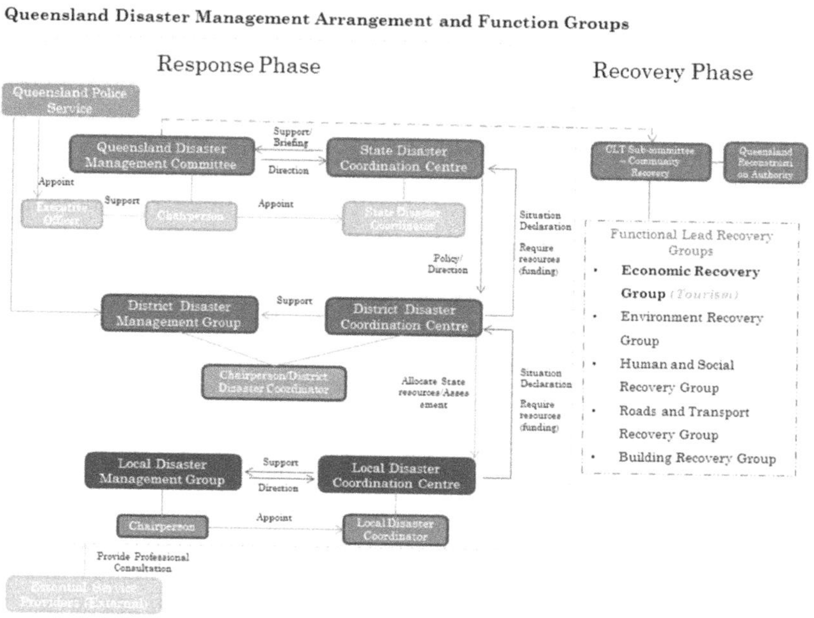

Queensland Disaster Management Arrangement and Function Groups

Figure 8.2 Queensland disaster management arrangement and function groups (developed by the authors based on Public Safety Business Agency (2015) and Queensland Police Service (2015))

corresponding functions are stated at different management levels, as demonstrated in Figure 8.2. Principal components (Public Safety Business Agency, 2015) in the structure that make up the Queensland Disaster Management Arrangement (QDMA) are:

(1) *Disaster management groups*: responsible for the planning, organisation, coordination and implementation of all measures to mitigate/prevent, prepare for, respond to and recover from disaster situations.
(2) *Coordination centres*: support disaster management groups in coordinating information, resources and services necessary for disaster operations.
(3) *Functional lead agencies*: through which the functions and responsibilities of the State Government in relation to disaster management are managed and coordinated.

Five functional recovery groups report through the CEO Leadership Team (CLT) Sub-committee to the Queensland Disaster Management Committee (Queensland Police Service, 2015). Tourism is part of the 'Economic Recovery Group'.

Within this system, Disaster Coordination Centers (DCCs) at the local, district and state levels play a critical role in retaining communication links between all levels of the system. DCCs are activated as the need arises to coordinate resources, information and provide support, which helps to maintain the flexibility of the QDMA system in responding to a disaster (Public Safety Business Agency, 2015). This coordination function can be referred to as collaboration 'procedures' that bring together organisations to ensure effective disaster management before, during and after the event. This coordination operates both horizontally and vertically across organisations. It is argued that a tiered management system with resource support from higher level stakeholders could help destinations with more effective resource utilisation across various management levels, such as funds support (tangible recovery) and post-disaster marketing (intangible recovery).

However, as each disaster is different and unique, the actual operational management framework could be different from case to case (Miller & Ritchie, 2003). Campbell (1999) has pointed out that much crisis planning tends to be impracticable as it is only directed towards a certain type of crisis. Similarly, Augustine (1995) highlighted that a plan should be able to deal with a variety of undesirable crises. Campiranon and Scott (2014) indicated that a crisis management plan is only a basic guideline – the plan needs to be adapted to the situation, location and market (Henderson, 2007; Tiernan et al., 2007). In turn, a disaster plan cannot be based on a standard set of critical decisions that determine specific success and must instead be flexible and able to cope with a broad range of disaster types. Therefore, destinations need to be prepared with a plan but remain flexible in how it is implemented based on the context. The following section discusses the specific collaboration structure for Cyclone Marcia.

Management structure and connections for Tropical Cyclone Marcia

Based on the interviews with major tourism stakeholders who were involved directly in tourism disaster management, this research further examined the actual disaster management structure from the perspective of tourism. Some results are well-supported by the secondary data displayed above. A tiered collaborative structure across various management levels is proposed based on participants' responses and the review of government reports (Figure 8.3). As one participant noted:

> You have sort of a three-tiered approach. You have the national government who supports us with some personnel, but they support us with funding ... You have a state structure which supports you through police, emergency services, fire and rescue, so they have quite a number of agencies to support us. Then you have local government which is primarily concerned about restoring services and the agencies. (RO)

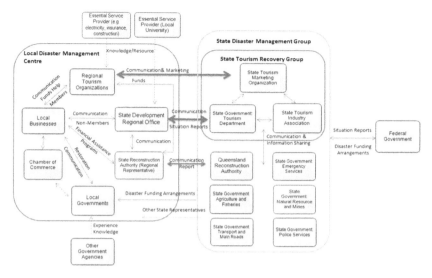

Figure 8.3 Collaborative structures and relationships for tourism disaster management (developed by the authors based on interviews and government reports)

Communications across levels within the structure relied on regular meetings and the use of teleconference to engage remote members to collaborative management (Public Safety Business Agency, 2015). In the case of Cyclone Marcia, communication ensued before the cyclone and continued during and after the disaster event to update information and the progress of tasks' implementation, as participants noted: 'I think it's very effective. There's regular minutes being taken, there's milestones being set. You revisit those milestones every meeting and you make sure every single one is done' (RG).

Joint partnership structure at local and state level

Effective stakeholder collaboration for tourism disaster management relies on the collaborative working structure and relationships among stakeholders on different levels. The basic collaboration structure was a joint partnership through setting up disaster management groups at both state and local levels. These management groups were established based on existing networks and past management systems. Stakeholders involved in the management groups shared information with each other and developed management plans together to solve problems, as indicated by one participant: 'The Deputy Mayor chaired the Disaster Management Center. So it's a committee and it's got members on it from both local and state government agencies. It's responsible for disseminating information about the disaster' (LG).

Participants indicated that their collaborative management occurred through setting up an affiliated program at both local (Local Disaster Management Center) and state level (State Disaster Management Group). 'Economic recovery groups' or 'Disaster Management Centers' were mentioned by local government as the key structure that helped tourism collaborative management after the cyclone. These local disaster management groups were established to coordinate effective disaster management at the local level, as it is regarded as the key focus of the disaster management arrangements and all other levels of management need to provide support to the local level (Public Safety Business Agency, 2015). Several local disaster management groups were separated from each other based on different political and geographical boundaries. This is also supported by the formal arrangements that 'local disaster coordination center may be temporary facilities provided within each local government area during disasters' (Public Safety Business Agency, 2015).

'Weakened' coordination at regional level

Stakeholders located in a regional/district level played an important role in bridging and communication among local and state stakeholders. This is supported by Queensland Disaster Management Framework, which indicates that 'District disaster coordination centers are established to coordinate the provision of State Government assets to local disaster management groups, and to provide information to the SDCC and LDCC' (Public Safety Business Agency, 2015). However, different from a formal district structure, there was no regional disaster management group established in this case. Instead, regional stakeholders were invited and took part in different local economic recovery groups/disaster management centers established by each local government, in which they shared information and developed action plans for disaster recovery. As demonstrated by one participant:

> Our agency has been involved in the economic recovery side of things with the [LG1], [LG2], and the [LG3] … We're a panel member of the economic recovery group … [LG1] had a recovery mechanism/committee, they've for the five headings for disasters and we're on the economic one… Those meetings were held at regular intervals and there was a record kept and there was an action plan and people went off and did stuff. (RG)

It can be argued consistently with past research (Henderson, 2003; Sönmez et al., 1999) that each crisis/disaster situation is unique and difficult to resolve with simple standard management structure. Findings from the specific case of Cyclone Marcia have verified this view by showing the 'weakened' regional/district coordinative management. The adjusted structure focused more on local management and active engagement of regional representatives. A district could contain several local areas managed by different local governments. In this case, the impacts on different local areas within the same district were different due to the weakening of the cyclone after landfall (Department of Infrastructure, Local Government and Planning (DILGP), 2015). Therefore, different local disaster management groups were established and led by local governments respectively, without a united regional management approach. Regional stakeholders were invited to join each local group and maintained frequent communication with the State Disaster Management Group.

Leading organisations' roles in collaborative management

Leading tourism organisations (such as DMOs) should play an important role in securing resources for the affected local tourism destinations and can become catalysts in coordinating initiatives (Hystad & Keller, 2008; Paraskevas & Arendell, 2007). This view is supported by the research findings as three key tourism-related organisations (State Government of Tourism, State Tourism Industry Association and State Tourism Marketing Organization) communicated actively and frequently representing the tourism industry at the State Management Level. Their collaborative efforts helped to achieve a faster recovery for local tourism operators. Furthermore, at the regional/district level, the Regional Tourism Organization (RTO) played an extremely significant role in disseminating the information between local and state level and strived to attract resources from the State Government. Mutual trust and positive relationships had been established between the RTO and other key stakeholders (e.g. state DMO, local governments, local businesses), which facilitated the tourism industry recovery (Jiang & Ritchie, 2017).

The leading role of tourism organisations should be highlighted and reinforced in the broader disaster management structure. They should actively (1) facilitate communication and coordination among tourism stakeholders before, during and after the disaster, (2) encourage and support local tourism businesses to strengthen capability in management over hidden risks of disasters, and (3) collaborate with essential service providers from other sectors (e.g. infrastructure, electricity, construction, insurance) to perfect information systems and knowledge formation for disaster response. Governments or industry associations could create incentives to encourage businesses to build their disaster management capabilities and integrate into the local disaster management structure. Examples could include regular free workshops on disaster capability building and sharing best practices across industry to learn from past disaster experience.

External stakeholders in the collaborative structure

It is also worth noting that the 'Essential Service Providers' are displayed for both standard structure and actual operational structure. In the standard framework, disaster management stakeholders could consult essential services to help with performing relevant functions (Queensland Police Service, 2015). Examples of these essential services are gas, electricity, telecommunication, etc. In this case, key service providers such as a local electricity supplier, major insurance company, highway and street construction company actively participated in the local economic recovery group. A local university also joined to assist in analysing disaster impacts by collecting statistical data and qualitative information for further decision-making. Therefore, tourism disaster recovery as part of the broader disaster management structure also relies on multi-sector collaboration to provide various insights and knowledge for more comprehensive and effective planning and decision-making.

Collaborative actions in various stages of tourism disaster management

Management circle of tourism disaster recovery

Collaboration can be utilised throughout all phases of disaster management. This research has developed a 'Management Circle of Tourism Disaster Recovery' based on participants' responses of their actions in different stages of tourism disaster management (Figure 8.4). Different from linear disaster management models, this pattern is a closed circulation connected by knowledge flowing from disaster reflection to pre-planning for the next potential incident. Experience and knowledge have been developed from Cyclone Marcia, which are intended to inform preparation for future natural disasters. As participants indicated: 'with this one we've learnt, or we're learning about how might we do that better... we then assess what we do and what have we learnt and how can we do it

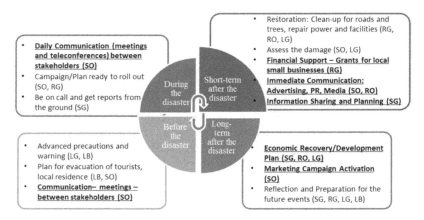

Figure 8.4 Management circle of tourism disaster recovery

better' (SG) and 'I think as long as the lessons are learnt and the preparations are made to get ready for the next one' (LG).

Major actions for tourism disaster management happened in the response (short-term after the disaster) and recovery (long-term after disaster) stages of disaster management, which supports the idea that tourism organisations and businesses play a primary role in post-disaster management (Hystad & Keller, 2008). Stakeholders worked closely with each other on accessing financial assistance, immediate communication, and timely advertising in the short-term response stage. This supports the literature that highlights the importance of information- and resource-sharing in the response phase of tourism disaster management (Pennington-Gray et al., 2014).

However, it is found that less tourism collaborative management occurred during the long-term recovery stage. In this case, the collaborative relationship broke down in the longer-term with some organisations pulling out from the collaboration or stopping management actions for disaster recovery. This is because the long-term goals of regional tourism recovery have a longer time horizon than individual goals and this leads to reduced shared interests and a need for stakeholder collaboration beyond the short term. Furthermore, some management organisations argued that the long-term disaster recovery is simply seen as a component of their economic development plan and thus no longer the main goal for collaboration. Some stakeholders regard the disaster as a turning point for future economic development and seek further growth (a new start) rather than a recovery (back to original level):

> ...we all have an interest in economic development for the region, so we tend to meet either on individual projects or mechanisms or something like that. So disasters are simply a component of how regions work. We all tend to work together as well as we can, basically it's about growth rather than about disaster recovery. (RG)

Although the tourism industry can do little before and during the disaster, active and consistent communication among stakeholders is still vital throughout all stages of disaster management and helps to develop quicker and more effective plans for post-disaster management. Communication before and during the disaster mainly focuses on information-sharing within the system, while communication after the disaster includes destination-marketing, information-sharing and strategy-making. For example, stakeholders first communicate potential threats before the disaster for further planning, and then keep in regular communication through a regular situation update during the disaster to help plan their response; finally, they coordinate communication and information-sharing across management levels after the disaster for effective marketing and recovery. This supports past literature that indicated good communication and information-sharing as the key component of successful bouncing back to pre-disaster conditions (Becken & Hughey, 2013; de Sausmarez, 2007; Stafford *et al.*, 2002).

Key collaborative actions in tourism disaster management

Taskforces were established soon after Cyclone Marcia based on both the state and local Recovery Plans. At the state level, five 'Functional Recovery Groups' (FRGs) are responsible for leading and coordinating the planning and implementation of recovery tasks. Tourism is included in the Economic Recovery Group which is in charge of economic recovery activities and chaired by the Department of State Development (DSD) (DILGP, 2015). At the local level, the Livingstone Shire Council established four separate taskforces to focus on each area and include relevant stakeholders for more recovery contribution. Tourism is included in the Regional & Economic Development Taskforce, which is liaised by the Local Government Economic Development Manager and Regional Tourism Organisation (RTO) CEO (Livingstone Shire Council, 2015).

Some activities were clearly identified and provide directions for effective disaster recovery. Four tourism-related collaborative activities, which were extracted from interviews and government reports, are discussed next.

Communication and Information-Sharing (Before, During and After)

For the tourism industry, key stakeholders formally participated in this collaborative structure immediately after the disaster, but the informal collaborative communication started even before the disaster. Participants from the state and regional level showed close and frequent communication across management levels when they saw a high probability of natural disasters: 'When we see something approaching, when it becomes a real, likely event, we start to communicate… Then as the threat becomes more real or gets closer, maybe the meetings become more frequent, maybe specific issues have to be addressed, depending on where it is' (SO).

During the disaster, there was little that the tourism industry could do apart from maintaining regular communication on situation updates and issuing reports. Leading tourism organisations play a more important role in exchanging information from other sectors to the tourism industry, such as transportation, infrastructure and facilities: 'We're saying that we're not involved in the actual disaster management (emergency management) … but we're aware of it. It's just sharing information. That's most important. Everybody does their own thing, but we share the information' (SO).

After the disaster, the communications were still active across the management levels (from local to state), focusing on task coordination and information-sharing between various management groups. This is because one of the key tasks of the State Economic Recovery Group is to maintain consultation and intelligence gathering with economic stakeholders and peak industry bodies (DILGP, 2015). As one participant from the state government demonstrated: 'We have a signed agreement with State Development as an agency that they represent us, because we don't have regional staff at that level. So all the reports they do they will feed straight to us, so we get all that information. So the coordination is really good between the levels and it works' (SG).

At the local level, business operators were invited to join a series of post-cyclone forums facilitated by local governments to share the information of available resources and situation updates from state representatives, local governments and related organisations (Livingstone Shire Council, 2015). As one local business owner stated: 'We had briefings from those people about what was happening, what help was available. Where we could go to get the help, where we could go to get information about who we can get help from' (LB).

Disaster Planning (Public vs. Private)

A clear, systematic Disaster Management Act and Guideline were developed prior to Cyclone Marcia. As noted by participants from governments and tourism-related organisations, this plan was updated frequently and was flexible with different locations and impacts:

> Internally we would have a plan in terms of where our staff are going to be and what locations and what's going to work best for the sectors that have been affected. (RG)

> There's a state recovery plan, and there are local recovery plans and they'll be different depending on terrain, nature of the location, and where that's impacted. (RO)

However, compared with management parties, local small businesses were less prepared for natural disasters with little or no pre-planning. Even though they received information from local government about the upcoming Cyclone Marcia, there was little which could be done due to their limited capability and preparedness: 'It was in 24 hours they'd said it's now going to be a category 5. So we had no chance to gear up for a category 5 in 24 hours. It was just too much to do' (LB).

This finding is in line with other studies showing that disaster management planning is well-managed in the public sector, but still lacking for the private sector, including local small tourism businesses (de Sausmarez, 2004). Reasons for this could be both internal and external:

(1) internally, small businesses lack resource and capability to prepare an effective contingency plan and they tend to focus on day-to-day operations (Coles, 2004; de Sausmarez, 2004); (2) externally, natural disasters are hard to predict and therefore become a major barrier for effective preparation (Faulkner, 2001; Prideaux *et al.*, 2003).

Active involvement (empowerment) of the private sector in collaborative public disaster management through communicating and information-sharing can reduce this deficiency. After the disaster, empowerment of local tourism businesses is emphasised to facilitate collaborative disaster planning and management, as demonstrated in local recovery groups' major tasks list: 'ensuring businesses and industry groups are involved in the decision making process' (Livingstone Shire Council, 2015). Furthermore, the importance of improving the capability of local businesses in dealing with natural disasters is highlighted. Free workshops were provided after the disasters in this case. 'Over the last six months all those workshops we've just delivered free of charge to businesses to help them kind of start to build themselves up again; and that includes the tourism industry…' (RG).

Funding

In order to help tourism recover from the disaster, 'facilitating business assistance, access to funds and loans and employer subsidies' is one of the major tasks of local economic recovery groups (Livingstone Shire Council, 2015). Natural Disaster Relief and Recovery Arrangements (NDDRA) were activated soon after the disaster for all affected local areas (DILGP, 2015). Queensland Reconstruction Authority and the RTO helped with the funding process, while the representative at the regional level actively communicated with affected local businesses, leading organisations and governments to help the effective release of supporting funds:

> Our role is a liaison role. So we assist them with determining eligibility, accessing the necessary application forms and assisting them to prepare those and the necessary attachments. So we help them in – we initially sat out in a recovery center. We had staff from our Brisbane office assisting. (RG)

As clearly indicated in the State Disaster Management Guideline, lower-level disaster coordination groups can request support from the higher-level if the resources are not available or are exhausted at the lower-level (Public Safety Business Agency, 2015), as one participant noted: 'We do the activation up to the federal government. So we prepare the business case for that so the federal government to get the funding will rely on what we put forward from the state government' (SG).

However, the process of funds assistance was claimed to be too bureaucratic and ineffective in achieving fast disaster recovery, which could be improved in the future: '... because the government was asking for numbers of dollar value of what the effect was on businesses, two days after the cyclone. A lot of businesses weren't able to say what dollar figure, until their assessors came out from the insurance companies' (RO).

Advocating and Marketing

For effective tourism recovery, it was important that information and advocacy should be provided by one voice on behalf of the entire tourism industry. State-level stakeholders (government and marketing bodies) are responsible for leading communication with the media and the public:

> The best position we can put the tourism industry in is being able to collectively get as much information together as we can to advocate on their behalf. That might be advocating to media about the issue. (SO)

> The more data we can collect and send to the Minister for Tourism that makes it easier for her to put a press release out saying and here's what we're doing. (RG)

Implementing a marketing campaign to provide positive messages about Queensland tourism is one of the key tasks of the State Economy Recovery Group (DILGP, 2015). In order to mitigate booking cancellations and re-attract tourists, a marketing campaign at the state level was released two weeks after the disaster to promote business as usual in many locations. 'We developed a campaign while the crisis was happening and we had that campaign ready to roll out within about two weeks of the event...we needed to have marketing activity in market to ensure people would return' (SO). Immediately after the disaster, advocating and marketing activities were released at the local level by communicating through media outlets, such as TV and radio, the message that businesses had reopened.

The marketing campaign was altered at the state level based on local situation reports and active communication between regional representatives and state marketing stakeholders. For an uncertain situation such as a natural disaster, the information sent out needs to be accurate and responsible. Therefore, marketing activity and messages need to be built upon active collaboration and communication, as demonstrated by the participants:

> ...we had put a hold on it because we felt that prior to the event it would be wrong to be sending people the message to travel to the region, when so many things were closed. So we liaised very closely with the RTO and others to say when do you feel that it's ready for us to put this campaign back into market? Then we switched the campaign on. At that point we also assessed the campaign for the key messages: are they still relevant? Or do they need to be changed? (SO)

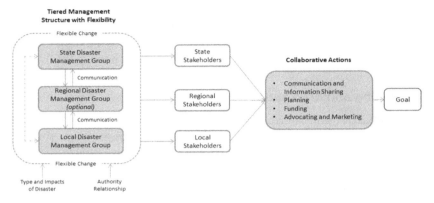

Figure 8.5 Simplified model of findings summary

In summary, findings are shown in Figure 8.5 in line with the structure concept (Figure 8.1). The tired management structure can be regarded as the prescribed operating procedure established before the disaster. With the influence of different types or impacts of disasters, and the changing relationship between authorities, this procedure could be adjusted with flexibility to adapt to the specific management context.

Conclusion

This study discusses the critical role of stakeholder collaboration in tourism disaster management, with a focus on collaborative structures and major actions throughout the disaster stages. A standard tiered management structure was established in advance in the local and regional area, but it remained flexible in operation for the specific disaster context. Four key collaborative actions were identified within this structure: communication (all stages), planning (before and after), funding (post-disaster), advocating and marketing (post-disaster). The findings suggest a cross-sector and tiered collaborative management structure for tourism disaster management and highlight the critical role of effective communication facilitated by leading tourism organisations.

Future research on structure could further examine the effectiveness of different structures in different disaster situations and possible factors (e.g. management culture, political environment, types of disasters) that could influence the development and operation of structures. Additionally, structures are likely to be dynamic due to the inherent ambiguity and complexity in collaborations (Huxham & Vangen, 2005). Membership turnover could be one of the critical factors when powerful players leave and join (Crosby & Bryson, 2005). Thus, there is a need to study external and internal factors that could affect the stability of collaborative structures in a tourism disaster context.

Active communication was found to be the most important action throughout the collaboration stages; thus, further research should focus on how to improve the effectiveness of communication within the collaborative tourism disaster management system. For example, Cioccio and Michael (2007) highlighted the importance of DMOs in destination disaster management because of their role in crisis communication and recovery marketing activities on behalf of the tourism industry. Similarly, Orchiston and Higham (2016) argued that crisis communication is based on well-developed information and knowledge. A focus on knowledge management concepts and organisational learning in tourism disaster management (Blackman *et al.*, 2011) could be used to examine how knowledge is created, transmitted and used by tourism organisations to recover from natural disasters.

References

Abrahams, J. (2001) Disaster management in Australia: The national emergency management system. *Emergency Medicine* 13 (2), 165–173.

Arklay, T.M. (2012) Queensland's State Disaster Management Group: An all agency response to an unprecedented natural disaster. *Australian Journal of Emergency Management* 27 (3), 9–19.

Armstrong, E.K. and Ritchie, B.W. (2008) The heart recovery marketing campaign: Destination recovery after a major bushfire in Australia's national capital. *Journal of Travel and Tourism Marketing* 23 (2–4), 175–189.

Atkinson, S., Schaefer, A. and Viney, H. (2000) Organizational structure and effective environmental management. *Business Strategy and the Environment* 9 (2), 108–120.

Augustine, N. (1995) Managing the crisis you tried to prevent. *Harvard Business Review* (November–December), 75 (6), 147–158.

Becken, S. and Hughey, K.F. (2013) Linking tourism into emergency management structures to enhance disaster risk reduction. *Tourism Management* 36, 77–85.

Blackman, D., Kennedy, M. and Ritchie, B.W. (2011) Knowledge management: The missing link in DMO crisis management? *Current Issues in Tourism* 14 (4), 337–354.

Bryson, J.M., Crosby, B.C. and Stone, M.M. (2006) The design and implementation of Cross-Sector collaborations: Propositions from the literature. *Public Administration Review* 66 (s1), 44–55.

Campbell, R. (1999) Controlling crisis chaos. *Australian Journal of Emergency Management* 14 (3), 51–54.

Campiranon, K. and Scott, N. (2014) Critical success factors for crisis recovery management: A case study of Phuket hotels. *Journal of Travel and Tourism Marketing* 31 (3), 313–326.

Carlsen, J. (2006) Post-tsunami tourism strategies for the Maldives. *Tourism Review International* 10 (1–2), 69–79.

Carlsen, J.C. and Hughes, M. (2008) Tourism market recovery in the Maldives after the 2004 Indian Ocean tsunami. *Journal of Travel and Tourism Marketing* 23 (2–4), 139–149.

Cioccio, L. and Michael, E.J. (2007) Hazard or disaster: Tourism management for the inevitable in Northeast Victoria. *Tourism Management* 28 (1), 1–11.

Coles, T. (2004) A local reading of a global disaster: Some lessons on tourism management from an Annus Horribilis in South West England. *Journal of Travel and Tourism Marketing* 15 (2–3), 173–197.

Coombs, W.T. (2007) Attribution theory as a guide for post-crisis communication research. *Public Relations Review* 33, 135–139.

Creswell, J.W. (2014) *Research Design: Qualitative, Quantitative, and Mixed Methods Approaches*. CA: Sage Publications.

Crosby, B.C. and Bryson, J.M. (2005) *Leadership for the Common Good: Tackling Public Problems in a Shared-power World* (2nd edn). San Francisco: Jossey-Bass.

Department of Infrastructure, Local Government and Planning (DILGP) (2015) *Severe Tropical Cyclone Marcia Recovery Plan March 2015*. [pdf] Available at: http://www.dilgp.qld.gov.au/resources/plan/local-government/tc-marcia-recovery-plan.pdf

de Sausmarez, N. (2004) Malaysia's response to the Asian financial crisis: Implications for tourism and sectoral crisis management. *Journal of Travel and Tourism Marketing* 15 (4), 217–231.

de Sausmarez, N. (2007) Crisis management, tourism and sustainability: The role of indicators. *Journal of Sustainable Tourism* 15 (6), 700–714.

Eden, C. and Ackermann, F. (1998) *Making Strategy: The Journey of Strategic Management*. Thousand Oaks, CA: Sage.

Evans, N., Campbell, D. and Stonehouse, G. (2003) *Strategic Management for Travel and Tourism*. Oxford: Butterworth-Heinemann.

Faulkner, B. (2001) Towards a framework for tourism disaster management. *Tourism Management* 22 (2), 135–147.

Fink, S. (1986) *Crisis Management*. New York: American Association of Management.

Gibbs, G.R. (2007) Analysing qualitative data. In U. Flick (ed.) *The Sage Qualitative Research Kit*. Thousand Oaks, CA: Sage. https://doi.org/10.4135/9781849208826

Granot, H. (1997) Emergency inter-organizational relationships. *Disaster Prevention and Management* 6 (5), 305–310.

Gray, B. (1989) *Collaborating: Finding Common Ground for Multiparty Problems*. San Francisco: Jossey-Bass.

Harmon, A. (2015) Cyclone Marcia hits QLD tourism hard. *The Byte*, 4 March. [online] Available at: http://www.thebyte.com.au/cyclone-marcia-hits-qld-tourism-hard/

Heath, R. (1998) *Crisis Management for Managers and Executives*. London: Financial Times Management.

Henderson, J.C. (1999) Managing the Asian financial crisis: Tourist attractions in Singapore. *Journal of Travel Research* 38 (2), 177–181.

Henderson, J.C. (2003) Communicating in a crisis: Flight SQ 006. *Tourism Management* 24 (3), 279–287.

Henderson, J.C. (2007) Corporate social responsibility and tourism: Hotel companies in Phuket, Thailand, after the Indian Ocean tsunami. *Hospitality Management* 26 (1), 228–239.

Huang, Y.C., Tseng, Y.P. and Petrick, J.F. (2008) Crisis management planning to restore tourism after disasters: A case study from Taiwan. *Journal of Travel and Tourism Marketing* 23 (2–4), 203–221.

Huque, A.S. (1998) Disaster management and the inter-organizational imperative: The Hong Kong disaster plan. *Issues and Studies* 34 (2), 104–123.

Huxham, C. and Vangen, S. (2005) *Managing to Collaborate: The Theory and Practice of Collaborative Advantage*. New York: Routledge.

Hystad, P.W. and Keller, P.C. (2008) Towards a destination tourism disaster management framework: Long-term lessons from a forest fire disaster. *Tourism Management* 29 (1), 151–162.

Jamal, T. and Stronza, A. (2009) Collaboration theory and tourism practice in protected areas: Stakeholders, structuring and sustainability. *Journal of Sustainable Tourism* 17 (2), 169–189.

Jamal, T.B. and Getz, D. (1995) Collaboration theory and community tourism planning. *Annals of Tourism Research* 22 (1), 186–204.

Jiang, Y. and Ritchie, B.W. (2017) Disaster collaboration in tourism: Motives, impediments and success factors. *Journal of Hospitality and Tourism Management* 31, 70–82.

Johnson, G. and Scholes, K. (1993) *Exploring Corporate Strategy*. Oxford: Butterworth-Heinemann.

Laws, E. and Prideaux, B. (2005) Crisis management: A suggested typology. *Journal of Travel and Tourism Marketing* 19 (2–3), 1–8.

Livingstone Shire Council (2015) *Community Relief and Early Recovery Activities – February 2015 to August 2015*. [online] Available at: https://www.livingstone.qld. gov.au/DocumentCenter/Home/View/5366

Mansfeld, Y. (1999) Cycles of war, terror, and peace: Determinants and management of crisis and recovery of the Israeli tourism industry. *Journal of Travel Research* 38 (1), 30–36.

Miller, G.A. and Ritchie, B.W. (2003) A farming crisis or a tourism disaster? An analysis of the foot and mouth disease in the UK. *Current Issues in Tourism* 6 (2), 150–171.

Moore, T. (2015) Cyclone Marcia leaves thousands of tourism jobs at risk. *Brisbane Times*, 26 February. Available at: http://www.brisbanetimes.com.au/queensland/cyclone-marcia-leaves-thousands-of-tourism-jobs-at-risk-20150225-13oxn6.html

Niininen, O. and Gatsou, M. (2008) Crisis management: A case study from the Greek passenger shipping industry. *Journal of Travel and Tourism Marketing* 23 (2–4), 191–202.

Orchiston, C. and Higham, J.E.S. (2016) Knowledge management and tourism recovery (de) marketing: The Christchurch Earthquakes 2010–2011. *Current Issues in Tourism* 19 (1), 64–84.

Paraskevas, A. and Arendell, B. (2007) A strategic framework for terrorism prevention and mitigation in tourism destinations. *Tourism Management* 28 (6), 1560–1573.

Pennington-Gray, L., Cahyanto, I., Schroeder, A. and Kesper, A. (2014) Collaborative communication networks: An application in Indonesia. In B. Ritchie and K. Campiranon (eds) *Tourism Crisis and Disaster Management in the Asia-Pacific* (pp. 77–94). Wallingford: CAB International.

Pforr, C. and Hosie, P.J. (2008) Crisis management in tourism: Preparing for recovery. *Journal of Travel and Tourism Marketing* 23 (2–4), 249–264.

Prideaux, B. (1999) Tourism perspectives of the Asian financial crisis: Lessons for the future. *Current Issues in Tourism* 2 (4), 279–293.

Prideaux, B., Laws, E. and Faulkner, B. (2003) Events in Indonesia: Exploring the limits to formal tourism trends forecasting methods in complex crisis situations. *Tourism Management* 24 (4), 475–487.

Proulx, K.E., Hager, M.A. and Klein, K.C. (2014) Models of collaboration between nonprofit organizations. *International Journal of Productivity and Performance Management* 63 (6), 746–765.

Provan, K.G. and Kenis, P. (2005) Modes of network governance and implications for public network management. In *Eighth National Public Management Research Conference*, Los Angeles, CA, September 29–October 1.

Provan, K.G. and Kenis, P. (2008) Modes of network governance: Structure, management, and effectiveness. *Journal of Public Administration Research and Theory* 18 (2), 229–252.

Public Safety Business Agency (2015) *Queensland Disaster Management Arrangements Participant Guide*. [pdf] Available at: http://www.disaster.qld.gov.au/About_Disaster_Management/documents/QDMA-PG.pdf

Queensland Police Service (2015) *Queensland State Disaster Management Plan – Reviewed May 2015*. [pdf] Available at: http://www.disaster.qld.gov.au/Disaster-Resources/Documents/State-Disaster-Management-Plan_WEB.pdf

Ritchie, B.W. (2004) Chaos, crises and disasters: A strategic approach to crisis management in the tourism industry. *Tourism Management* 25 (6), 669–683.
Roberts, V. (1994) Flood management: Bradford paper. *Disaster Prevention and Management* 3 (2), 44–60.
Rockhampton Regional Council (2015) *Cyclone Marcia: Business Recovery and Resilience Plan.* [pdf] Available at: http://fitzroyridges.com.au/Fitzroy_Ridges/cyclone/Rockhampton_Cyclone_Business_Recovery_Plan.pdf
Santana, G. (2004) Crisis management and tourism: Beyond the rhetoric. *Journal of Travel and Tourism Marketing* 15 (4), 299–321.
Sönmez, S.F., Apostolopoulos, Y. and Tarlow, P. (1999) Tourism in crisis: Managing the effects of terrorism. *Journal of Travel Research* 38 (1), 13–18.
Stafford, G., Yu, L. and Armoo, A.K. (2002) Crisis management and recovery: How Washington, DC, hotels responded to terrorism. *Cornell Hospitality Quarterly* 43 (5), 27–40.
Tew, J.P., Lu, Z., Tolomiczenko, G. and Gellatly, J. (2008) SARS: Lessons in strategic planning for hoteliers and destination marketers. *International Journal of Contemporary Hospitality Management* 20 (3), 332–346.
Tiernan, S., Igoe, J., Carroll, C. and O'Keefe, S. (2007) Crisis communication response strategies: A case study of the Irish Tourist Board's response to the 2001 European foot and mouth scare. In E. Laws, B. Prideaux and K. Chon (eds) *Crisis Management in Tourism* (pp. 310–326). Wallingford: CABI Publishing.
Veal, A.J. (2011) *Research Methods for Leisure and Tourism: A Practical Guide.* Harlow: Pearson Education.
Viljoen, J. (1994) *Strategic Management: Planning and Implementing Successful Corporate Strategies* (2nd edn). Melbourne: Longman.
Waugh, W.L. and Streib, G. (2006) Collaboration and leadership for effective emergency management. *Public Administration Review* 66 (1), 131–140.
Williams, C. and Ferguson, M. (2005) Recovering from crisis: Strategic alternatives for leisure and tourism providers based within a rural economy. *International Journal of Public Sector Management* 18 (4), 350–366.
Xu, J. and Grunewald, A. (2009) What have we learned? A critical review of tourism disaster management. *Journal of China Tourism Research* 5 (1), 102–130.
Zeng, B., Carter, R.W. and De Lacy, T. (2005) Short-term perturbations and tourism effects: The case of SARS in China. *Current Issues in Tourism* 8 (4), 306–322.

9 Disaster in #Paradise: The Tourism Riskscape of Tropical Cyclone Winston, Fiji

Cecilia Möller

Introduction

> The ocean was coming inland 70 meters, bringing with it all the debris. I had such big rocks in my swimming pool that I had to get an excavator to get them out. I had chunks of concrete from my swimming pool deck … you know, this big, inside the rooms. All by the ocean. And we had the waves coming up, the swirl coming up and burst our barriers in here. And it was trying to take the furniture out that backdoor. (Owner resort K, Taveuni)

On 20 February 2016, the Fiji Islands were hit by the severe Tropical Cyclone Winston (TC Winston), the most intense cyclone on record to make landfall in the country. TC Winston left significant devastation to local communities, infrastructure, and communications. 44 people were killed, 30,000 houses were destroyed and 250,000 people were in need of immediate emergency assistance such as shelters, water and sanitation (Robinson *et al.*, 2016). For the tourism sector, 19% of the resorts reported significant damage to their properties, mainly in the northern and eastern parts of the islands (Government of Fiji, 2016). The high disaster risk profile of Fiji, manifested through TC Winston, challenges the destination's image as a tropical island paradise of comfort, luxury and authenticity. Following the cyclone, media reports of devastation and flooding spread globally, as well as stories of tourists 'fearing for their lives' in the storm (Murray-Atfield, 2016). Travel warnings were issued for the main tourist markets in Australia and New Zealand. Still, through social media, positive stories of rebuilding and fundraising were communicated by resorts and tourism organisations, sending unifying messages of Fiji being #strongerthanwinston and 'back in business', while launching the social media marketing campaign #*Fijinow* (Möller *et al.*, 2018).

Previous studies of crisis communication show how mobile technology and social media become important tools to provide warnings, updates, damage reports, and mobilisation of assistance and resources (Austin & Jin, 2018). Yet in tourism research few studies have explored the role of social media in disaster situations, and previous studies have been business and management oriented, discussing brand restoration and crisis communication strategies (Hvass, 2013; Ketter, 2016; Liu *et al.*, 2015). This chapter aims to make *tourists* visible as actors in the disaster communication process alongside other destination stakeholders. Previous studies have portrayed tourists as particularly 'vulnerable' to disasters due to their visits to unfamiliar environments (Becken & Hughey, 2013; Wang & Ritchie, 2012). Tourists have also been labelled as 'privileged' groups compared to local residents, since they can choose to avoid or exit the disaster area (Pezzullo, 2009; Syssner & Khayati, 2016). This chapter uses the concept of *'tourism riskscape'* as the 'scene' to analyse the spatial contexts of disaster communication through social media following TC Winston. This allows for an actor approach, where tourists are acknowledged as active producers and consumers in disaster communication. The study is based on interviews with Australian tourists visiting Fiji during, or shortly after, TC Winston, as well as with Fijian resort and destination representatives. Two research questions are addressed: How did tourists and destination stakeholders communicate, interpret and handle travel-related risks through social media? How was social media used to mobilise resources for tourists, destination stakeholders and local communities following the cyclone?

Tourism Riskscapes

The chapter draws inspiration from the communicational turn in human geography and the emerging interdisciplinary field of geomedia studies, which is a way of studying *'the role of media in organizing and giving meaning to processes and activities in space'* (Fast *et al.*, 2018: 3). This allows for a less technology-centred analysis of the use of digital media within tourism, illustrating the complex relations between media and communication on the one hand, and the production, representation and performance of tourism spaces and mobilities on the other. The mediatisation of mobility and everyday life may be both emancipating and empowering through increased accessibility, but also carries traits of inequalities (Fast *et al.,* 2018; Jansson, 2018).

Risks and disasters

Despite being associated with pleasure and hedonism, travelling in a 'global risk society' means that tourists cannot be cut off from risks and uncertainties (Balaz *et al.*, 2015; Beck, 2008). *Risk* has been explored extensively in tourism research, for example in relation to travel as way of experiencing 'adventure' or 'thrills' within extreme tourism and backpacking (Elsrud, 2004; Cater, 2006). Risks have also been studied as part of disaster and crisis management, as a way for tourism businesses and other actors to mitigate, handle and control risks following natural disasters (Huang *et al.*, 2008; Pforr, 2009; Ritchie & Campiranon, 2015). Still, few studies have explored travel-related risks in relation to the use of social media in times of crisis (Björk & Kauppinen-Räisänen, 2012; Mizrachi & Fuchs, 2016). In this chapter, I refer to travel-related risks as both actual visible risks and imagined/perceived risks related to natural *disasters* (Balaz *et al.,* 2015; Seabra *et al.*, 2013). A common definition of a disaster is:

> A serious disruption of the functioning of a community or a society involving widespread human, material, economic or environmental losses and impacts, which exceeds the ability of the affected community or society to cope using its own resources. (United Nations International Strategy for Disaster Reduction (UNISDR), 2009: 9)

Quarantelli (2005) describes natural disasters as rooted within societal and cultural systems, revealing flaws of insufficient risk mitigation and planning, rather than merely being affected by external forces of nature. Thus, a disaster can be interpreted as 'a window upon the inner workings of society' (Alexander, 2005: 25). Still, disasters are global events, mobilising complex networks of emergency and mobilities (Sheller, 2016). Disasters also carry symbolic traits and narratives, communicated through different media channels that sometimes transform the events into entertainment and voyeurism due to their news value (Alexander, 2005).

In this chapter, the term 'tourism riskscapes' is used for analysing the spatial dimensions of risks and disasters associated with tourism destinations (Müller-Mahn, 2013). The term is inspired by Appadurai's (1996) ideas of global cultural flows, connecting the local and global into more fluid (land)scapes as 'imagined worlds'. Appadurai (1996) identifies five different *'scapes'*: ethnoscapes, technoscapes, mediascapes, ideoscapes and financescapes. By using the suffix *scapes*, the localising and globalising forces of tourism can be analysed in terms of how both people and material objects are 'on the move' and mobilised following disasters (van der Duim, 2005, 2007). Rather than merely viewing the disaster as a 'locality', placed at a particular geographical site, disasters may trigger political uprising, fundraising and consequences for mobility on a global scale (Müller-Mahn, 2013). Thus, tourism riskscapes are not as isolated or 'fixed' in space or time, but dynamic and *'implicated within complex networks by which hosts, guests, buildings, objects and machines are contingently brought together to produce certain performances in certain places at certain times*' (Hannam *et al.*, 2006: 13).

The forces of globalisation play a significant role in this process, making disaster response reliant on global networks and systems of interconnectivity, communication and resource mobilisation (Smith, 2005; Urry, 2003). This is also related to issues of *mobility* as being at the 'centre-stage' during disasters (Hannam *et al.*, 2006). Disasters may both trigger and disable different forms of mobility, including virtual/digital mobility (e.g. media and information) and physical mobility (e.g. people and technology). Disasters may contribute to a decrease in tourist arrivals, or immobility during the emergency phase (Cresswell, 2006; Sheller, 2016).

Communicating disasters

The complexity of tourism riskscapes means that different actors are involved in dealing with, responding to, and communicating disaster events. Disasters include collective sense-making processes, revealing contested geographical understandings of the world (Boin, 2005). Media in general, and social media in particular, has an important role in this sense-making process, continuously affecting our (mis)understanding of global risks and crisis events (Finn & Palis, 2015). Previous studies have shown how access to mobile devices and social media have transformed the conditions for crisis communication, providing both opportunities and challenges (Bratu, 2016; Liu *et al.*, 2016). On the one hand, the participatory nature of social media may involve faster ways of sharing and responding to urgent crises, both by distributing warnings and initiating crowd sourcing and fundraising (Cho *et al.*, 2013). On the other hand, it may also give rise to false information, lack of accountability, and lack of control over information flows (Bunce *et al.*, 2012).

In tourism studies, research about social media and crisis communication has been scarce and has evolved around themes of brand and image reputation, and best practices for crisis communication strategies (Austin & Jin, 2018; Zeng & Gerritsen, 2014). I use the concept 'disaster communication' rather than 'crisis communication', as a way of including other actors apart from tourism businesses and organisations in the communication process (Fraustino *et al.*, 2018). I argue that tourists themselves are important actors for responding to and communicating disasters. The tourist is here conceived of as a 'prosumer', who actively takes part in both the production and consumption of risks and media through tourism (Ritzer & Jurgenson, 2010).

Social media has the potential to increase transparency and participation in disaster communication, but previous research has suggested that communications tend to be unevenly produced and consumed following a disaster (Ooi & Munar, 2013; Sheller, 2016). Thus, I also raise questions of *agency* and control in my analysis of how the tourism riskscape is communicated. Smith (2005) applies an actor approach for analysing disaster response, and describes how agency is affected by sociocultural and political contexts in which they are placed: *'Once we see disasters as human-centric, then the interplay of space-place-time and the subtleties around human networks and agencies takes on a new dimension'* (Smith, 2005: 228). Using the CATWOE framework. Disasters root definition, based on the CATWOE (Customers, Actors, Transformations, *Weltanshuung* (worldviews of people), Operators, Environment) dramework, riginally developed by Checkland (1981). Smith (2005) identifies three main groups of actors involved in the disaster response and sense-making process: *victims*, *rescuers* and *agents*. Even though these concepts have been used in an organisational setting, they also address the overlapping roles of tourists and destination stakeholders as both 'victims' and 'rescuers/agents' when tourism riskscapes are communicated and mobilised. Smith (2005) describes *'victims'* as individuals or groups who are directly affected by a disaster event, not as passive targets, but as those who may influence and take actions in its outcomes. *'Rescuers'* involve actors who respond to the emergency (emergency services, disaster agencies) by aiding others, while the *'agents'* are those who make crucial decisions and play an active role for the development and emergence of the disaster. These groups may be overlapping and have different functions in the emergency and recovery processes, including interpreting, communicating and making sense of the disaster events (Smith, 2005).

Tourism and Disasters in Fiji

The Fiji Islands comprise 332 islands and a population of 884,887 of which a majority are indigenous Fijians (56.8%) and Indo-Fijians (37.8%) (Fiji Bureau of Statistics, 2019). Tourism has been the main foreign exchange earner in Fiji since the 1990s, and the number of tourists has increased steadily (Kaufmann & Nakagawa, 2015). Fiji had 792,000 international visitors in 2016, mainly from the Australian, New Zealand and US markets (Fiji Bureau of Statistics, 2019). Tourism's direct contribution to GDP was 14.5% in 2016, constituting 16% of direct employment (Harrison & Pratt, 2015; World Travel and Tourism Council (WTTC), 2017). Apart from its economic benefits, previous research has highlighted a number of sociocultural challenges for tourism development, including political instability, local resistance towards tourism development due to native land ownership conflicts, poor working conditions in the tourism sector, limited sociocultural benefits for indigenous communities, and the use of exotic and subordinate stereotypes of the local population in destination marketing campaigns (Kanemasu, 2013, 2015; Movono *et al.*, 2015). Frequent natural disasters in Fiji, such as cyclones, flooding, drought and seismic activity, also constitute challenges for tourism development. Fiji is affected by at least one cyclone per year, and the urban and informal settlements in coastal areas make the communities vulnerable to flooding (Bryant-Tokalau & Campbell, 2014). Poor tourism planning and land use have in turn had effects on the outcomes of the storms, such as severe flooding (Bernard & Cook, 2015).

TC Winston started its path near Vanuatu in the South Pacific at the beginning of February 2016, moving past Fiji towards Tonga but suddenly changing its track westward and developing into a Category 5 cyclone through Fiji. Its impact included wind gusts exceeding 300km/hour, flash flooding, landslides and storm surges, leaving significant devastation to infrastructure, housing and the agricultural sector. A national state of emergency was declared for 60 days, and Australia and New Zealand provided humanitarian aid relief. Around 80% of the population lost power, and in the worst-hit areas, disruptions in fixed-line and cellular communication services continued several months after the cyclone. TC Winston had a large impact on the Fijian national economy, comprising a total value of F$1.99 billion in disaster effects of which the tourism sector represented F$120 million, including both physical damage and economic losses (Government of Fiji, 2016). The cyclone did not have a high impact on the main tourism areas (e.g. the Coral Coast or Nadi), but left significant damage to resort properties, landscaping and coral reefs in the northern parts of Viti Levu (the main island), Vanua Levu and Taveuni (Government of Fiji, 2016).

Interview Study

Fieldwork was conducted in Australia and Fiji during April and June 2016, including semi-structured interviews with (1) Australian tourists who visited Fiji during and shortly after the cyclone; (2) tourism destination stakeholders, consisting of Fijian resort representatives and the tourism organisation Tourism Fiji. The study has a qualitative approach aimed at gaining a more in-depth understanding of the respondents' own narratives, interpretations and experiences of the events of the cyclones in relation to risks, mobility and communication (Merriam, 2009). Using an interpretivist inquiry approach, the interview material has been analysed by identifying common themes and patterns, but also paradoxes and contradictions in the material, while analysing and theorising its socio-cultural context (Braun & Clarke, 2006; Phillimore & Goodson, 2004).

Interviews with Australian tourists

Australia is the main tourism source market in Fiji and represented 44% of all tourism arrivals in 2016 (Fiji Bureau of Statistics, 2019). The interviewees were recruited through strategic sampling, combining a mix of snowballing, contact through social media (Tripadvisor messages and a Facebook survey) and during fieldwork in Fiji. The survey was distributed in public Facebook groups, including Fiji travel groups and Fijian Australian community groups, with permission from the group administrators. The survey was a way of distributing information about the study while providing consent from the interview participants.

16 interviews were conducted, involving 19 respondents, of whom five were in Fiji during TC Winston and 14 visited Fiji after the cyclone for holiday purposes or volunteer work. Three group interviews were conducted at resorts in Savusavu (Vanua Levu) and Taveuni, while others were conducted via telephone or Skype. The respondents are from different parts of Australia. 14 of the respondents were returning visitors to Fiji. Three of the respondents identified themselves as active participants in a Fijian Australian community, having been born in Fiji or having relatives in Fiji. The interview themes included the use of social media in everyday life, the role of social media when planning the trip, handling the events of the cyclone, post-cyclone fundraising and donations, and travel-related risks associated with Fiji.

Interviews with destination stakeholders - Tourism Fiji and resorts

Tourism Fiji is the main tourism organisation in Fiji, serving under the Department of Tourism to promote and develop Fiji as a tourism destination (Tourism Fiji, 2018). An interview was conducted with a public relations representative to gain insight into how crisis communication in general and social media in particular was used by the organisation following TC Winston.

The resorts included in the interview study were selected geographically, partly based on the degree of impact from TC Winston, and partly based on the destinations' different scale and niches of tourism. Two main areas were identified: (1) Nadi and Denarau Island (Viti Levu), which represent less cyclone-affected areas while constituting one of the main tourism destinations with large-scale resorts. (2) Savusavu (Vanua Levu) and Taveuni, areas that were severely affected by the cyclone which contain more niche and small-scale forms of tourism, including diving resorts. The resorts were initially contacted by email, and snowballing sampling was used. Twelve semi-structured interviews were conducted: Denarau Island (3), Nadi (2), Savusavu (2), Taveuni (5), with a total of 16 respondents. Four of the interviews were group interviews including different representatives from the hotel (e.g. owner, marketing and sales director, manager, staff members). The interview themes focused on crisis management and communication strategies, how social media was used before, during and after TC Winston, risks related to communication practices, and the role of social media for fundraising and donation initiatives (see Möller *et al.*, 2018).

The Tourism Riskscape of TC Winston

The following two sections discuss the results of the interview study based on two main themes: (1) *Communicating tourism riskscapes*, which involves how tourists and tourism actors use social media to monitor, interpret and respond to risks associated with (im)mobility as 'victims' of the disaster; (2) *Mobilising tourism riskscapes*, illustrating how social media was used to respond to the disaster events, making tourists and resorts 'rescuers' and 'agents', by providing assistance for local communities 'at risk'.

Communicating tourism riskscapes

It took me seven days to get them (the tourists) off the island. Because there was nowhere to go … No boats, no planes, anything. So when they finally cleared the road, I got into a car and I drove towards the north … and I see a plane approaching the airport, and it turned out to be a medevac (medical evacuation) plane that was coming to evacuate … and I told the pilot like 'I have eight people here, they'll pay you to get out of the island, can you please come back?' And he came back and took my guests the same day. (Manager, Resort I, Taveuni)

Emergencies like TC Winston trigger sudden immobility, people become stranded, and communications are blocked. However, disaster events also enable certain types of mobilities, such as medical emergency actions and humanitarian aid, as well as alternative forms of communication (Adey, 2016; Sheller, 2016). The interview citation above also highlights how mobility may be unequal in its character, providing means for movement for some groups, including tourists, while being restricted for others. Below I discuss how social media was used to handle risks of *(im) mobility*, *disconnectedness* and *(un)controlled* communication.

Risks of (im)mobility

The state of 'immobility' due to TC Winston was associated with both 'safety' and 'risks' by the respondents. Despite being 'trapped' in the cyclone, tourists described the resorts as safe places for shelter. The large-scale resorts' implementation of 'lock-down' procedures were considered as well-functioning by both tourists and managers. However, some of the smaller resorts in high impact areas were less prepared and more vulnerable to the effects of the cyclone. In Taveuni, guests and staff of one of the resorts were forced to take shelter in a 20-foot shipping container when other parts of the resort flooded.

The respondents describe social media as an important tool for handling risks of both mobility and immobility. They tracked the mobility of TC Winston closely through social media weather news updates and hashtags as a way of estimating the path and impact of the storm. When possible, tourists in Fiji used social media to stay in contact with family and friends overseas and registered as 'safe' through Facebook's Safety Check function. Other respondents who were planning their trips to Fiji monitored the cyclone from Australia by analysing travel-related risks through social media forums, before making their decision to cancel or proceed with their travel. In line with previous research results, different types of risks were emphasised when searching for information online (Björk & Kauppinen-Räisänen, 2012; Boksberger & Craig-Smith, 2006). The interviewees stressed *financial* and *functional* risks, since postponing or cancelling their trips would include financial losses. Some respondents reflected on the risks of not 'getting their money's worth', due to potential damage to the islands and resorts. This included risks of 'paradise being lost', a worry that their previous aesthetic images of Fiji would not be fulfilled when realising their dream holiday. Consequently, one of the aims of using social media was to pinpoint and select locations and resorts that had been less affected by the cyclone. *Physical* risks were also mentioned in the interview study, including diseases such as Zika virus, and potential health related risks associated with poor water and food quality and lack of electricity.

Tourists travelling to more remote areas of Fiji emphasised the lack of information about the effects of the cyclone through regular news and from the resorts. One family travelling with younger children had planned their trip to Fiji carefully before the cyclone hit and had to reconsider their route and choice of resorts:

> The regular online news sites was not really reporting what I needed to know. So I had to rely on Facebook, which to me, I didn't feel… I was sort of perplexed. In this day and age I couldn't get the information that I needed from regular newspapers … So all of a sudden I'm looking at some new sites that I never look at, rarely look at, trying to get information … So then you have to rely on people. (John, visiting Savusavu and the Yasawa Islands)

In this case, the lack of information about the cyclone and the reliance on social media was in itself associated with risk taking and uncertainty. However, a majority of the respondents had previous travel experience to Fiji, which made them less inclined to cancel their trips. For Fijian Australians, potential travel-related risks were considered low, having knowledge and experience from travelling to Fiji after previous cyclones.

Risks of disconnectedness

Access to communication during TC Winston had large geographical variations. Some tourists struggled to get in contact with families overseas, while others could access social media throughout the storm. Ellen describes the 'lock-down' in a ballroom area of one of the large hotels, where there was no internet or phone reception for 48 hours:

> There were people crying, everyone was trying to use their phones but there was no power. And obviously no reception. There was a lot of people, I don't know, just hundreds and hundreds of people just in this area ... And it was very worrying, but... And being close to the ocean, we were actually sitting with probably 50 meters from the actual ocean. That was one concern of mine. (Ellen, Denarau Island)

For the resorts, the cyclone brought challenges of communication with guests overseas, including loss of electricity, disruption of phone lines, and damaged mobile phone towers. Still, some of the larger hotels in the less affected destinations could maintain wi-fi access throughout the cyclone, and social media was described as a more reliable alternative for communication. Resorts in more remote and high-impact areas encountered major challenges with mobile or internet communications for weeks after TC Winston, and had few back-up alternatives such as generators or satellite phones:

> On the Thursday, I could get reception on the roof of my house. I spent like a couple of hours up there, just calling everyone. The first people to have physically made contact with me was the Australian High Commission. And they were the first people to physically come into this property and see if we were okay. No one else from the Government of Fiji, DISMAC, not one person has actually come into this property to see if we were okay. You know, which is ... we're Fijian citizens. (Owner, Resort K, Taveuni)

In order to combat the communication challenges, some of the larger resorts, as well as Tourism Fiji, were able to mobilise 'digital teams' abroad when power and wi-fi were lost. This possibility was a result of previous strategies to outsource PR and social media marketing agencies. Thus, during and after the cyclone, a majority of all social media updates and communication were handled from other countries. This was described as an advantage since it meant that resort staff and management could focus on taking care of in-house guests. Nevertheless, it still required having people 'on the ground', reporting on the effects of the cyclone:

> If we were to moderate and do a lot of things online, we wouldn't have been able to do it from here. We had a generator here, but then it runs out of fuel, and then it needs power. So having them there (in Australia) ... they were responding to queries, they kept everyone calm. This (area) was under water. (Staff) had to go into the office, work overnight. So for us, having someone over there and making sure that someone is constantly communicating updates to Australia, it worked for us. (PR representative, Tourism Fiji)

(Un)controlled communication

For tourists in Fiji during the cyclone, social media became a way of gaining control in a risky situation. Even though they expressed confidence in the resorts' preparedness, they also worried that the staff were not taking the threat of an arriving Category 5 cyclone seriously. The respondents emphasised that the cyclone arrived earlier than first predicted, and that the information provided by resort staff was not up to date:

> I actually had more information through social media than the Fijian people had. They didn't seem to be as aware or using the information, we were telling them information, as tourists. We seemed to know a lot more than they did. They just like 'oh, yeah, another cyclone coming', you know they're used to cyclones there, but I don't think they'd realized that this was a Category 5 that was forecast and just what level of destruction it could do. (Sue, Nadi)

The respondents also contributed to the social media information flows by posting images and movies of the storm and its physical devastation as *'eye-witness reports'*. Posts made on Twitter spread to traditional media and got picked up by TV shows and newspapers in Australia. Doreen posted pictures of a damaged resort on Instagram but was contacted by the staff and asked to remove the resort's hashtag, since it was considered as damaging for the resort's image:

> People on Instagram, a lot of people contacted me, because they were going to be staying on (island) resort in the next like month or two, so they wanted to know like 'how bad is it?' … Because (island) is really well known for its vegetation … but the gardens were just so demolished, it was just crazy. It was just nothing left. So I just told people that the vegetation wouldn't be very good, but it's still a very beautiful place to go. (Doreen, Mamanuca Islands)

Attempts to control the reputation of Fiji through social media were also discussed by the resorts. One resort gave an example of how disappointed guests chose to evaluate the resort's service during the cyclone in social media forums, rather than making direct complaints to the staff and management teams. In this case, the guests were contacted by staff and asked to remove their social media posts.

For tourists visiting Fiji post-cyclone, damage reports through social media were described as less 'trustworthy', and the respondents emphasised the need for applying 'critical eyes' due to the possible manipulation of content. Consequently, they used their social networks and contacted the resorts by email or phone to control the information. One holidaying couple followed the *#FijiNow* campaign on Instagram and emphasised the advantage of experiencing Fiji 'through the eyes of the bloggers' but struggled to interpret the trustworthiness of Instagram images:

> They would always post heaps and heaps of photos with the hashtag #Fijinow. But then still even a part of us was like 'I don't know if they're just doing that just to make people come there again kind of thing'. But what if it actually does look like that. Because some of the photos were amazing like, because we were all thinking like all the palm trees wouldn't have any leaves on them. And then like you'd see photos like that and you'd think 'is it real?' (Hannah, Taveuni)

Mobilising Tourism Riskscapes

> The resort was absolutely smashed. Big time. It was actually quite sad to see something that you know, absolutely beautiful and then you go there and the mango trees are on the ground and, you know, it was just devastating, unbelievable. And the village, just everything you know, the place was just ripped apart. I've never experienced something like that in my life. It was like jaw-dropping. (Ben, volunteer, Vanua Levu)

Ben followed the path of TC Winston through social media from Australia, realising that the resort that he and his family had visited for several years had suffered a direct hit. He got in contact with staff members through Facebook to check the effects of the cyclone in their village. 12 days after the cyclone, Ben and other volunteers travelled to Fiji to rebuild staff housing after raising money through a Facebook page and GoFundMe initiative.

In the interview study, social media was described as a crucial tool for responding to the effects of the cyclone by mobilising different resources from outside of the disaster area, including fundraising, donations and labour. Below, I will discuss examples of how the tourism riskscape was mobilised through social media, including *mobilising mobilities*, *mobilising network capital* and *mobilising communities*.

Mobilising mobilities

For tourism, immobility may in itself constitute a 'disaster', generating impaired economic and sociocultural effects for the destination. Thus, destination actors such as government agencies and tourism businesses are responsible for getting things 'moving again' following a disaster event (Adey, 2016). In Fiji, a 'crisis-group' (Tourism Action Group) was activated after TC Winston, including destination and resort representatives, to proactively combat the risks of decreasing visitor numbers. The social media marketing campaign *#FijiNow* was launched to convey positive messages of Fiji being 'back in business' and encourage tourists to post images of their post-cyclone experiences using the hashtag *#FijiNow*. Moreover, a

selection of well-known social media influencers was invited to Fiji to reinforce the aesthetic image of Fiji as a 'tropical paradise':

> These are people who have 50,000 or even over a million followers … So
> these are people who are travelling the world, promoting destinations …
> We brought them in, took them around, got them to take nice images and
> post them on their Instagram accounts. And their followers would obvi-
> ously see them, like them. So obviously, using the hashtag, like 'I'm here
> in this beautiful place, sipping a Piña Colada…' (PR representative,
> Tourism Fiji)

The campaign was especially used by the large-scale hotels in destinations
less affected by the cyclone, which stated the importance of avoiding 'keep
hammering in the message' of the devastating cyclone through traditional
media channels.

The need to maintain tourism arrivals was also emphasised by the tourists themselves. Fiji's dependence on tourism was used as an argument for
travelling to Fiji, in order to continue supporting the local population's work
and income from tourism. The respondents also stressed the importance of
bringing donations into Fiji. Social media was used to coordinate and distribute donations, ranging from large-scale projects of shipping containers
to Fiji, to micro-initiatives of packing extra clothes or food items in suit-
cases. Transporting goods and supplies into Fiji was also crucial for volunteer work, since equipment in Fiji was both expensive and scarce:

> We took about 400 kilograms of supplies with us, we ended up having to
> pay excess baggage on it which is a bit annoying, considering that we were
> doing it out of our own pockets to help people. We took over about 9,000
> roofing screws … We took over our own power tools … And threw in a
> little clothes, 8 t-shirts, just the bare minimum stuff that we need. (Ben,
> volunteer, Vanua Levu)

The barriers for mobility were highlighted, including customs regulations,
fees and long delays. In most cases, the donations were informal and non-
profit initiatives. This reflected a distrust towards established aid organisations due to previous failures of bringing in aid to Fiji and problems
with corruption. Thus, social media initiatives were considered as more
reliable, and the tourists expressed a wish for 'delivering the donations
themselves'. The resorts also posted updates through their Facebook
pages of what the tourists could bring, and the donations were distributed
by the staff to affected villages.

Mobilising network capital

Previous research has defined *network capital* as key 'instruments for
mobility' during disasters, including for example legal documents,

vehicles, communications, and the ability to create networks (Sheller, 2016; Urry, 2012). According to Urry (2012: 27), 'Network capital is the capacity to engender and sustain social relations with those people who are not necessarily proximate and which generates emotional, financial and practical benefits'.

Network capital is considered to be a result of people's work and mobile lifestyles, as 'over and above their possession of economic or cultural capital' (Urry, 2012: 27). Urry (2012: 27) claims that network capital entails eight different elements: (1) documents, visas, money; (2) people who can offer hospitality; (3) movement capacities; (4) location free information; (5) communication devices; (6) safe and secure meeting points; (7) access to multiple systems; (8) time and resources to manage system failures. The networks also tend to be 'on the move', and can be activated in different places through mobile technologies. The access to network capital also tends to reflect social inequalities, for example between poor and immobile local communities and the well-connected mobile foreign aid workers (Sheller, 2016; Urry, 2012).

The respondents who were travelling to Fiji for volunteer purposes described how they mobilised both private and professional networks through social media for planning and coordinating their work. In Australia, local fundraising events were organised through churches and Fijian Australian communities, coordinated through Facebook and GoFundMe pages. The fundraising and donation initiatives on social media spread onwards to TV and newspapers. Dialogue with affected resorts and local villages in Fiji were also maintained through social media:

> We tried to get some photos of the village, which she (resort owner) put on the social media so that we could see, you know, the impact on the village through photos posted on Facebook. And then we set up a GoFundMe page. And we managed to raise around 15,000 dollars. Yeah, it happened quite quickly ... I think, it was three weeks from us first kind of talking about it, then we were on the plane ready to go. (Stephen, volunteer, Vanua Levu)

The volunteer work included different forms of non-profit work, from project management to manual labour when rebuilding houses or distributing donations, such as clothes, toys and health items. The respondents emphasised the importance of bringing together people's different skills, and their professional networks were used to raise sponsorship and donations, such as building material and tools. Chloe describes how she coordinated her volunteer work from her local community in Queensland, while mobilising her contacts from around the world:

> I didn't know how to build a house. But we built it. I'm a business analyst. I do like process design. Being able to use social media to connect with

people and for people to be able to see what you've been doing and what you are doing. It's like we've got an architect in Toronto. We've got an architect in Sydney. We've got a structural engineer in Indonesia at the moment. (Chloe)

Mobilising communities

The small-scale resorts in high-impact areas stated how they became 'first responders' to the devastation affecting staff members' villages following the cyclone. They contributed with emergency assistance to the villagers, such as food, water and clothes, before the arrival of national and foreign disaster relief aid. The resort representatives expressed little confidence in the abilities for national aid initiatives and started their own social media fundraising campaigns for the needs of local villages, together with local aid organisations, previous tourists, and their personal networks.

The respondents highlighted the unifying powers of social media following the cyclone as a way of bringing people in both Australia and Fiji closer together. For the Fijian Australian interviewees, coordinating donation campaigns through social media provided a new platform for collaboration in communities which previously had been dispersed due to religious and ethnic conflicts. As Fijian Australians, they emphasised the responsibilities to make updates on social media following the delivery of donations, acting as 'spokespersons' for their communities:

I think that the fact that they knew someone that returned there was really what themselves feel connected, because I'm a good friend and I'm there, it affected me, they felt were affected, they were happy because we were happy. (Laisa)

The resorts also acknowledged how social media became a way of bringing tourists, staff and communities together as a 'fan resort community'. The resorts described how they posted 'heroic' stories of tourists as helpers and rebuilders following the cyclone, showing both the economic contributions made by tourists and also their work efforts as volunteers.

The respondents described it as their responsibility to assist Fijian 'friends and family', with whom they had established a relationship during their travels to Fiji. The interviews also made sociocultural inequalities between tourists and the local population visible. Both tourists and resort managers described the staff and local communities as being resilient, relaxed, welcoming and smiling despite the disaster events, while putting the needs of the tourists first before their own families and friends. Social media became a way of promoting resilience, emphasising that the resorts and their staff were back in business and 'stronger than Winston' (Irons & Paton, 2017; Möller *et al.*, 2018):

> No one showed how concerned and worried they were, they just delivered and kept on connecting with the guests and being all smiles and singing. It was crazy to see, everyone was still smiling, I remember one photo in particular, the landscaping guy, doing a quick nap in the bathrobe, just all smiles, and it looked like the perfect day in Fiji but it wasn't, it was the day after the cyclone, it was like terrible, it was so much to do but, yeah... I guess, that's what's Fiji is all about, and what the Fijian people are all about. (Director of sales and marketing, Resort A, Denarau Island)

The narratives of the tourists as volunteers and donors bear colonial traits, highlighting the distinctions between hosts and guests. They portray the Fijian population as living 'simple and poor traditional lives', and in need of external 'expert' assistance due to dysfunctional building standards, work culture and the lack of know-how and skills for rebuilding their communities. Some respondents described the Fijians as well-connected through internet and social media, while other respondents stressed the stereotypical image of the Fijian people as living traditional and isolated lives:

> Do they have social media? Or, you don't need to have them on social media, they're just friendly anyway kind of thing. And they're so welcoming, I'm sure they wouldn't turn your back if you did want to help them kind of thing (Hannah, Taveuni)

Discussion and Conclusions

In this chapter, I have discussed how social media was used to negotiate travel-related risks for both tourists and resorts following TC Winston, as well as to mobilise assistance and resources for tourism stakeholders and the local population 'at risk'. I argue that there is a need to make tourists visible in the disaster communication process, as actors and participants for handling and responding to disaster events. In my analysis, tourists emerge as both *'victims'* and *'rescuers/agents'* of the disaster (Smith, 2005). In the first case, social media was used to negotiate agency and control for action rather than passivity to prepare and handle the events of TC Winston. Secondly, tourists used social media as a tool for showing action and response in the post-cyclone period, including planning, coordinating and bringing in immediate assistance and aid, such as building materials, donations and health supplies, which traditionally are handled by aid organisations or disaster relief agencies. Thus, the traditional roles and definitions of tourists in relation to other stakeholders are blurred, including the distinctions between leisure/everyday life, tourist/worker, guest/host, home/away.

The results show how social media tended to provide a *unifying* force between tourism stakeholders following the cyclone, reinforcing established links of friendship between the tourists and resort staff and their local communities, turning tourists into commercial 'destination brand carriers' in the recovery phase, activating Fijian Australian communities overseas, and mobilising the resort's 'fan communities' both virtually and physically. However, my analysis also reveals more *ambivalent, unequal patterns* of mobility and communication. The tourism riskscape of Fiji following TC Winston can be analysed as a *disaster space of the in-between,* revealing spatial contradictions of liminality in the shifts between, for example, centrality/marginality, mobility/immobility, safety/risk (Andrews & Roberts, 2012). Thus, the tourism riskscape is reclaimed as a space for consumption and touristic pleasure on the one hand, and (de)constructed as a disaster space of utter devastation on the other hand. A disaster event like TC Winston brings issues of inequalities and exploitation to a head, while renegotiating issues of mobility, communication and risks, which may also provide opportunities to promote change, agency and redistribution of power (Balaz *et al.*, 2015). Below, I discuss different examples of 'in-betweenness'.

The local/global

The boundaries of the tourism riskscape are not 'fixed' but 'fluid' as defined by diverse layers of narratives and representations through social media (Ooi & Munar, 2013). TC Winston did not merely have local effects, but generated a global response, including fundraising, donations and mobilities. On the one hand, tourists used social media to pinpoint the specific 'risky' location of the disaster, but on the other hand, social media activated complex global networks of virtual and physical communities and resources.

Mobility/immobility

The mobility of TC Winston, making its way towards Fiji, was monitored by aerial satellite images and weather updates from Fiji as well as overseas. Social media updates and hashtags added to rumours and misinformation about when the cyclone was supposed to hit. The impact of the cyclone generated both immobility and mobilities of people, goods, donations and money. Navigating the tourism riskscape through social media made both privileged exit and entry to the destination possible. As temporary visitors, tourists could choose to leave the disaster area and return as volunteers or post-cyclone visitors. Still, the prevailing immobility of the local population constitutes a crucial component of the tourism riskscape, which in turn also spurs tourism mobilities as a way of supporting and assisting Fijians 'at risk'.

Connected/disconnected

The impact of TC Winston reveals uneven geographies of both physical damage and access to communications. For tourism, the impact reinforced existing centre-periphery relations of the destination. Some of the small-scale resorts in more remote areas of Fiji were shattered by the storm, while large-scale resorts in the main tourism destinations had limited impact. This affected their potential to use social media. Some resorts were placed in 'void' communication pockets, while others had wi-fi and cellular phone reception throughout the storm. Still, the networked spaces of disaster communication also provided alternative ways of communication through outsourced social media agencies located overseas.

Controlled/uncontrolled

The tourism riskscape constitutes a contested space, which raises questions of control and uncontrol, and of who benefits from spreading information and generating action through social media. The results of the study show the ambivalent roles of tourists in this process, partly as 'victims' of temporary disconnectedness, immobility and risks, and partly as regaining control and access to information and communication in the safe spaces of the resorts. Social media is described as uncontrolled by both tourists and the resorts themselves, raising questions of trustworthiness and how the image of the destination was 'filtered' by tourism stakeholders following the cyclone.

Mobilisation/immobilisation

Donations and fundraising were described as a reaction towards other actors' inability to respond to the disaster, including Fijian government agencies and international aid organisations. This also included the local Fijian communities, which were not considered able to rebuild and respond to the disaster events on their own. On the one hand, the Fijian communities were described as resilient, smiling and strong, having the capacity to withstand and 'bounce back' following the cyclone. On the other hand, they were portrayed as vulnerable, suffering and in need of external assistance as victims of the disaster. Thus, initiatives of rebuilding and fundraising can be interpreted as indirectly immobilising local communities' rebuilding capacities.

References

Adey, P. (2016) Emergency mobilities. *Mobilities* 11 (1), 32–48.
Alexander, D. (2005) An interpretation of disaster in terms of changes in culture, society and international relations. In R.W. Perry and E.L. Quarantelli (eds) *What Is A Disaster?: New Answers to Old Questions* (pp. 25–38). Philadelphia: Xlibris.

Andrews, H. and Roberts, L. (2012) *Liminal Landscapes: Travel, Experience and Spaces In-between*. Abingdon: Routledge.

Appadurai, A. (1996) *Modernity at Large: Cultural Dimensions of Globalization*. Minneapolis: University of Minnesota Press.

Austin, L.L. and Jin, Y. (2018) *Social Media and Crisis Communication*. New York, NY: Routledge.

Balaz, V., Williams, A.M. and Balaz, V. (2015) Tourism risk and uncertainty: Theoretical reflections. *Journal of Travel Research* 54 (3), 271–287.

Beck, U. (2008) *World Risk Society*. Cambridge: Polity Press.

Becken, S. and Hughey, K.F.D. (2013) Linking tourism into emergency management structures to enhance disaster risk reduction. *Tourism Management* 36, 77–85.

Bernard, K. and Cook, S. (2015) Luxury tourism investment and flood risk: Case study on unsustainable development in Denarau island resort in Fiji. *Interntional Journal of Disaster Risk Reduction* 14 (3), 302–311.

Björk, P. and Kauppinen-Räisänen, H. (2012) A netnographic examination of travelers' online discussions of risks. *Tourism Management Perspectives* 2–3, 65–71.

Boin, A. (2005) From crisis to disaster: Towards an integrative perspective. In R.W. Perry and E.L. Quarantelli (eds) *What Is A Disaster?: New Answers to Old Questions* (pp. 153–172). Philadelphia: Xlibris.

Boksberger, P.E. and Craig-Smith, S.J. (2006) Customer value amongst tourists: A conceptual framework and a risk-adjusted model. *Tourism Review* 61 (1), 6–12.

Bratu, S. (2016) The critical role of social media in crisis communication. *Linguistic and Philosophical Investigations* 15, 232–238.

Braun, V. and Clarke, V. (2006) Using thematic analysis in psychology. *Qualitative Research in Psychology* 3 (2), 77–101.

Bryant-Tokalau, J. and Campbell, J. (2014) Coping with floods in urban Fiji: Responses and resilience of the poor. In M. Sakai, E. Jurriëns, J. Zhang and A. Thornton (eds) *Disaster Relief in the Asia Pacific: Agency and Resilience* (pp. 132–146). Abingdon: Routledge.

Bunce, S., Partridge, H. and Davis, K. (2012) Exploring information experience using social media during the 2011 Queensland Floods: A pilot study. *Australian Library Journal* 61 (1), 34.

Cater, C.I. (2006) Playing with risk? Participant perceptions of risk and management implications in adventure tourism. *Tourism Management* 27 (2), 317–325.

Checkland, P. (1981) *Systems Thinking, Systems Practice*. Chichester: Wiley.

Cho, S.E., Jung, K. and Park, H.W. (2013) Social media use during Japan's 2011 earthquake: How Twitter transforms the locus of crisis communication. *Media International Australia* 149 (1), 28–40.

Cresswell, T. (2006) *On the Move: Mobility in the Modern Western World*. New York: Routledge.

Elsrud, T. (2004) Taking Time and Making Journeys: Narratives on Self and the Other Among Backpackers. Lund Dissertations in Sociology Vol. 56. Lund: Lund University.

Fast, K., Jansson, A., Tesfahuney, M., Bengtsson, L.R. and Lindell, J. (2018) Introduction to Geomedia Studies. In K. Fast, A. Jansson, J. Lindell, L.R. Bengtsson and M. Tesfahuney (eds) *Geomedia Studies: Spaces and Mobilities in Mediatized Worlds* (pp. 1–17). New York: Routledge.

Fiji Bureau of Statistics (2019) *Visitor Arrivals Statistics: Summary of Visitor Arrivals and Departures*. [online] Available at: http://www.statsfiji.gov.fj/statistics/tourism-and-migration-statistics/visitor-arrivals-statistics

Finn, J.C. and Palis, J. (2015) Introduction: The medium, the message, and media geography in the 21st century. *GeoJournal* 80 (6), 781–790.

Fraustino, J.D., Liu, B.F. and Jin, Y. (2018) Social media use during disasters. In L.L. Austin and Y. Jin (eds) *Social Media and Crisis Communication* (pp. 283–295). New York: Routledge.

Government of Fiji (2016) *Fiji Post-Disaster Needs Assessment. Tropical Cyclone Winston, February 20, 2016.* [pdf] Available at: https://www.gfdrr.org/sites/default/files/publication/Post%20Disaster%20Needs%20Assessments%20CYCLONE%20WINSTON%20Fiji%202016%20(Online%20Version)pdf

Hannam, K., Sheller, M. and Urry, J. (2006) Editorial: Mobilities, immobilities and moorings. *Mobilities* 7 (1), 1–22.

Harrison, D. and Pratt, S. (2015) Tourism in Pacific Island countries. Current issues and future challenges. In S. Pratt and D. Harrison (eds) *Tourism in Pacific Islands: Current Issues and Future Challenges* (pp. 3–21). Abingdon: Routledge.

Huang, Y.-C., Tseng, Y.-P. and Petrick, J.F. (2008) Crisis management planning to restore tourism after disasters: A case study from Taiwan. *Journal of Travel & Tourism Marketing* 23 (2–4), 203–221.

Hvass, K.A. (2013) Tourism social media and crisis communication: An erupting trend. In A.M. Munar, S. Gyimóthy and L. Cai (eds) *Tourism Social Media: Transformations in Identity, Community and Culture* (pp. 177–192). Bingley: Emerald Group Publishing.

Irons, M. and Paton, D. (2017) Social media and emergent groups: The impact of high functionality on community resilience. In D. Paton and D.M. Johnston (eds) *Disaster Resilience: An Integrated Approach* (pp. 194–211, 2nd edn). Springfield: Charles C Thomas Publisher.

Jansson, A. (2018) *Mediatization and Mobile Lives: A Critical Approach.* Abingdon: Routledge.

Kanemasu, Y. (2013) Social construction of touristic imagery: Case of Fiji. *Annals of Tourism Research* 43, 456–481.

Kanemasu, Y. (2015) Fiji tourism half a century on: Tracing the trajectory of local responses. In S. Pratt and D. Harrison (eds) *Tourism in Pacific Islands: Current Issues and Future Challenges* (pp. 87–108). Abingdon: Routledge.

Kaufmann, U. and Nakagawa, H. (2015) Recent developments and changes in demand for tourism in Fiji. In S. Pratt and D. Harrison (eds) *Tourism in Pacific Islands: Current Issues and Future Challenges* (pp. 196–218). Abingdon: Routledge.

Ketter, E. (2016) Destination image restoration on facebook: The case study of Nepal's Gurkha earthquake. *Journal of Hospitality and Tourism Management* 28, 66–72.

Liu, B., Kim, H. and Pennington-Gray, L. (2015) Responding to the bed bug crisis in social media. *International Journal of Hospitality Management* 47, 76–84.

Liu, B.F., Fraustino, J.D. and Jin, Y. (2016) Social media use during disasters: How information form and source influence intended behavioral responses. *Communication Research* 43 (5), 626–646.

Merriam, S.B. (2009) *Qualitative Research: A Guide to Design and Implementation.* San Francisco: Jossey-Bass.

Mizrachi, I. and Fuchs, G. (2016) Should we cancel? An examination of risk handling in travel social media before visiting ebola-free destinations. *Journal of Hospitality and Tourism Management* 28, 59–65.

Möller, C., Wang, J. and Nguyen, H.T. (2018) #strongerthanwinston: Tourism and crisis communication through Facebook following tropical cyclones in Fiji. *Tourism Management* 69, 272–284.

Movono, A., Pratt, S. and Harrison, D. (2015) Adapting and reacting to tourism development. A tale of two villages on Fiji's Coral Coast. In S. Pratt and D. Harrison (eds) *Tourism in Pacific Islands. Current Issues and Future Challenges* (pp. 101–117). Abingdon: Routledge.

Müller-Mahn, H. (2013) *The Spatial Dimension of Risk: How Geography Shapes the Emergence of Riskscapes.* New York: Routledge.

Murray-Atfield, Y. (2016) Cyclone Winston: Australian holidaymakers 'feared for their lives' in Fiji's category five storm. *ABC News,* 21 February. [online] Available at: http://www.abc.net.au/news/2016-02-21/australians-describe-tropical-cyclone-winston/7187608

Ooi, C.S. and Munar, A.M. (2013) Digital social construction of a tourist site: Ground zero. In A.M. Munar, S. Gyimóthy and L. Cai (eds) *Tourism Social Media: Transformations in Identity, Community and Culture* (pp. 159–175). Bingley: Emerald Group Publishing.

Pezzullo, P.C. (2009) 'This is the only tour that sells': Tourism, disaster, and national identity in New Orleans. *Journal of Tourism and Cultural Change* 7 (2), 99–114.

Pforr, C. (2009) Crisis management in tourism: A review of the emergent literature. In C. Pforr and P. Hosie (eds) *Crisis Management in the Tourism Industry: Beating the Odds?* (pp. 37–52). Farnham: Ashgate.

Phillimore, J. and Goodson, L. (2004) The inquiry paradigm in qualitative research. In J. Phillimore and L. Goodson (eds) *Qualitative Research in Tourism: Ontologies, Epistemologies and Methodologies* (pp. 30–45). London: Routledge.

Quarantelli, E.L. (2005) A social science research agenda for the disasters of the 21st century: Theoretical, methodological and empirical issues and their professional implementation. In R.W. Perry and E.L. Quarantelli (eds) *What Is A Disaster?: New Answers to Old Questions* (pp. 325–396). Philadelphia: Xlibris.

Ritchie, B.W. and Campiranon, K. (2015) *Tourism Crisis and Disaster Management in the Asia-Pacific [Elektronisk resurs]*. Wallingford: CABI.

Ritzer, G. and Jurgenson, N. (2010) Production, consumption, prosumption: The nature of capitalism in the age of the digital 'prosumer'. *Journal of Consumer Culture* 10 (1), 13–36.

Robinson, C., Harris, C., Ray, S., Morrison, I. and Cross, R. (2016) Case study: How a disaster simulation helped red cross prepare for Cyclone Winston. *Australian Journal of Emergency Management* 31 (3), 12–14.

Seabra, C., Dolnicar, S., Abrantes, J.L. and Kastenholz, E. (2013) Heterogeneity in risk and safety perceptions of international tourists. *Tourism Management* 36, 502–510.

Sheller, M. (2016) Connected mobility in a disconnected world: Contested infrastructure in postdisaster contexts. *Annals of the American Association of Geographers* 106 (2), 330– 339.

Smith, D. (2005) In the eyes of the beholder? Making sense of the system(s) of disaster(s). In R.W. Perry and E.L. Quarantelli (eds) *What Is A Disaster?: New Answers to Old Questions* (pp. 201–236). Philadelphia: Xlibris.

Syssner, J. and Khayati, K. (2016) Veni, Vidi, Adios: The tourist and the three privileges. In M. Tesfahuney and K. Schough (eds) *Privileged Mobilities: Tourism as World Ordering* (pp. 31–46). Newcastle upon Tyne: Cambridge Scholars Publishing.

Tourism Fiji (2018) About Tourism Fiji. [online] Available at: www.fiji.travel/about-tourism-fiji

United Nations International Strategy for Disaster Reduction (UNISDR) (2009) 2009 UNISDR Terminology on Disaster Risk Reduction. [pdf] Available at: https://www.unisdr.org/files/7817_UNISDRTerminologyEnglish.pdf

Urry, J. (2003) *Global Complexity*. Cambridge: Polity.

Urry, J. (2012) Social networks, mobile lives and social inequalities. *Journal of Transport Geography* 21, 24–30.

van der Duim, R. (2005) Tourismscapes. An Actor-network Perspective on Sustainable Tourism Development. PhD, Wageningen University.

van der Duim, R. (2007) Tourismscapes an actor-network perspective. *Annals of Tourism Research* 34 (4), 961–976.

Wang, J. and Ritchie, B.W. (2012) Understanding accommodation managers' crisis planning intention: An application of the theory of planned behaviour. *Tourism Management* 33 (5), 1057–1067.

World Travel and Tourism Council (WTTC) (2017) *Travel & Tourism: Economic Impact 2017 Fiji*. London: WTTC.

Zeng, B. and Gerritsen, R. (2014) What do we know about social media in tourism? A review. *Tourism Management Perspectives* 10, 27–36.

10 Damage to Inland Tourism from Rain-Derived Floods

Diego Toubes, Noelia Araújo-Vila and
José Antonio Fraiz-Brea

Introduction

Studies analysing the impact of floods on tourism normally approach the activity as one of the affected industries (Merz *et al.*, 2010; Yeo, 2002) and focus on marine and coastal floods (Kellens *et al.*, 2011; Toubes *et al.*, 2017). The tourism sector, by nature, depends on territorial and environmental attributes, and is closely related to local societies. Moreover, it is highly sensitive to weather conditions and global climate change (De Freitas, 2003; Scott & Lemieux, 2010). Therefore, tourism is a vulnerable sector, and it may suffer severe loss due to natural phenomena such as floods (Agnew & Viner, 2001; Espiner & Becken, 2014). This phenomenon offers risks to the population in general, including both residents and tourists (Sayers *et al.*, 2013). Mountain areas are the most vulnerable due to their higher exposure to sudden rises in the water levels, which may cause flash floods. This was the case in the flood of the *Grand Bonnard* campsite in the French Alps in 1987, which killed 23 people (Meunier, 1990) as well as that in the *Las Nieves* campsite in the Pyrenees in 1996, which killed 87 people (Gutiérrez *et al.*, 1998).

Any area where recreational activities are carried out in fresh water by a significant number of people is vulnerable to flooding (World Health Organization (WHO), 2003). In inland areas, the most common recreational uses of fresh water are bathing/swimming, recreational fishing, recreational sailing and boating, and uses related to medicinal properties of thermal water (Ministry of Agriculture and Fisheries, Food and Environment (MAPAMA), 2017; Hall & Härkönen, 2006). An increasing body of literature has addressed the impact of floods with a focus on affected assets, such as campsites, caravan parking lots, river beaches, water sports, resorts and accommodation establishments (Bernard & Cook, 2015; Fitchett *et al.*, 2016; Southon & van der Merwe, 2018; Yeo, 2003), and Faulkner and Vikulov (2001) refine the model of disaster management in tourism and apply it to the case of flooding in Katherine

(Australia). However, the issue remains underexplored, and more research is needed on inland rain-derived floods to analyse the potential and indirect impacts on tourist activity as a result of damage to heritage sites, natural spaces, tourist facilities and local infrastructure. Flood experiences may also influence risk perceptions and, thus, become a threat to tourist destinations (Walters et al., 2014).

Flood Damage Assessment in Inland Tourism

The assessment of flood damage is necessary for the development of vulnerability analysis tools, such as risk maps, as well as for calculating insurance prices. Besides the economic aspects, such evaluation must consider the social, cultural, environmental and political dimensions of flooding. Damage evaluation is a complex endeavour, not least because it relates to heterogeneous elements that affect vulnerability, such as climatic oscillations and socioeconomic factors that might intensify or mitigate damage (Khan, 2011; Yu et al., 2009). In this context, the present work follows Merz et al.'s (2010) suggestions regarding flood damage evaluation and applies them to the context of inland tourism, focusing on the case of river floods.

The chapter evaluates the damage of individual elements at risk (micro-scale approach) and employs an empirical method, which allows for the collection of precise information. This approach facilitated adaptation to the vulnerability that arise from different situations, i.e. flood type, flooded elements, previous experiences, and warning time. A major limitation faced when employing such an approach is the application of the results of the study to other tourist destinations and flood scenarios (Smith, 1994). Due to the difficulty in obtaining data on the value of affected assets, the study employed absolute damage functions and estimated the direct monetary damage caused by the floods (Messner, 2007). Furthermore, as the damage depends on the affected elements' value, considering that such value may increase due to new investments, future periodic calibrations will be necessary to maintain accurate assessments (Penning-Rowsell & Green, 2000).

Types of flood damage

Flood impacts on the tourism industry include a decline in visitor numbers and consequent business loss, damage to facilities and infrastructure, and rebuilding costs (Bernard & Cook, 2015; Fatti & Patel, 2013; Hamzah et al., 2012). Floods may cause direct and indirect damage to tourism. Direct damage refers to the interruption of business activities due to the physical impacts of flood water on facilities (Merz et al., 2011). Indirect damage is caused by a flood, but not in the same time period and place as the disaster. Flood damage can also be classified as tangible and intangible. Tangible damage includes both direct and indirect damage that can be evaluated in monetary terms without any significant difficulty. Despite the clarity of planning, there are practical difficulties and potential confusion in the classification of damage as direct or indirect, as well as tangible or intangible (Jonkman *et al.*, 2008).

The indirect costs are difficult to quantify and may have effects over months or even years. In the short term, floods cause indirect economic damage through decreased tourist consumption and, consequently, of income due to the interruption of business activities. Floods may also cause indirect impacts over the long term through changes in tourist behaviour and destination choice (Jeuring & Becken, 2013; Scott *et al.*, 2012), communication and promotion channels, the local community, local jobs and public budgets. In this context, in order to effectively evaluate the damage caused by floods, it is necessary to carry out a dynamic adjustment, which is normally not included in the existing damage evaluation models (Merz *et al.*, 2010). In order to measure the indirect costs, some studies employ data from public aid and insurance companies. However, such data is of limited use, as it does not include the biggest part of indirect effects. Moreover, many companies do not have business interruption insurance (Merz *et al.*, 2010).

Exposure and susceptibility analysis

The first step to estimate the cost of flood damage on the tourism sector is defining the study's spatial and temporal limits, as the damage evaluation results may change according to such limits. For example, a flood may negatively affect the tourist activity in a particular locality but cause an increase in visits to neighbouring destinations. In this context, from a broad enough temporal and spatial perspective, the economic damage caused by the disaster in one locality is compensated by the increase caused in others. On the other hand, an evaluation adopting a narrower spatial perspective would overestimate the total damage by focusing on the directly affected destination.

Once these limits are defined, it is necessary to establish the baseline. As each sector has specific characteristics, it is important to identify the assets of tourism that have been affected (Economic Commission for Latin America and the Caribbean (ECLAC), 2003). The assets' susceptibility also differs according to the sector. For instance, the elements at risk included in the 'infrastructure' and 'public utilities' categories are common to many sectors. However, there are important differences to be considered when evaluating the impact of damage to those assets on tourism, agriculture or the manufacturing industry. Therefore, it is necessary to have detailed information on the elements at risk, namely: number, capacity and relevance, as the distribution of damage and affected elements

Table 10.1 Elements at risk in tourism sector with river flood event

Service sector	Facilities	Infrastructure	Others
hotels restaurants travel agencies tour operators	spas campsite and caravan parks rest and recreation areas swimming pools sports centres	transportation communications water supply sewerage and drainage gas and power supply	ecosystems, cultural heritage clean-up costs cost of promotional campaigns increase in insurance damage to flood defence structures

Adapted and extended from ECLAC (2003) and Merz *et al.* (2010).

often follows a Pareto distribution. This means that 20% of the affected elements correspond to 80% of the total damage (Merz *et al.*, 2010). The grouping and classification of elements at risk tends to be based on the judgement of specialists in the field. Table 10.1 presents the elements at risk in the tourism industry for rain-derived floods.

Damage evaluation is carried out homogeneously in terms of the elements of each class and considering the different types of damage: direct and indirect; tangible and intangible. Adopting this classification, Merz *et al.* (2011) propose the following list of elements at risk in the tourism industry:

- *Direct, tangible*: damage to accommodation establishments, restaurants, bars and facilities; destruction of infrastructure, such as paths, roads and railroads; business interruption inside the flooded area; evacuation and rescue measures; clean-up costs.
- *Direct, intangible*: damage to cultural heritage; negative effects on ecosystems.
- *Indirect, tangible*: disruption of public services outside the flooded area; business losses to companies outside the flooded area, e.g. cancellation of tour operators and suppliers of flooded camping and hotels.
- *Indirect, intangible*: media coverage; negative perception; business closure due to lack of resilience.

Besides the nature of the affected elements, other factors influence the damage caused by a flood. For instance, in the case of tourism, the time of the year (high season or low season) and duration of the flood are particularly relevant for the evaluation of its impacts (Förster *et al.*, 2008). The damage functions relate the damage (to each element at risk) to its main influencing factors and to the flood characteristics (Table 10.2). Damage-influencing factors can be classified as impact parameters and resistance parameters (Thieken *et al.*, 2005). Impact parameters reflect the specific characteristics of a flood event to the object of study and depend on the type and magnitude of the flood. Resistance parameters represent the capacity of an element to resist the impact of

Table 10.2 Damage-influencing factors considered in river flood damage assessments for tourism

Impact parameters	Description
Duration of inundation	Direct and indirect damage to the tourism industry in the affected area are directly proportional to the duration of the flood.
Inundation depth	The likeliness of damage to assets and property is directly proportional to the inundation depth.
Frequency of inundation	The frequency of flood events may have negative effects on destination image. On the other hand, the destination improves its capacity to face future floods, as flood experience may also be considered a resistance parameter.
Timing	The time of the year in which a flood event happens influences the magnitude of the damage. Floods during the high season and vacation time affect a higher number of tourists and cause greater business loss.
Resistance parameters	Description
Use and type of building	State/level of preparation. For example, a flood in a recreation area with a pool presents lower damage potential than one at a restaurant.
Precaution/ Mitigation measures	Measures that may significantly mitigate the damage caused by the flood, such as construction of dikes and transportation of elements at risk to higher altitude areas.
Early warnings	With enough warning time, the mitigation measures may be particularly effective, as the water levels are still low.

Adapted and extended from Merz *et al.* (2010).

a flood. They depend on the characteristics of the element at risk and their likeliness to flood (Ghaderi *et al.*, 2015). Considering that the various influencing factors are not independent from each other, a multivariate analysis is necessary (Merz *et al.*, 2010).

In certain cases, there are two additional impact parameters and corresponding damage to be considered: the possible water contamination, for example, in the case of flood reaching engine rooms or fuel tanks; and potential debris or sediment in recreation areas on riverbanks, which increase the costs of cleaning and repairing the affected areas.

Case Study: Miño River, Ourense, Spain

Floods are the most significant natural disasters in Europe (European Environment Agency (EEA), 2004). In the case of Spain, floods caused by torrential rain, alongside droughts, are the natural hazards with the greatest socioeconomic and territorial effects (Olcina Cantos, 2008). In Spain, there are on average 20 deaths each year as a result of flooding as well as 800 million euros worth of economic loss (Ministry of Agriculture, Good and Environment (MAGRAMA), 2016). Flood effects may be mitigated. However, they cannot be completely avoided. In the case of river floods, the risk may be decreased by reducing water flows through reservoirs and dams. In contrast, the risk may be increased by a combination of climatic factors. Accordingly, the vulnerability of territories may be aggravated by socioeconomic issues (Alfieri *et al.*, 2016). Studies on this phenomenon in the Iberian Peninsula (Roudier *et al.*, 2016) and in the north of Spain (Alfieri *et al.*, 2015; Arnell & Gosling, 2016; Hirabayashi *et al.*, 2013) show that global warming will increase the risk of flooding in a return period of 100 years.

The case study analyses the urban section of the Miño River that passes through the Ourense Municipality in Spain, from the Velle dam to the thermal and recreational area of Outariz (Figure 10.1). The Velle reservoir is situated at the head of the examined area. On its Normal Maximum Level (NML), the reservoir occupies an area of 263ha and has a capacity of 17hm^3 (iAgua, 2018). Downstream, a stretch of 7.1 km, qualifies as a zone of moderate risk (overall risk assessment 2.6 out of 5) (Miño-Sil Hydrographical Confederation (CHMS), 2015), and features more than ten thermal and recreational facilities.

An analysis of damage to the tourism industry was undertaken in the first six months of 2016. The study was based on data regarding precipitation levels, the river's water level and average flow, and the floods that affected the examined destination during the data collection period. Additionally, data on tourist arrivals has also been examined in order to establish possible connections between periods of high tourist arrival rates with floods and the consequent closing of facilities. Such data was complemented by semi-structured interviews with local government representatives and the manager of the company responsible for the thermal facilities. The analysis of the collected data allowed for the evaluation of strategies adopted by the affected businesses, prevention policies and maintenance

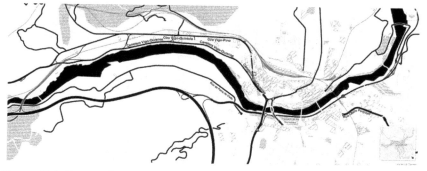

Figure 10.1 Ourense location and study area (Miño river)
Source: ©OpenStreetMap contributors. This map is made available under the Open Database License: http://opendatacommons.org/licenses/odbl/1.0/

actions carried out by the responsible organisations, and coordination mechanisms developed by the various institutions involved.

Elements at risk

Ourense is promoted as *provincia termal* as the province features thermal pools, spas, sports and recreational areas, and mineral-medicinal springs all located on the banks of Miño River. There are more than 70 hot springs registered in the municipality, providing more than three million litres of thermal water per day (European Historic Thermal Towns Association (EHTTA), 2018). Many of those springs are currently exploited, and host infrastructure includes public pools and thermal stations under private concession. Except for one spring, all the thermal facilities are located on the river's north bank (Table 10.3). There is a train tour departing from Ourense's old town, which features a 12th century cathedral, to the thermal facility. Along the way, the tour also includes the Roman Bridge, which was originally built in the first century A.D., and is still in use. During summer, nine tours are undertaken daily, but the frequency drops to four a day in winter.

Floods did not directly affect hotels as they are outside the flood zone. However, some spa restaurants were closed, which significantly affected the operation of spa facilities. Chavasqueira Spa's restaurant was closed for five days from 14 to 19 February 2016; and Outariz Spa closed for 11 days, from 14 to 25 February 2016. In the case of the latter, the main reason for the duration of the shutdown was the flooding of the engine room. Outariz Spa has 83 pumps and, therefore, takes longer to repair. This was only the second time these two spas have closed due to floods in 15 years, the first being in February 2009. However, the pools flood every year as they are closer to the river and less protected.

Table 10.3 Facilities that are susceptible to flooding

Name	Type	Management	Water temperature
Outariz	thermal pool	public	45° C
Canedo	thermal pool	public	45° C
Outariz	spa	private	50° C
Muiño da Veiga	thermal pool	public	72° C
Chavasqueira	spa	private	41° C
Chavasqueira	thermal pool	public	67° C
O Tinteiro	hot spring	public	45° C
Reza	hot spring	public	32° C
Oira	swimming pools	public	cold water

Source: Concellería de Termalismo (2017).

Types of damage

The floods within the examined section of the river are normally fluvial floods. Therefore, the damage caused by flood impacts has been relatively homogeneous, which facilitates the evaluation of socioeconomic damage (Kreibich & Dimitrova, 2010). Thermal facilities are open to residents and tourists throughout the year, which helps respond to issues of seasonality that are a common problem in the tourism industry. However, the pools and swimming areas of Oira close during winter. Therefore, the only costs caused by flood damage are those of cleaning and services repair. In this context, the City Hall has spent €22,547 to repair the thermal baths and recreational areas, €15,000 to recover access roads, and €24,623 in 2016 to rebuild slopes (X. Araujo, personal communication, 9 February, 2017). In previous years, costs reached much higher values of €300,000 in 2010, and €600,000 in 2011 (Rapela Freire *et al.*, 2015).

Flooding normally happens in winter during a period that coincides with Carnival and Easter, which are two important holidays for local tourist activities. Nevertheless, the negative effect on tourist arrivals has been moderate and of short duration. During the flood period (January to March, 2016), there were 46,456 overnight stays in the city of which 4231 were international tourists (National Institute of Statistics of Spain (INE), 2017). These figures are similar to those of previous years. The only variations are caused by Easter falling in either March or April.

Damage-influencing factors

The total precipitation in the examined river section during the first six months of 2016 is 679.9 mm according to CHMS (2017) and 763 mm according to MeteoGalicia (2017). The first three months included the heaviest rainfall events and had a total precipitation of 457mm and 509mm

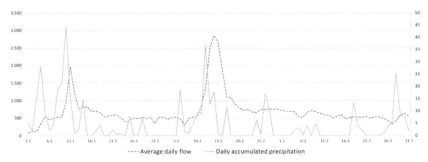

---- Average daily flow   —— Daily accumulated precipitation

Figure 10.2 Miño River's flow (m³/s) and precipitation level (mm) in Ourense during the first three months of 2016

Source: Adapted from CHMS (2017).

according to the same sources (which represents 67% of the total precipitation for the six-month period) (Figure 10.2).

The main damage-influencing factors for the case study, differentiating impact and resistance parameters, are detailed in Table 10.4.

Table 10.4 Impact and resistance parameters

Impact parameters

Duration of inundation	In January 2016, two flood periods were registered: 6–11 January and 14–20 February.
Inundation depth	The river's average daily water level from January to June 2016 was 2.81m (CHMS, 2017). On 10 January, when the highest precipitation in the six-month period was registered (44.7mm), the water level reached 6.57m. On 11 January, the average flow was slightly lower than 2000 m^2 per second, and slowly decreased during the next few days (CHMS, 2017). The heavy rain that occurred between 12 and 14 February, combined with that of previous days, resulted in significant floods along the examined section. From 11 to 19 February, the average water level fell to 4.13m. The maximum (7.27m) was registered on 15 February. The flow during the period 13–15 February was higher than 2500 m^2 per second (CHMS, 2017).
Frequency of inundation	The examined section is classified as an Area with Potential Significant Flood Risk (APSFR). 34 historical floods have been registered in the area, and they normally occur between October and March, especially in December (13 floods since 1909) (CHMS, 2011).
Timing	The two floods of the first six months of 2016 happened in holiday periods: Epiphany (6 January) and Shrove Tuesday (9 February). Those dates are important for the local tourism calendar. The most serious moments of the February flood happened right after the end of Carnival on 10 February (Ash Wednesday), so their impact on tourism was less intense.

Resistance parameters

Use and type of building	Floods affect mainly thermal and swimming pools, which are simple to clean and repair. Occasionally, spas' engine rooms are also flooded.
Precaution/ Mitigation measures	Transferring elements at risk from the flood level zones to higher areas is not always possible as the tourism and leisure resources are often directly linked to their geographical location (e.g. geothermal sources). Therefore, relocation would imply a significant loss of attractiveness to visitors.
Early warning	In the case of Ourense, reliable meteorological information is available. However, inundations are often caused by the opening of the upstream dam's floodgates. Several local governmental institutions and authorities of the river basin organisation work together, both in the implementation of preventive measures and in the warning phase, as well as in the subsequent repair actions.
Flood experience	Prior to floods, maintenance work is carried out in green areas, access roads, and thermal facilities. Cleaning tasks authorised by the basin organisation are also carried out on the banks of the river, aiming at facilitating its natural flow. Once a flood threat is detected, technicians from the *Velle* dam send a discharge increase warning to Civil Protection, which is responsible for evacuating the inflow zones. Such communication is also coordinated by the basin organisation. Finally, once the flood has happened, repair measures are carried out (X. Araujo, personal communication, 9 February, 2017).

Conclusion

Floods affect recreational areas and thermal facilities located on Miño River's banks, temporarily preventing their use. The constant need for flood-related repairs in the study area represents a weakness of Ourense's tourism sector. The regular floods imply the interruption of many tourism-related businesses in the affected areas following inundation. In this context, the goal of mitigating seasonality in the tourism sector by attracting more visitors during times other than the holidays becomes very difficult to achieve. However, the damage is concentrated in the zones directly affected by the floods. As a result, neighbouring destinations may benefit from the temporary unavailability of such areas for tourist use, as well as from the consequent damage to destination image as a result of closures and an increased perception of risk. The main damage is a result of the specific characteristics of the tourism sector (ECLAC, 2003). Tourism's dependency on natural, thermal resources, combined with the fact that such attractions are located in flood zones, increases the sector's vulnerability to inundation.

In terms of communication, providing precise and accessible information on the affected facilities is essential. The media and local policymakers must distinguish between affected resources as they differ significantly in relevance. For example, in this case, potential tourists perceived the area as being totally flooded even though only the pools are periodically inundated. In contrast, the spas, which are significantly more relevant to tourism, are rarely affected. The generic use of the term 'flooding of the thermal facilities' by media, officials and others is imprecise and leads to an overestimation of the damage and impacts of floods. As a result, it leads to a negative perception from potential visitors and thus negatively affects tourism-related businesses, such as hotels and restaurants.

The main limitation of the present study is the difficulty in directly applying the obtained results to other destinations and inundation scenarios. Such a limitation is caused by the scarcity of available data, as well as by differences in the types of flooding, affected resources, and influencing flood factors. Nevertheless, issues relating to the effective communication of actual versus perceived flood impact will remain relevant to many destinations affected by floods and storms.

Acknowledgement

Portions of this chapter have been previously published in an article titled 'Factors influencing the assessment of tourism damage caused by river floods' which appeared in *Revista Turismo & Desenvolvimento* 36 (1), 51–61. https://doi.org/10.34624/rtd.v1i36.8917.

References

Agnew, M.D. and Viner, D. (2001) Potential impacts of climate change on international tourism. *Tourism and Hospitality Research* 3 (1), 37–60.

Alfieri, L., Burek, P., Feyen, L. and Forzieri, G. (2015) Global warming increases the frequency of river floods in Europe. *Hydrology and Earth System Sciences* 19 (5), 2247–2260.

Alfieri, L., Feyen, L. and Di Baldassarre, G. (2016) Increasing flood risk under climate change: A pan-European assessment of the benefits of four adaptation strategies. *Climatic Change* 136 (3–4), 507–521.

Arnell, N.W. and Gosling, S.N. (2016) The impacts of climate change on river flood risk at the global scale. *Climatic Change* 134 (3), 387–401.

Bernard, K. and Cook, S. (2015) Luxury tourism investment and flood risk: Case study on unsustainable development in Denarau island resort in Fiji. *International Journal of Disaster Risk Reduction* 14 (3), 302–311.

Concellería de Termalismo (2017) *Ruta Termal. Concello de Ourense*. [online] Available at: http://termalismo.ourense.es/gl/descarga-folletos/

De Freitas, C.R. (2003) Tourism climatology: Evaluating environmental information for decision making and business planning in the recreation and tourism sector. *International Journal of Biometeorology* 48 (1), 45–54.

Economic Commission for Latin America and the Caribbean (ECLAC) (2003) *Handbook for Estimating the Socio-economic and Environmental Effects of Disasters*. ECLAC, Mexico City.

Espiner, S. and Becken, S. (2014) Tourist towns on the edge: Conceptualising vulnerability and resilience in a protected area tourism system. *Journal of Sustainable Tourism* 22 (4), 646–665.

European Environment Agency (EEA) (2004) *Mapping the Impacts of Recent Natural Disasters and Technological Accidents in Europe, Environmental Issue Report n.35*. EEA, Copenhagen, Denmark.

European Historic Thermal Towns Association (EHTTA) (2018) *Ehtta's Towns Ourense-Spain*. [online] Available at http://www.ehtta.eu/index.php?option=com_zoo&task=item&item_id=3

Fatti, C.E. and Patel, Z. (2013) Perceptions and responses to urban flood risk: Implications for climate governance in the South. *Applied Geography* 36, 13–22.

Faulkner, B. and Vikulov, S. (2001) Katherine, washed out one day, back on track the next: A post-mortem of a tourism disaster. *Tourism Management* 22 (4), 331–344.

Fitchett, J., Hoogendoorn, G. and Swemmer, T. (2016) Economic costs of the 2012 floods on tourism in the Mopani District Municipality, South Africa. *Transactions of the Royal Society of South Africa* 71 (2), 187–194.

Förster, S., Kuhlmann, B., Lindenschmidt, K.E. and Bronstert, A. (2008) Assessing flood risk for a rural detention area. *Natural Hazards and Earth System Science* 8 (2), 311–322.

Ghaderi, Z., Mat Som, A.P. and Henderson, J.C. (2015) When disaster strikes: The Thai floods of 2011 and tourism industry response and resilience. *Asia Pacific Journal of Tourism Research* 20 (4), 399–415.

Gutiérrez, F., Gutiérrez, M. and Sancho, C. (1998) Geomorphological and sedimentological analysis of a catastrophic flash flood in the Arás drainage basin (Central Pyrenees, Spain). *Geomorphology* 22 (3–4), 265–283.

Hall, C.M. and Härkönen, T. (eds) (2006) *Lake Tourism: An Integrated Approach to Lacustrine Tourism Systems*. Clevedon: Channel View Publications.

Hamzah, J., Habibah, A., Buang, A., Jusoff, K., Toriman, M.E., Mohd Fuad, M.J., Er, A.C. and Azima, A.M. (2012) Flood disaster, impacts and the tourism providers' responses: The Kota Tinggi experience. *Advances in Natural and Applied Sciences* 6 (1), 26–32.

Hirabayashi, Y., Mahendran, R., Koirala, S., Konoshima, L., Yamazaki, D., Watanabe, S., Hyungjun, K. and Kanae, S. (2013) Global flood risk under climate change. *Nature Climate Change* 3 (9), 816–821.

iAgua (2018) *Presa de Velle*. [online] Available at: https://www.iagua.es/data/infraestructuras/presas/velle

Jeuring, J. and Becken, S. (2013) Tourists and severe weather – An exploration of the role of 'Locus of Responsibility' in protective behaviour decisions. *Tourism Management* 37, 193–202.

Jonkman, S.N., Bočkarjova, M., Kok, M. and Bernardini, P. (2008) Integrated hydrodynamic and economic modelling of flood damage in the Netherlands. *Ecological Economics* 66 (1), 77–90.

Kellens, W., Zaalberg, R., Neutens, T., Vanneuville, W. and De Maeyer, P. (2011) An analysis of the public perception of flood risk on the Belgian coast. *Risk Analysis* 31 (7), 1055–1068.

Khan, A.N. (2011) Analysis of flood causes and associated socio-economic damages in the Hindukush region. *Natural Hazards* 59 (3), 1239–1260.

Kreibich, H. and Dimitrova, B. (2010) Assessment of damages caused by different flood types. In D. de Wrachien, D. Proverbs, C.A. Brebbia and S. Mambretti (eds) *Flood Recovery, Innovation and Response II* (pp. 3–12). Southampton: WIT Press.

Merz, B., Kreibich, H., Schwarze, R. and Thieken, A. (2010) Assessment of economic flood damage. *Natural Hazards and Earth System Sciences* 10 (8), 1697–1724.

Merz B., Thieken A. and Kreibich H. (2011) Quantification of socio-economic flood risks. In A. Schumann A (ed.) *Flood Risk Assessment and Management. How to Specify Hydrological Loads, Their Consequences and Uncertainties* (pp. 229–248). Dordrecht: Springer.

Messner, F. (2007) Evaluating flood damages: Guidance and recommendations on principles and methods. *Hydraulic Engineering Report T09-06-01*. [online] Available at: http://resolver.tudelft.nl/uuid:5602db10-274c-40da-953f-34475ded1755

MeteoGalicia (2017) *Observación. Estación meteorológica Ourense-Estación*. [online] Available at: http://www2.meteogalicia.gal/galego/observacion/estacions/estacions.asp?request_locale=gl#

Meunier, M. (1990) La catastrophe du Grand Bornand: Crue torrentielle du Borne le 14 juillet 1987. *Revue de Géographie Alpine* 78 (1), 103–113.

Ministry of Agriculture and Fisheries, Food and Environment (MAPAMA) (2017) *Planificación hidrológica Miño Sil. Usos recreativos*. [pdf] Available at: https://www.chminosil.es/images/fichas/2120-Ficha_11_Ed02.pdf

Ministry of Agriculture, Food and Environment (MAGRAMA) (2016) *Gestión de los riesgos de inundación*. [online] Available at: http://www.magrama.gob.es/es/agua/temas/gestion-de-los-riesgos-de-inundacion/

Miño-Sil Hydrographical Confederation (CHMS) (2015) *Plan de gestión del riesgo de inundación Ciclo 2016 – 2021*. Anexo1. Caracterización de las ARPSIS.

National Institute of Statistics of Spain (INE) (2017) *INEbase/Encuesta de ocupación hotelera*. [online] Available at: http://www.ine.es/jaxiT3/Datos.htm?t=2078

Olcina Cantos, J. (2008) *Prevención de riesgos: Cambio climático, sequías e inundaciones*. Fundación Nueva Cultura del Agua, Panel Científico-Técnico de seguimiento de la Política de Aguas.

Penning-Rowsell, E.C. and Green, C. (2000) New insights into the appraisal of flood-alleviation benefits: (1) Flood damage and flood loss information. *Water and Environment Journal* 14 (5), 347–353.

Rapela Freire, L., Toubes, D.R. and De Uña-Alvarez, E. (2015) La gestión de riesgo de riadas: el caso de Ourense. Congreso Internacional del Agua. Termalismo y Calidad de Vida, Ourense, Spain, November 2015.

Roudier, P., Andersson, J.C., Donnelly, C., Feyen, L., Greuell, W. and Ludwig, F. (2016) Projections of future floods and hydrological droughts in Europe under a +2C global warming. *Climatic Change* 135 (2), 341–355.

Sayers, P., Yuanyuan, L., Galloway, G., Penning-Rowsell, E., Fuxin, S., Kang, W., Yiwei, C. and Quesne, T.L. (2013) *Flood Risk Management: A Strategic Approach*. Paris: UNESCO.

Scott, D., Hall, C.M. and Gössling, S. (2012) *Tourism and Climate Change: Impacts, Adaptation and Mitigation*. Abingdon: Routledge.

Scott, D. and Lemieux, C. (2010) Weather and climate information for tourism. *Procedia Environmental Sciences* 1 (1), 146–183.

Smith, D.I. (1994) Flood damage estimation – A review of urban stage damage curves and loss functions. *Water SA* 20 (3), 231–238.

Southon, M.P. and van der Merwe, C.D. (2018) Flooded with risks or opportunities: Exploring flooding impacts on tourist accommodation. *African Journal of Hospitality, Tourism and Leisure* 7 (1), 1–27.

Thieken, A.H., Müller, M., Kreibich, H. and Merz, B. (2005) Flood damage and influencing factors: New insights from the August 2002 flood in Germany. *Water Resources Research* 41 (12), doi.org/10.1029/2005WR004177.

Toubes, D.R., Gössling, S., Hall, C.M. and Scott, D. (2017) Vulnerability of coastal beach tourism to flooding: A case study of Galicia, Spain. *Environments* 4 (4), 83. https://doi.org/10.3390/environments4040083

Walters, G., Mair, J. and Ritchie, B. (2014) Understanding the tourist's response to natural disasters: The case of the 2011 Queensland floods. *Journal of Vacation Marketing* 21 (1), 101–113.

World Health Organization (WHO) (2003) *Guidelines for Safe Recreational Water Environments. Volume 1: Coastal and Fresh Waters*. Geneva: WHO.

Yeo, S. (2003) Flood risk management for caravan parks in New South Wales. *Australian Geographer* 34 (2), 195–209.

Yeo, S.W. (2002) Flooding in Australia: A review of events in 1998. *Natural Hazards* 25 (2), 177–191.

Yu, G., Schwartz, Z. and Walsh, J.E. (2009) A weather-resolving index for assessing the impact of climate change on tourism related climate resources. *Climatic Change* 95 (3–4), 551–573.

11 Should I Stay or Should I Go? Hurricane Sandy and Second Home Tourism on Fire Island, New York

Bailey Ashton Adie

Introduction

Hurricane Sandy hit Fire Island on the 29 October 2012 and left a wave of devastation in its wake. According to data from the US Army Corps of Engineers (2013), approximately 50% of all housing on Fire Island experienced some level of damage from the storm. Nonetheless, regardless of the destruction, many second homeowners returned to Fire Island. What was the impetus for returning, particularly for those who received more significant damage? While there are several previous studies on decision-making post-hurricane, these have only focused exclusively on permanent residents (Bukvic *et al.*, 2015; Bukvic & Owen, 2017; Bukvic *et al.*, 2018). Therefore, there is a significant gap in post-disaster studies and coastal second home tourism. This is especially relevant as coastal second homes are at an increasingly high risk of disaster-related damage. Given this risk, it becomes necessary to understand the implications of these disasters for coastal second home communities. This chapter addresses this knowledge gap through a discussion of the relationship between place attachment and the post-disaster decision-making surrounding continued second homeownership within a second home community on Fire Island, New York, USA.

A Home Away From Home: Second Home Tourism and Place Attachment

The discussion of second homes is incredibly complex and has been for decades, as can be seen in Coppock's (1977b) *Second Homes: Curse or Blessing?*, which was, until recently, the leading volume on second home research (Müller & Hoogendorn, 2013). Coppock (1977a: 2) stated that 'second homes do not constitute a discrete type, sharply distinguished from other kinds of accommodation, but form a somewhat arbitrarily identified group within a continuum'. Therefore, the complexity of defining what is and is not a second home is not a new concept but has been complicated by the growth of second home literature, particularly in relation to the number of fields that engage with the concept. This has led to various definitions that are based on the context within which the second home is situated, the field in which it is being studied, as well as with modern conceptualisations of mobility (Hall & Müller, 2004; McIntyre, 2006; Müller, 2014). In this chapter, the term 'second home' is defined as a dwelling which is not the owner's legal permanent residence, and which is primarily used for leisure purposes.

The motivations for owning and meanings attached to second homes are a common theme within the second home literature (Hall & Müller, 2018; Kaltenborn, 1998; McIntyre, 2006; Müller, 2014). Some individuals purchase their second homes as a form of escape (Chaplin, 1999; Nouza et al., 2018; Perkins & Thorns, 2006; Stedman, 2006a; Williams & Van Patten, 2006) or as a way to 'get back to nature' (Jaakson, 1986; Müller, 2002, 2006; Tuulentie, 2006). Others wish to leave a legacy for their children and grandchildren (Jansson & Müller, 2004; Williams & Van Patten, 2006) and, unsurprisingly, still others inherit their homes (McIntyre et al., 2006; Williams & Van Patten, 2006). However, this may in fact result in lower levels of satisfaction in comparison to those who chose that location independently (Lundmark & Marjavaara, 2013). Kaltenborn (1998: 133) highlights how important a vacation home can become, specifically that 'life revolving around the recreation home can gradually become the ordinary life that provides the desired meaning, while the modern, urban life represents the extraordinary existence'. Given these varied motivations and meanings, it becomes necessary to understand the second homeowner's place attachment as 'the use of second (recreational) homes...is often the locus of long-lasting relationships with particular places' (Kaltenborn, 1997: 177).

Stedman (2006b: 192) states that 'second homes are homes: There are relationships with neighbours, maintenance activities and worries about local issues.' How then do permanent residents and second homeowners differ? One of the distinctions drawn in the literature is connected to the impetus behind this place attachment. In a study on resident and non-resident homeowners in three communities in the north-west of the United States, Nielsen-Pincus et al. (2010) observed that the permanent residents had higher levels of place attachment than the non-residents. In contrast, Stedman (2006a, 2006b), in his study on property owners in northern Wisconsin, USA, found that while second homeowners may have higher levels of place attachment than permanent residents, this attachment is derived from different sources: community for permanent residents and the environment and escape from the quotidian for second homeowners. According to Kaltenborn (1997: 186):

> place attachment is not attachment solely to landscape or to social conditions or experiences. The sense of place or sets of meaning associated with the recreation homes and the surrounding settings are intertwined with natural, social, historical, and cultural processes.

This relationship between second homeowners and the second home's context then could result in alterations with regards to the reason for the place attachment (Nouza *et al.*, 2018). In other words, place attachment is variable and very context dependent.

One such context is coastal second home tourism, which can be understood as its own subtype of second home tourism. In Back and Marjavaara's (2017: 607) work mapping second homeownership in Sweden, coastal locations were noted as being a hotspot where second homeowners 'are prepared to both travel farther and pay more for their second homes in these areas than in others'. In North America, Paris (2009: 300) found that 'second homes [in the US] were an element of *making places*, often in previously unsettled coastal areas'. Historically, coastal second homes were more common on the west Coast in New England and across the Mid-Atlantic states in comparison to the Southeast, though this region has since experienced a growth in coastal second homeownership (Timothy, 2004). A similar historical trend towards domestic, coastal, second homeownership can be noted in Australia (Frost, 2004; Selwood & Tonts, 2004) and South Africa (Visser, 2004). Thus, it can be stated that coastal second homes are of particular importance given their higher pull factor and importance for tourism.

Coastal second home tourism and place attachment have been discussed in several studies. McIntyre and Pavlovich (2006) found that while coastal residents, both seasonal and permanent, in a community in New Zealand valued the local natural amenities, second homeowners, regardless of their length of ownership, attached lower levels of importance to community values in comparison with permanent residents. Kelly and Hosking (2008) also observed an attachment to the natural qualities of their Australian study site. However, in contrast to McIntyre and Pavlovich (2006), the coastal second homeowners in Kelly and Hosking's (2008: 589) study felt 'a deep attachment to the place and its community'. Selwood and Tonts (2006) observed a similar trend with longer-term residents exhibiting a strong sense of place tied to memories; this resulted in the expression of displeasure with the changing coastal community, particularly with regards to the aesthetics of the built environment. This is unsurprising given Anton and Lawrence's (2014: 459) research on place attachment, which indicated that individuals who 'move to places because they find them more physically appealing... may be more open to forming emotional and functional attachments to that place'. How then does place attachment in these coastal areas, particularly those considered high risk, affect decision-making processes post-disaster?

When Disaster Strikes: Decision-Making Post-Disaster by Coastal Homeowners

Coastal communities and, by extension, coastal second homeowners must confront location-specific risks due to their proximity to the sea/ ocean, e.g. sea level rise, tidal flooding, hurricanes, typhoons, tsunamis. While these natural hazards have always existed, in many locations they will only be exacerbated by the continued impact of climate change (IPCC, 2014; UNEP, 2008). In particular, sea level rise poses a notable risk as it increases the vulnerability of coastal destinations to erosion, flooding, and submergence (IPCC, 2014). Therefore, second homeowners in coastal areas, which may have once been at a relatively low risk of disaster, will note a rise in the probability of disaster-related damage.

Often an attempt to minimise these risks through the construction of man-made coastal protective features can cause greater problems as it disrupts the natural coastal ecosystem, as was observed in the case of Ireland (Cooper & Boyd, 2018). The disruption in this case was the result of the misinterpretation of the term 'coastal protection', which was understood as the need to safeguard the existing coastal infrastructure and local built environment (Cooper & Boyd, 2018; Cooper & McKenna, 2008). The alternative, though, is to allow natural coastal erosion to occur with the caveat that homeowners on the coastline may be required to eventually retreat inland (Abel et al., 2011; Bukvic et al., 2015). This is generally undesirable to property owners who would much rather install artificial defence systems in order to protect their private property (Cooper & McKenna, 2008), which only shifts the erosion further down the coastline creating a negative cycle of coastal disruption (Abel et al., 2011). However, these defences can fail in the event of a disaster, which in turn leaves the built infrastructure of the coastal community more vulnerable. Hurricanes in particular can cause widespread damage as a result of storm surges, high winds, and flooding, which can weaken or destroy the existing defence systems. This allows for secondary damage from smaller, though not insignificant, storms. Therefore, to what extent does this danger impact coastal homeowners' decision-making processes after a disaster event?

Several studies illustrate that individuals are aware of the various natural hazard risks inherent in owning coastal property, particularly after a hurricane (Binder et al., 2015; Bukvic et al., 2015; Bukvic & Owen, 2017; Bukvic et al., 2018). Bukvic and Owen (2017: 120) noted that 'extreme weather and sea-level rise are most likely to prompt [a community member] to consider relocation', a decision which is undertaken independent from the community as a whole. In a similar study, Bukvic *et al.* (2018) determined that those who live closer to the ocean are less likely to consider relocation when compared to those nearer to the bay. Bukvic *et al.* (2018: 14) speculate that this is due to the fact that ocean-facing homeowners may have 'purchased homes primarily for the personal gratification of having the ocean views or beach access', which, in turn, leads to an assumption that these individuals may be more 'financially stable' (Bukvic *et al.*, 2018: 14). Thus, it is unsurprising that the decision-making process focused on rebuilding or relocating is further impacted by financial factors such as tax and insurance increases or potential loss in housing value due to low Federal Emergency Management Agency (FEMA) pay-outs (Bukvic *et al.*, 2015; Bukvic & Owen, 2017).

While these works focused on decision-making, only Binder *et al.*'s (2015) study, which analysed two coastal communities that were impacted by Hurricane Sandy and subsequently offered home buyouts, was the only one that incorporated a discussion of place attachment. According to their findings, the residents of Rockaway Park were more likely to rebuild as their identity was tied to the geographic location, whereas Oakwood Beach homeowners took the buyout as theirs was predicated on the concept of homeownership (Binder *et al.*, 2015). Thus, place attachment can be seen as an important aspect of decision-making post-disaster (Bonaiuto *et al.*, 2016; De Dominicis *et al.*, 2015). However, it would appear that individuals in coastal locations predominantly base their decision-making on concrete aspects, i.e. future risk or financial issues. Perhaps a better approach towards an interpretation of the results of these various studies is through Henry's (2013) understanding of post-disaster decision-making as a rational process composed of both objective and subjective factors.

The Context: Fire Island, New York, USA

Fire Island is a long, narrow barrier island off the southern coast of Long Island, New York State, in the United States, stretching approximately 31 miles in length but only a quarter of a mile across at its widest point. While used for various activities throughout its history, including wampum production and whaling by the local Native American tribes, with the latter also undertaken by later European settlers, it was generally uninhabited throughout its history (Koppelman & Forman, 2008). However, this changed in the mid-19th century, when the first resort, the Surf Hotel, was constructed on the island in what is now the community of Kismet. While this resort eventually was sold in 1892 during the cholera epidemic, the use of the island as a beach destination continued, with the first community Point O'Woods established in 1894 (Koppelman & Forman, 2008). The island continued to attract recreational development activity, which resulted in the creation of what are, today, 17 distinct communities. These communities are all located within the Fire Island National Seashore, which was established in 1964 as the result of a grassroots movement to protect the island and prevent the development of a road through the middle of the island.

Today, the national seashore spans 26 miles and, in the summer, the Fire Island communities can only be reached by boat from the mainland or by foot from elsewhere on the island. According to the US Census Bureau (2010a, 2010b, 2010c), the number of second homes on Fire Island in 2010 totalled 4262, or 95.5% of all homes on the island. Ocean Beach is the largest community with 562 second homes (US Census Bureau, 2010b) as well as what can be described as a small, yet vibrant, commercial centre. This community was established in 1908 and then incorporated as a village in 1921, and it is considered the unofficial capital of Fire Island (Koppelman & Forman, 2008).

Hurricane Sandy made landfall on Fire Island on the 29 October 2012 and is considered the worst hurricane to hit the island since the 'Long Island Express' of 1938. According to the National Hurricane Center's report:

> Sandy's extensive storm surge inundated New York's 32-mile long Fire Island with water and sand, destroyed or washed away 200 homes, and obliterated protective sand dunes. Atlantic Ocean water breached the island in three places, but about 4000 homes survived because of the protection offered by the dunes. (Blake *et al.*, 2013: 18)

However, these homes did not escape unscathed as approximately 2200 were damaged in Sandy (US Army Corps of Engineers, 2013). Furthermore, the US Geological Survey reported that the storm resulted in a loss of 54.4% of the total pre-storm beach and dune volume and 'profoundly impacted the morphology of Fire Island...that has left the barrier island vulnerable to future storms' (Hapke *et al.*, 2013: 1). Therefore, not only was the damage to Fire Island substantial, but it is also more likely to occur again.

Method

Interviews were conducted over the long weekend of 4 July 2017 as this was determined to be the period in which the second homes were most likely to be occupied. This observation was based on both anecdotal evidence as well as similar research conducted by Stewart and Stynes (2006). The interviews were semi-structured as the overall focus was on allowing the respondents to have a free space to express themselves, providing for a breadth of responses. Respondents were initially selected from the researcher's own network as a community insider with additional interviews secured through snowball sampling. While this is acknowledged as being problematic in that it may not have resulted in a representative sample, it also allowed the respondents to talk freely as they were comfortable with 'someone whose family has been here forever'. In total, 14 second homeowners were interviewed with interviews lasting anywhere from 7 to 35 minutes. These second homeowners were predominantly from Ocean Beach, with two from the neighbouring community of Seaview.

Findings

The second homeowners were predominantly over 65 years old and retired, with slightly more women interviewed than men. They were also highly educated with most having at least some university-level education and slightly less than half having completed a degree at postgraduate level. Additionally, only eight of the respondents had purposely purchased their houses as adults with the other six currently residing in houses that used to belong to previous generations. Furthermore, all of the respondents were broadly aware of the potential dangers associated with continuing their homeownership. However, regardless of these factors, no interviewed owner indicated that they had considered selling as a direct result of Sandy. In fact, throughout the interviews, three dominant themes emerged in regard to most of the second homeowners' decisions to retain and, when necessary, repair and refit their homes: the importance of the community, the importance of the house as a centre for family memories, and the desire to leave it for future generations.

Community ties

Certain respondents emphasised the importance of the community (R6, R7, R8). For R8, this, as well as the fact that they sustained no real damage, was the main motivation for not considering selling their home:

> We have several friends out here that are part of the community, and, you know, we have a lot of community dinners and get-togethers. It didn't even cross our minds to sell.

In comparison with R8, who was focused on his specific social circle, R6, who has been coming to the island for the shortest period of time, spoke of community as a whole, with the concepts of home and community intertwined:

> So that's why it's home. And it's not just a home, but it's a home that's part of a community. And that's what's important.

Community was also very important for her husband, R7, who has been coming to Fire Island since he was a child:

> This is a special place because of the people, whether you like them or you don't. At least we know the people we don't like, and we get to see the people we don't like every day and it's ok. That's ok. It's ok. ... You know, I sit on the bench in the town, and I get to see people that I love every day or people that I don't like every day. And I get to not like them every day or I get to like them every day. And it's, you know, there's something beautiful about that ... Everybody stands together in this community, the people you like and the people you don't like. It's incredible.

He mentioned the community several times in his interview, highlighting how it was special and unique. Community, then, in both its personal and broader meanings can be a source of strong place attachment for second homeowners.

Family memories

Family history and memories were the most common motivating factor for retaining the second home (R3, R4, R5, R11, R12, R14). It is interesting to note that these respondents include not only individuals who have been coming to Fire Island for most of their lives, if not their whole life, but also those who only began visiting as adults and self-selected their second homes. Both R3 and R4 bought their houses on Fire Island as vacation homes when they had young children. R3 made a point of emphasising that he did not care about the value fluctuation of his home and instead stressed its importance to his entire family, including his grandchildren:

> And, you know, we had the house basically so we could enjoy it, and, you know, it became the center of my whole family until I had grandchildren. Now of course I can't invite any of my family anymore because my grandchildren are always here. You know, they won't leave, and they fight over whose getting which week.

A similar scenario can be seen within R4's family. She spoke about how her children, now adults, have friends who still come to Fire Island:

> This place is very special not only to, you know, to my family, to my children, but to their children. In fact, a few of them are coming in just to see each other ... to reconnect.

In both situations, the second home functions as a source of happy family memories as well as a place wherein multiple generations can meet.

This phenomenon of the second home as a meeting place is also present among the homeowners whose houses had been purchased or built by past family members. For example, R11 also had multiple generations, including grandchildren, visiting during the interview period. For her, the house is an important source of family memories and history:

> As my brother says, they'll have to bury him in the house. No, but you know what I mean, it's just- it's a family member. It's part of our family.

The idea of a family home was also emphasised by R5:

> This is the house I grew up in. My father built this house ... It's my home, and, really, in every regard, it's my primary residence except that I don't live here in the winter.

Additionally, while R5 indicated that she would never sell her second home, she, in conjunction with her family, did sell the other house that she owned:

> Because it was becoming more and more difficult to financially maintain it, and it needed a lot of work which we just didn't you know have the money to put into it. So it's kind of a relief.

As can be seen, there is a noted difference in relation to attachment to individual properties given how they are identified by the owner, i.e. work vs. home.

Similarly, family memories were highlighted by R12, who emphasises her own personal recollections surrounding coming to the island as a child:

> It means a lot. I mean, I have such great memories. We were here – My mother was a schoolteacher, and we were here every summer since 1945 except once when we were married and living in California. We didn't make it. But it means a whole lot to us. A lot of happy memories and you know our six kids come and the grandchildren and they all love it. So it does mean a lot.

R14 also discussed her long family history on Fire Island, even recalling the official date that her grandfather had closed on the house. When asked what it meant to her, she replied simply: 'I love it. I love this house'. While these four respondents have personal, childhood memories that link them strongly to their second homes, it is interesting to note that, regardless of when they first began visiting Fire Island, for over half of the owners, the house appears to function in a similar way, as a meeting point for multiple generations.

For the kids

While the previously discussed factors dealt more directly with the individual homeowner's attachment, the final theme that emerged from the interviews involved the attachment of the successive generations (R1, R2, R9). R1 and R2, a married couple, both underscored how much their grandchildren cared about their second home:

> My grandkids grew up out here, and there are people ... who raised their kids or had their kids here during the summer or for a couple of weeks for vacation or something like that. Listen, my grandson is 21. He's been coming out here his entire life, and he loves it. Any opportunity that he gets, he wants to be here. So ... you know, that's what it's about. It's not about me anymore. It's not about me anymore. It's about them, you know. You know, I realize where I am in the age spectrum, but, you know, he's 21. He has another 60, 70 years of his life left. Let him enjoy it.

His wife, R1, echoed these sentiments and, in order to illustrate how much her grandchildren love the house, she included an anecdote about how her granddaughter would not allow her to change any aspect of her room in the house. R9 took it one step further:

> My daughter would kill me if I sold the house. It's really not my house anymore. It's her house and, you know, when you're brought up here and you're circle of friends is here- She has a much deeper attachment to the island than I do although I have a lot of friends out here and a lot of acquaintances. Her closest friends are out here so there's just no way ... Yeah, I technically own the house. I pay the bills, but it's not my house.

For all three of these second homeowners, there is an obvious relinquishing, at least symbolically, of ownership to the future generation who are acknowledged as having a much stronger connection to Fire Island than the current owners possess themselves.

Discussion

The Fire Island interviewees had a very strong negative response when asked whether or not they had considered selling their homes after Sandy. One would assume that this was due in part to either a lack of damage or a surplus of capital. However, regardless of the individual respondent's financial situation and if there was or was not any damage to their house, there was no hesitation in the negative response. This contrasts with the findings of most previous studies wherein finances played a significant role in a community member's decision to remain or rebuild after Sandy (Bukvic *et al.*, 2015; Bukvic & Owen, 2017; Bukvic *et al.*, 2018). The results presented in this chapter are closer to those observed by Binder *et al.* (2015) with respect to place attachment's impact on decision-making post-disaster. Nevertheless, none of these previous studies have specifically addressed the impact of place attachment on the decision-making processes of second homeowners following a natural disaster. In fact, what became evident throughout the interview process was the level of place attachment that was felt by most of the respondents, although this exhibited itself in different ways. More specifically, the respondents stressed their ties to the community, the importance of their house for their family, past and present, and the place attachment felt by the next generations.

Several Fire Island second homeowners emphasised the significance of the local community when discussing why they chose to return to Fire Island. This contrasts with the findings reported by McIntyre and Pavlovich (2006) and Stedman (2006a, 2006b), whose second homeowners' place attachment was almost entirely based on the concept of escape. Interestingly, this level of community-based place attachment is evident in the research of Kelly and Hosking (2008) as well as Selwood and Tonts (2006), which both analysed Australian coastal communities. However, in contrast to Selwood and Tonts (2006), the respondents did not exhibit a difference in terms of length of ownership on, or visitation to, Fire Island, similar to the findings of Kelly and Hosking (2008). The significance of community-based place attachment at Fire Island can perhaps be attributed to the American tradition of building second homes in previously uninhabited areas (Paris, 2009). Communities on the island are a result of a process of second home and vacation destination development that originated in the mid-19th century. Therefore, the local community in this case is composed almost entirely of second homeowners, particularly as the number of 'year-rounder' homes account for less than 5% of the total homeownership on Fire Island.

The largest group of respondents spoke of their second homes on Fire Island in relation to their families, both as a source of memories as well as a current gathering place for multiple generations. This same type of familial attachment was observed by Selwood and Tonts (2006) and Williams and Van Patten (2006). It is interesting to note that the ways in which respondents spoke of their homes did not alter based on how they had acquired their second home (i.e. purchased outright, inherited, or bought from family/friends). This partially contrasts with Lundmark and Marjavaara's (2013) findings related to second homeowner satisfaction with their second homes. While their data specifically focused on satisfaction, they did allow for the possibility that place attachment might override this satisfaction level. Based on the results from the Fire Island interviews, it can be supposed then that, at least in this particular instance, place attachment tied to family memories and history can nullify any potential lower levels of satisfaction with the second home, particularly when taking into account that these were dominant factors in a discussion of why the individuals had decided not to sell their Fire Island homes.

Given the importance of family for many of the interviewed second homeowners, it is unsurprising that there were respondents who no longer saw themselves as the owners of their second homes, referencing instead their children and/or grandchildren. The idea of leaving a second home to either children or grandchildren is not a new concept (McIntyre *et al.*, 2006; Williams & Van Patten, 2006). However, the framing used by the second homeowners to describe this phenomenon is tied to their acknowledgement of the future generation's place attachment, highlighting the importance of their personal relationships with both the house itself as well as the local community. This can be tied to Jaakson's (1986) conceptualisation of the second home as an emotional home, providing a sense of continuity which is not common in the modern mobile world. This aspect can be read as an expansion of the two previously discussed place attachment themes as these are noted as the reasons for the place attachment of the next generation. As can be seen, the strength of interpersonal connections to Fire Island have acted as a strong motivational force directly, or by proxy in the case of the next generations, on the decision-making processes of these specific second homeowners.

Conclusions

While coastal second homeowners have generally experienced some level of natural hazard risk, global climate change will lead to a higher probability of disaster-related property damage in the long term. Therefore, it becomes necessary to understand the implications of these disasters for coastal second home communities. While this phenomenon is multi-faceted, this chapter has highlighted the influence that place attachment can have on the decision-making process of coastal second homeowners post-disaster, which has not as yet been covered in the literature. Overall, the Fire Island second homeowners exhibited strong levels of place attachment, particularly in relation to community and family connections, which had a direct impact on their eventual decision to retain and, if necessary, rebuild their second home. Therefore, it can be asserted that, in certain cases, second homeowners may not only exhibit place attachment in a similar manner to that traditionally ascribed to permanent residents but will also be highly influenced by this attachment. This is best expressed by R6, who stated:

> This is our home. It's our home. We are not giving it up. We are here to stay. We're here to deal with what the environment hurls at us, and hopefully that won't ever happen again.

While these findings are of note, it is important to acknowledge the limitations of this research. Most importantly, in this study, only individuals who still owned their home on Fire Island were interviewed. This can partly be attributed to the use of the researcher's extended network, which did not include anyone who had sold. Future research needs to include these individuals in order to understand what the differentiating factor was between those who sold and those who stayed. Additionally, the interviews were only taken from predominantly one community on Fire Island. In order to develop a better conceptualisation of the decision-making process post-Sandy on Fire Island, it would be of interest to have a more representative sample from across the various communities. Finally, it should be noted that a common constraint in second home research is its limited application in a broader international sense due to the 'importance of place' (Müller & Hoogendorn, 2013: 365). Therefore, future work should also look at similar coastal locations globally to understand if this type of place attachment and its influence on decision-making is universal.

References

Abel, N., Gorddard, R., Harman, B., Leitch, A., Langridge, J., Ryan, A. and Heyenga, S. (2011) Sea level rise, coastal development and planned retreat: Analytical framework, governance principles and an Australian case study. *Environmental Science & Policy* 14 (3), 279–288.

Anton, C.E. and Lawrence, C. (2014) Home is where the heart is: The effect of place of residence on place attachment and community participation. *Journal of Environmental Psychology* 40, 451–461.

Back, A. and Marjavaara, R. (2017) Mapping an invisible population: The uneven geography of second-home tourism. *Tourism Geographies* 19 (4), 595–611.

Binder, S.B., Baker, C.K. and Barile, J.P. (2015) Rebuild or relocate? Resilience and post-disaster decision-making after Hurricane Sandy. *American Journal of Community Psychology* 56 (1&2), 180–196.

Blake, E.S., Kimberlain, T.B., Berg, R.J., Cangialosi, J.P. and Beven, J.L. (2013) *Tropical Cyclone Report: Hurricane Sandy. (AL182012) 22 – 29 October 2012.* Miami: National Hurricane Center.

Bonaiuto, M., Alves, S., De Dominicis, S. and Petruccelli, I. (2016) Place attachment and natural hazard risk: Research review and agenda. *Journal of Environmental Psychology* 48, 33–53.

Bukvic, A. and Owen, G. (2017) Attitudes towards relocation following Hurricane Sandy: Should we stay or should we go? *Disasters* 41 (1), 101–123.

Bukvic, A., Smith, A., and Zhang, A. (2015) Evaluating drivers of coastal relocation in Hurricane Sandy affected communities. *International Journal of Disaster Risk Reduction* 13, 215–228.

Bukvic, A., Zhu, H., Lavoie, R. and Becker, A. (2018) The role of proximity to waterfront in residents' relocation decision-making post-Hurricane Sandy. *Ocean and Coastal Management* 154, 8–19.

Chaplin, D. (1999) Consuming work/productive leisure: The consumption patterns of second home environments. *Leisure Studies* 18 (1), 41–55.

Cooper, J.A.G. and Boyd, S.W. (2018) Case study Ireland: Coastal tourism and climate change in Ireland. In A. Jones and M. Phillips (eds) *Global Climate Change and Coastal Tourism: Recognizing Problems, Managing Solutions and Future Expectations* (pp. 92–110). Wallingford: CABI.

Cooper, J.A.G. and McKenna, J. (2008) Working with natural processes: The challenge for coastal protection strategies. *The Geographical Journal* 174 (4), 315–331.

Coppock, J.T. (1977a) Second homes in perspective. In J.T. Coppock (ed.) *Second Homes: Curse or Blessing?* (pp. 1–15). Oxford: Pergamon.

Coppock, J.T. (ed.) (1977b) *Second Homes: Curse or Blessing?* Oxford: Pergamon.

De Dominicis, S., Fornara, F., Cancellieri, U.G., Twigger-Ross, C. and Bonaiuto, M. (2015) We are at risk, and so what? Place attachment, environmental risk perceptions and preventive coping behaviours. *Journal of Environmental Psychology* 43, 66–78.

Frost, W. (2004) A hidden giant: Second homes and coastal tourism in south-eastern Australia. In C.M. Hall and D.K. Müller (eds) *Tourism, Mobility and Second Homes: Between Elite Landscape and Common Ground* (pp. 162–173). Clevedon: Channel View Publications.

Hall, C.M. and Müller, D.K. (2004) Introduction: Second homes, curse or blessing? Revisited. In C.M. Hall and D.K. Müller (eds) *Tourism, Mobility and Second Homes: Between Elite Landscape and Common Ground* (pp. 3–14). Clevedon: Channel View Publications.

Hall, C.M. and Müller, D. (eds) (2018) *The Routledge Handbook of Second Home Tourism and Mobilities.* Abingdon: Routledge.

Hapke, C.J., Brenner, O., Hehre, R. and Reynolds, B.J. (2013) *Coastal Change from Hurricane Sandy and the 2012–13 Winter Storm Season – Fire Island, New York.* U.S. Geological Survey Open-File Report 2013–1231.

Henry, J. (2013) Return or relocate? An inductive analysis of decision-making in a disaster. *Disasters* 37 (2), 293–316.

IPCC (2014) *Climate Change 2014: Impacts, Adaptation, and Vulnerability. Part A: Global and Sectoral Aspects. Working Group II Contribution to the Fifth Assessment Report of the Intergovernmental Panel on Climate Change.* Cambridge: Cambridge University Press.

Jaakson, R. (1986) Second-home domestic tourism. *Annals of Tourism Research* 13 (3), 367–391.

Jansson, B. and Müller, D.K. (2004) Second home plans among second home owners in Northern Europe's periphery. In C.M. Hall and D.K. Müller (eds) *Tourism, Mobility and Second Homes: Between Elite Landscape and Common Ground* (pp. 261–272). Clevedon: Channel View Publications.

Kaltenborn, B.P. (1997) Nature of place attachment: A study among recreation homeowners in Southern Norway. *Leisure Sciences* 19 (3), 175–189.

Kaltenborn, B.P. (1998) The alternate home – motives of recreation home use. *Norsk Geografisk Tidsskrift* 52 (3), 121–134.

Kelly, G. and Hosking, K. (2008) Nonpermanent residents, place attachment, and 'Sea Change' communities. *Environment and Behavior* 40 (4), 575–594.

Koppelman, L.E. and Forman, S. (2008) *The Fire Island National Seashore: A History.* Albany, NY: State University of New York Press.

Lundmark, L. and Marjavaara, R. (2013) Second home ownership: A blessing for all? *Scandinavian Journal of Hospitality and Tourism* 13 (4), 281–298.

McIntyre, N. (2006) Introduction. In N. McIntyre, D.R. Williams and K.E. McHugh (eds) *Multiple Dwelling and Tourism: Negotiating Place, Home and Identity* (pp. 3–14). Wallingford: CABI.

McIntyre, N. and Pavlovich, K. (2006) Changing places: Amenity coastal communities in transition. In N. McIntyre, D.R. Williams and K.E. McHugh (eds) *Multiple Dwelling and Tourism: Negotiating Place, Home and Identity* (pp. 239–261). Wallingford: CABI.

McIntyre, N., Roggenbuck, J.W. and Williams, D.R. (2006) Home and away: Revisiting 'escape' in the context of second homes. In N. McIntyre, D.R. Williams and K.E. McHugh (eds) *Multiple Dwelling and Tourism: Negotiating Place, Home and Identity* (pp. 114–128) Wallingford: CABI.

Müller, D.K. (2002) Second home ownership and sustainable development in Northern Sweden. *Tourism and Hospitality Research* 3 (4), 343–355.

Müller, D.K. (2006) The attractiveness of second home areas in Sweden: A quantitative analysis. *Current Issues in Tourism* 9 (4&5), 335–350.

Müller, D.K. (2014) Progress in second-home tourism research. In A.A. Lew, C.M. Hall and A.M. Williams (eds) *The Wiley Blackwell Companion to Tourism* (pp. 389–400). Chichester: John Wiley & Sons.

Müller, D.K. and Hoogendoorn, G. (2013) Second homes: Curse or blessing? A review 36 years later. *Scandinavian Journal of Hospitality and Tourism* 13 (4), 353–369.

Nielsen-Pincus, M., Hall, T., Force, J.E. and Wulfhorst, J.D. (2010) Sociodemographic effects on place bonding. *Journal of Environmental Psychology* 30 (4), 443–454.

Nouza, M., Ólafsdóttir, R. and Sæþórsdóttir, A.D. (2018) Motives and behaviour of second home owners in Iceland reflected by place attachment. *Current Issues in Tourism* 21 (2), 225–242.

Paris, C. (2009) Re-positioning second homes within housing studies: Household investment, gentrification, multiple residence, mobility and hyper-consumption. *Housing, Theory and Society* 26 (4), 292–310.

Perkins, H.C. and Thorns, D.C. (2006) Home away from home: The primary/secondary-home relationship. In N. McIntyre, D.R. Williams and K.E. McHugh (eds) *Multiple Dwelling and Tourism: Negotiating Place, Home and Identity* (pp. 67–81). Wallingford: CABI.

Selwood, J. and Tonts, M. (2004) Recreational second homes in South West of Western Australia. In C.M. Hall and D.K. Müller (eds) *Tourism, Mobility and Second Homes: Between Elite Landscape and Common Ground* (pp. 149–161). Clevedon: Channel View Publications.

Selwood, J. and Tonts, M. (2006) Seeking serenity: Homes away from home in Western Australia. In N. McIntyre, D.R. Williams and K.E. McHugh (eds) *Multiple Dwelling and Tourism: Negotiating Place, Home and Identity* (pp. 161–179). Wallingford: CABI.

Stedman, R.C. (2006a) Places of escape: Second-home meanings in Northern Wisconsin, USA. In N. McIntyre, D.R. Williams and K.E. McHugh (eds) *Multiple Dwelling and Tourism: Negotiating Place, Home and Identity* (pp. 129–144). Wallingford: CABI.

Stedman, R.C. (2006b) Understanding place attachment among second home owners. *American Behavioral Scientist*, 50 (2), 187–205.

Stewart, S.I. and Stynes, D.J. (2006) Second homes in the Upper Midwest. In N. McIntyre, D.R. Williams and K.E. McHugh (eds) *Multiple Dwelling and Tourism: Negotiating Place, Home and Identity* (pp. 180–193). Wallingford: CABI.

Timothy, D.J. (2004) Recreational second homes in the United States: Development issues and contemporary patterns. In C.M. Hall and D.K. Müller (eds) *Tourism, Mobility and Second Homes: Between Elite Landscape and Common Ground* (pp. 133–148). Clevedon: Channel View Publications.

Tuulentie, S. (2006) Tourists making themselves at home: Second homes as a part of tourist careers. In N. McIntyre, D.R. Williams and K.E. McHugh (eds) *Multiple Dwelling and Tourism: Negotiating Place, Home and Identity* (pp. 145–157). Wallingford: CABI.

UNEP (2008) *Disaster Risk Management for Coastal Tourism Destinations Responding to Climate Change: A Practical Guide for Decision Makers*. Paris: UNEP.

U.S. Army Corps of Engineers (2013) Fact Sheet – Fire Island Hurricane Sandy debris removal. [online] Available at: http://www.nan.usace.army.mil/Media/Fact-Sheets/Fact-Sheet-Article-View/Article/487616/fact-sheet-fire-island-hurricane-sandy-debris-removal/ (accessed 13 March 2018).

U.S. Census Bureau (2010a) Fire Island CDP, New York: General Population and Housing Characteristics. [online] Available at: https://factfinder.census.gov/faces/tableservices/jsf/pages/productview.xhtml?src=CF (accessed 15 April 2018).

U.S. Census Bureau (2010b) Ocean Beach Village, New York: General Population and Housing Characteristics. [online] Available at: https://factfinder.census.gov/faces/tableservices/jsf/pages/productview.xhtml?src=CF (accessed 15 April 2018).

U.S. Census Bureau (2010c) Saltaire Village, New York: General Population and Housing Characteristics. [online] Available at: https://factfinder.census.gov/faces/tableservices/jsf/pages/productview.xhtml?src=CF (accessed 15 April 2018).

Visser, G. (2004) Second homes: Reflections on an unexplored phenomenon in South Africa. In C.M. Hall and D.K. Müller (eds) *Tourism, Mobility and Second Homes: Between Elite Landscape and Common Ground* (pp. 196–214). Clevedon: Channel View Publications.

Williams, D.R. and Van Patten, S.R. (2006) Home *and* away? Creating identities and sustaining places in a multi-centred world. In N. McIntyre, D.R. Williams and K.E. McHugh (eds) *Multiple Dwelling and Tourism: Negotiating Place, Home and Identity* (pp. 32–50). Wallingford: CABI.

12 Reframing Sustainability and Resilience in the Recovery of the Cinque Terre following the October 2011 Flooding

Alberto Amore

Introduction

Over the last decade, the escalation of natural disasters affecting tourism destinations has brought scholars to acknowledge vulnerability and resilience as intrinsic elements of tourism destinations (Calgaro *et al.*, 2013; Cochrane, 2010; Jopp *et al.*, 2013). Such issues are clearly not just academic in nature and can have profound implications on the nature of policy interventions at different scales. This chapter builds on critical literature in sustainable tourism development and on recent advancements in the conceptualisation of resilience in tourism (Hall *et al.*, 2018; Lew & Cheer, 2017) to analyse planning and management in vulnerable destinations. The chapter frames the scales and dimensions of resilience within a theoretical framework that highlights the contraposition between the rhetoric of sustainable development and the ecological reality.

This chapter critically discusses the strategies and plans developed following the October 2011 flooding in the Cinque Terre, Italy. The focus of the chapter is on the land-use policies with relevance to tourism and the redefinition of the destination management strategy, which are assessed through the lenses of sustainability and resilience. Drawing on the destinations' response to natural disasters, this chapter critically analyses the recovery strategies put in place and instances of conflict among tourism-relevant stakeholders.

Research on the Cinque Terre as a tourism destination includes demand assessment and economic assessment of the site (Mondini & Bottazzi, 2006), the governance framework (Carlarne, 2007; Storti, 2005), and government-funded studies as part of the draft Site Operational Plan

(Ministero dei Beni e delle Attività Culturali e del Turismo (MIBACT), 2016) and the Interreg *Marittimo-IT-FR-Maritime* (ENEA, 2018). In terms of the issue of sustainability and tourism in the Cinque Terre, Patrucco (2008) highlights how pro-development rhetoric framed around the principle of economic sustainability outweighs the need to safeguard the local vulnerable landscape from the anthropic pressures caused by tourism. Patrucco (2008) further argues that two leading projects for the promotion of sound sustainable tourism in the Cinque Terre fell short of their original purpose, and that they were significantly downsized to pursue the pro-development agenda of the local Park Authority.

Literature

Tourism is an utterly complex phenomenon embracing a range of different socioecological features such as: natural resources, land use, planning, legislation, economy, community development, and marketing. These features are at the heart of sustainability, vulnerability, and resilience assessment models in tourism (Calgaro, 2010; Hall, 2008; Hall *et al.*, 2018). Ecological systems are context-specific, and 'place-based differences and context matter in determining differential levels of destination vulnerability and resilience' (Calgaro, 2010: 229). This logic also applies to the application of the sustainable development paradigm in tourism, as there are geopolitical and economic constraints at the local destination level (Mowforth & Munt, 2015).

Sustainability

The notion of sustainable tourism development has become a key feature in contemporary tourism planning discourse (Hall, 2008). Sustainability includes aspects such as protection of heritage, integration of environmental and sociocultural values, protection of biodiversity, and the achievement of balance and fairness through holistic planning strategies (Hall, 2008). There are key sociopolitical prerequisites to achieve an effective sustainable tourism development agenda. Ideally, a series of necessary conditions need to be met to successfully implement an integrated sustainable development strategy. These include environmental justice, equality, governance transparency, collaborative decision-making arrangements, and networking between tourism-related and tourism-relevant stakeholders (Bramwell & Lane, 1999; Dredge, 2015b).

Notwithstanding key postulates highlighted in sustainable tourism development literature (Lew & Hall, 1998), the conceptualisation of sustainable development in planning and destination management practices is much influenced by the current neoliberal doctrine (Dredge & Jenkins, 2012). As Hall (1998: 22) illustrates, 'there has been no easy middle path in attempting to find a balanced use of natural resources. Political reality, rather than ecological reality, has been the order of the day'.

Looking at tourism policy practices, national and international reports and guidelines for sustainable destination management tend to conceptualise tourism 'as an industrial system, and tourism policy as a mechanism to help balance supply–demand relationships' (Dredge & Jenkins, 2012: 246). This view of tourism has been called into question since the end of the 1990s (Hall, 1999, 2009; Higgins-Desbiolles, 2006), yet it still dominates mainstream rhetoric in tourism, sustainability and development. Concepts such as competitiveness, destination attractiveness, and sustainable economic growth are still predominant in policy documents at all scales (Bournemouth Tourism, 2017; Organization for Economic Cooperation Development (OECD), 2012; Regione Autonoma del Friuli Venezia-Giulia (RFVG), 2014; Tourism Industry Association of New Zealand (TIANZ), 2015; United Nations World Tourism Organization (UNWTO), 2011). For example, the *Estrategia Regional de Especializacão Inteligente do Alentejo*, Portugal, defines sustainable growth in the service, culture and tourism sectors in relation to the current trend in the demand for authenticity and experience in the tourism market (CCDR Alentejo, 2014). The rhetoric of sustainability in contemporary policy and planning in tourism legitimises exclusive and vested interests of tourism industry stakeholders (Dredge & Jenkins, 2012).

Undoubtedly, 'there are many contradictions within both the concept of sustainable development and the nature of tourism' (Hall, 2008: 62). Empirical evidence on tourism and planning practices around the world raises questions as to whether tourism stakeholders genuinely pursue sustainable development principles (Dredge & Jenkins, 2007). Many of these shortcomings can be attributed to the high fragmentation and poor coordination typical of tourism public policy (Hall & Jenkins, 1995). Also, there are contradictions between the priorities of the market and the instances for effective environmental conservation goals (Amore & Hall, 2017). This often results in poor policy integration, which represents one of the major constraints in the achievement of sustainable development in tourism (Hall, 2008).

Much current governance with regards to sustainable tourism can be seen as a policy failure characterised by market-obeying rhetoric (Hall, 2008, 2011). This point reflects those of Bernstein (2002) and Klein (2015) on how crucial environmental matters are side-lined in the name of allegedly effective (neo)liberal environmentalism. This calls for an alternative policy that acknowledges public perceptions around the environment and promotes actual sustainable development in tourism. The recent shift towards the resilience paradigm gives scope for a recalibration of genuine sustainable development in tourism (Hall et al., 2018) and the much-advocated third level of change with respect to paradigm shifts in tourism policymaking (Hall, 2011).

Resilience

The conceptualisation of resilience in tourism is mostly the result of increased research interest in the recovery of destinations following natural hazards (Hall, 2010). Most of the early works on resilience and tourism provided theorisations lacking empirical application and case studies that treat 'tourism as a separate enclave from its larger social and environmental system' (Lew, 2014: 16). Current advancements in the literature provide a multi-dimensional appraisal of resilience in tourism (Amore *et al.*, 2018; Hall *et al.*, 2018). Most of these works address the macro dimensions of resilience, with reference to tourism-induced stressors (Tyrrell & Johnston, 2008) as well as tourism-related issues such as climate change (Becken, 2013), spatial planning (Lew, 2014), community development (Strickland-Munro *et al.*, 2010) and business adaptation to ecological disturbances (Dahles & Susilowati, 2015).

Tourism destinations are highly vulnerable to natural disasters but are nevertheless able to show resilience and thrive in times of uncertainty (Biggs *et al.*, 2015; Buultjens *et al.*, 2014; Ghaderi *et al.*, 2014). The appraisal of resilience as a feature of sociopolitical, economic and ecological systems is addressed in relevant tourism literature (Amore, 2016; Becken, 2013; Calgaro *et al.*, 2014; Dredge, 2015a) and conceives of resilience and sustainability as complementary elements in destination development discourse (Cochrane, 2010).

Resilience strategies with relevance to tourism tend to overemphasise the socioeconomic dimension of destination recovery (see Hall *et al.*, 2018, 2022 for a review). The OECD, for instance, conceptualises resilience in relation to the economic recovery following the Global Financial Crisis and supports the adoption of long-term development policies rooted in the principle of green growth (Haxton, 2015). Moreover, it advocates for a particular policy mix as a key condition for the successful implementation of resilience in post-disaster destination policy and planning (Dredge, 2015a). Other international organisations instead view resilience as a synonym for risk reduction in the wake of natural and man-made disasters (e.g. United Nations International Strategy for Disaster Reduction (UNISDR), 2005; UNWTO, 2009), or emphasise disaster prevention (UNISDR, 2015). The asymmetry of the notion of resilience in tourism at the global level is reflected at national and local levels. On the one hand, Tourism England (2010) frames the concept of resilience with that of sustainable economic growth. On the other, the Great Barrier Reef Marine Park Authority (GBRMPA, 2007) understands resilience in relation to macro and micro ecological stressors, such as climate change and ecosystem vulnerability, and the vulnerability of the Great Barrier Reef to increased anthropic pressures.

As Hall (2016: 279) highlights, 'questions of power in the determination of the role, agenda setting and interpretation of resilience in policy making' need to be acknowledged when translating the notion of resilience to the socioeconomic dimension. Resilience – as defined in ecology – is neither positive nor negative (Hall, 2016). Rather, it implies nature's ability 'to absorb blows and get back up' (Klein, 2015: 447), regardless of human agency. Understanding the complex and reciprocal interdependencies of governance and meta-governance responses to natural disasters can shed light on issues with contemporary policymaking (Amore & Hall, 2016). Moreover, it is important to acknowledge how current development strategies are rooted in neoliberal and hyper-neoliberal paradigms (Amore & Hall, 2016, 2017) that claim to be 'green' but ultimately contribute to increasing environmental vulnerabilities (Klein, 2015).

   Therefore, the resilience of tourism destinations needs to be assessed within comprehensive frameworks of analysis (Amore et al., 2018; Hall et al., 2018). Only a greater understanding of the many facets of resilience can lead to an improvement of strategies, management and sustainable development of destinations in the long term. It is important to frame the discourses of resilience and sustainability as two sides of the same coin. Given the complex nature of tourism destinations, what occurs in a given destination and scale does not necessarily apply to others. As a rule of thumb, a destination is unlikely to be resilient without an environmentally sustainable strategy that is owned and shared among the wide spectrum of tourism stakeholders.

Sustainability and resilience in post-disaster contexts: A synthesis

   Figure 12.1 illustrates the relationship between sustainability and resilience at the destination level. It draws upon Moreno and Becken (2009) and Calgaro et al.'s (2013) frameworks on coastal vulnerability and destination vulnerability to climate change and natural disasters. Both frameworks are useful for the identification of ecological vulnerabilities and shortcomings in the planning and management of tourism destinations before a disaster. More importantly, the proposed framework permits the assessment of the post-disaster adaptiveness of destinations.

   Recent works on destination resilience and tourism (Amore et al., 2018; Hall, 2016; Hall et al., 2018) and mainstream literature in tourism policy and planning (Hall, 2008) are used here to assess strategies and action plans in the aftermath of a disaster. In particular, it is argued that policies and practices of land-use and destination management rooted in the rhetoric of economic sustainability heighten the vulnerability of both the local ecosystem and the local community. Conversely, policies promoting the safeguarding of the environment and of sociocultural systems are more likely to enhance the resilience of destinations against future disasters. This principle follows previous theories and empirical evidence from urban and rural environments (Gotham & Greenberg, 2014; Hall et al., 2018; Klein, 2015) and defies the current rhetoric of resilience in mainstream policymaking (Hall, 2016).

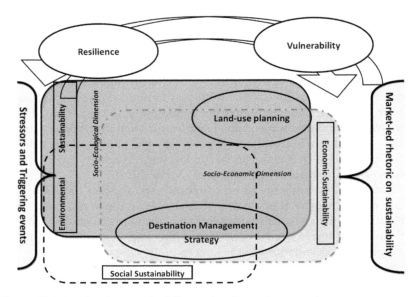

Figure 12.1 Destination sustainability and resilience framework

For the purposes of this study, the framework closely assesses the land-use planning and the destination management strategy in the Cinque Terre following the 2011 floods. The two elements are here conceived of as two sides of the same coin, as most of the political decisions concerning destinations are 'rarely exclusively devoted to tourism per se' (Hall, 2008: 14). The application of the framework in the Cinque Terre considers the multi-level regulatory framework in place. The area is listed as a World Heritage Site and follows guidelines from the United Nations Educational, Scientific and Cultural Organization (UNESCO) and the International Council on Monuments and Sites (ICOMOS). Moreover, the site is part of the Cinque Terre National Park (Italian: *Parco Nazionale delle Cinque Terre*) stretching from Monterosso to Portovenere and of the adjacent *Area Marina Protetta*. Therefore, the destination is subject to a range of restrictions that, in turn, are reflected in the tourism development strategy of the case study area. Finally, the framework permits the evaluation of whether land uses and policies for tourism labelled as 'sustainable' actually embrace the principles of sustainability and pursue the goal of sound resilient destination planning.

Context: The Cinque Terre

The Cinque Terre is a 15km-wide stretch of the Levantine coast of the Ligurian Sea, Italy (Figure 12.2). It consists of five small towns – Monterosso, Vernazza, Riomaggiore, Corniglia, and Manarola – and is a

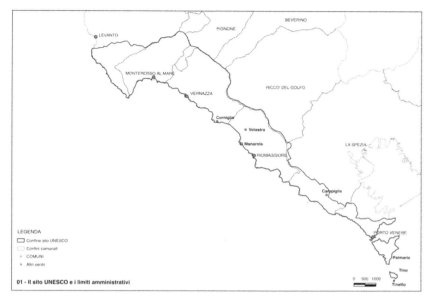

Figure 12.2 Map of the Cinque Terre (MIBACT, 2016)

core part of the Cinque Terre National Park. The area is named after the local wine (Cinque Terre D.O.C.) and was awarded World Heritage Site status in 1997 due to the 'exceptional scenic quality that illustrates a traditional way of life' (UNESCO, 1997: 10) and the unique old agricultural terraces retained by dry stone walls (Galve *et al.,* 2016). The area is home to an extensive network of dry-stone terraces (6729 km long), narrow walkways, and sanctuaries adjacent to fortresses originally built to resist Saracen raids (ICOMOS, 1996).

Until the 1960s, winegrowing and the production of olive oil represented the main outputs of the Cinque Terre. Since then, the agricultural areas have been progressively abandoned, with only 2.6% of the area (100ha) currently used for the cultivation of grapes and more than two thirds of the cultivable land listed as trees/bushes (Comune di Vernazza, 2018; Parco Nazionale delle Cinque Terre, 2014b). In parallel, tourism has steadily become the core economic output of the region. The area experienced the traditional curve of destination development, with an initial exploratory phase throughout the 1980s followed by a progressive increase of arrivals ever since (MIBACT, 2016). Nowadays, the Cinque Terre is a mature destination with strong appeal to international visitors that contributes greatly to boosting tourism in the wider Province of La Spezia (MIBACT, 2016).

Like the majority of World Heritage Sites worldwide, the Cinque Terre is exposed to geological hazards (Pavlova, Makarigakis, Depret & Jomelli, 2015). In October 2011, the Cinque Terre was hit by intense rainfall that ultimately led to large-scale flooding and landslides that severely damaged the towns of Vernazza and Monterosso. More than a quarter of the residents in the Cinque Terre were evacuated (Cevasco *et al.*, 2013) as hundreds of shallow landslides and inland flooding hit abandoned terraces, infrastructure and residential areas (Bartelletti *et al.*, 2017). Monterosso registered the highest precipitation in the Cinque Terre since 1951, with economic losses in the range of €130 million (Cevasco *et al.*, 2014). The UNESCO mission in the aftermath of the flooding reported that 'cloudbursts around the towns of Monterosso and Vernazza had been followed by landslides that had engulfed the settlements with water' (UNESCO, 2012: 9). While authorities were adamant that debris would be cleared in Monterosso and Vernazza before March 2012, the full reopening of key coastal routes and the recovery of historic buildings is likely to take years.

Despite ongoing vulnerability and haphazard recovery since the 2011 flooding, the Cinque Terre has been experiencing a steady increase of visitor arrivals (Parco Nazionale delle Cinque Terre, 2014b). Nonetheless, there are concerns about the current tourist pressure at the Cinque Terre, with the Mayor of Monterosso advocating for the adoption of measures to restrict visitor access and regulate the local tourism industry (Moggia, 2018).

Methodology

For the purposes of this study, an interpretive analysis of documents addressing sustainable development and resilience in the Cinque Terre area has been employed. Documents include the existing regulatory framework as identified in the Site Management Plan (MIBACT, 2016), the Cinque Terre National Park Authority and the *Regione Liguria*. Data collection also includes the *Adesione alla Carta Europea per il Turismo Sostenibile nelle Aree Protette* (Parco Nazionale delle Cinque Terre, 2014b) and the annual *Relazione sullo Stato dell'Ambiente* (Regione Liguria, 2013, 2016, 2017). The period of analysis covers all the relevant documents released following the October 2011 flooding.

The approach to data collection and analysis underpins previous research in tourism policy and planning and allows for a longitudinal research approach. Policy documents and reports are conceived of as the ultimate result of episodes of governance by stakeholders (Healey, 2003) and the most feasible research approach for this case study due to the ongoing judiciary investigations on the Cinque Terre National Park (ANSA, 2018). With regards to the method of analysis, the study developed a template for the analysis of archived sources. Findings were coded based on a matrix that was developed from existing literature in tourism planning, sustainable tourism development and destination resilience. A computer-assisted qualitative data analysis software (NVivo 12 Pro) was used to organise and code the collected data. This approach turned out to be the ideal compromise in light of previous research in post-disaster studies and tourism (Calgaro, 2010; Gotham & Greenberg, 2014).

Findings

Land use planning

Liguria and the Cinque Terre are among the regions in Italy most vulnerable to hydrogeological hazards (D'Onofrio & Trusiani, 2018), an issue authorities were well aware of prior to the 2011 flooding (Terranova *et al.*, 2006). Government authorities attempted to retain and reinforce abandoned terraces while introducing more effective water distribution networks for the few areas of cultivated land (ICOMOS, 1996), but they fell short of implementing a suitable land-use plan to recover abandoned terraces and enhance reforestation in the most remote localities. The 2003 operative plan foresaw the reintroduction of traditional terraces in declining and abandoned areas in the Cinque Terre as part of a wider rural tourism strategy, but it did not contemplate hydrogeological risk as a complementary factor in the safeguarding of the site (Parco Nazionale delle Cinque Terre, 2003).

Following the 2011 flooding, geological surveys by a research team based at the University of Florence showed that 90% of the landslides happened on abandoned terraces covered by pine trees and Mediterranean shrubs, while only 2% of the alluvial debris came from cultivated terraces. Detailed surveys in the Vernazza catchment area further suggest that the highest percentages of landslides occurred in recently abandoned dry stone terraces lacking proper maintenance (Cevasco *et al.*, 2014). Despite the existing framework for the protection and safeguarding of the natural and built environment in the Cinque Terre, 'the park management plan does not authorize the removal of the forests to restore the abandoned terraces, except in certain limited cases' (Agnoletti, 2014: 69). As a result, the area is still exposed to shallow yet highly dangerous landslides (Bartelletti *et al.*, 2017).

In light of current and potential vulnerabilities in the Cinque Terre, the Liguria region put in place 'a ban on new building and on work to existing buildings that goes beyond mere conservation work' (UNESCO, 2012: 29) and re-mapped the areas subject to hydrogeological risk (Regione Liguria, 2015). The maintenance of terraces and promotion of agricultural production represent an opportunity to repopulate abandoned areas and reduce erosion and landslides in the highly vulnerable site of the Cinque Terre (MIBACT, 2016). Nevertheless, the regional scheme for flooding risk reduction focuses almost exclusively on water regulation and maintenance of existing water streams in proximity to urban areas (Regione Liguria, 2013), with no established regulation on the recovery of abandoned terraces. The latter solution, in fact, is deemed as uneconomic and unlikely to reduce the risk of landslides in the future in contrast with more cost-effective solutions such as planned reforestation (Galve *et al.*, 2016).

Local authorities have done relatively little to effectively tackle the issue of abandoned terraces in the Cinque Terre following the 2011 flooding (Moggia & Marchese, 2012). Despite the area being under the Cinque Terre National Park Authority, the national heritage legislation and Cultural Heritage and Landscape Code, the initiative of retaining and restoring terraces still lies in the hands of private owners who lack the necessary resources to effectively restore the terraces (UNESCO, 2017). It should therefore not be a surprise that the few terrace refurbishment projects were carried out under the initiative of heritage trusts such as the *Fondo Ambiente Italiano (FAI)*, as in the case of the Casa Lovara (FAI, 2016).

According to a 2016 review of the existing land-use framework in the Cinque Terre, the plans currently in use in the five towns are out-dated (MIBACT, 2016). Moreover, these plans do not take into full consideration the extraordinary measures that need to be adopted for the retention of terraces and the reduction of vulnerability in the residential areas. Similarly, the land-use framework of the Cinque Terre National Park Authority is also out-dated (1999) and limited in action to the mere safeguarding of the cultural landscape (MIBACT, 2016). The 2012 UNESCO-ICOMOS mission further stressed the need for the Cinque Terre 'to develop a new World Heritage Plan, with a resource management perspective' (UNESCO, 2012: 24) and 'and incorporate within it a sustainable tourism strategy for the property, and an integrated risk management strategy' (UNESCO, 2013: 126). However, despite repeated recommendations from UNESCO on the matter, the revised Cinque Terre management plan is still not finalised.

An emblematic example of the delays in the redefinition of land-use in the Cinque Terre site is the so-called buffer zone. The UNESCO-ICOMOS mission of 2012 considered the buffer zone a key instrument 'to provide not only the preservation of the landscape from the visual point of view, but also from the perspective of the vulnerability of the property' (UNESCO, 2012: 23). The Ministry for Culture, Arts and Tourism similarly acknowledged the need to create a buffer zone within the Cinque Terre site and its importance in enhancing the preservation of the outstanding universal value of the Cinque Terre terraces against degradation and vulnerability post-flooding (MIBACT, 2016). Nevertheless, the establishment of a buffer zone is tied to the release of the new management plan. The draft simply identified the bodies in charge with the definition of the zone and its framing in the wider Coordinating Committee (UNESCO, 2017).

The lack of a defined coordinating body contributes significantly to the persistent state of fragmentation among local authorities and stakeholders. In a May 2018 Ministerial meeting, the Mayor of Monterosso advocated for the Cinque Terre National Park Authority to become the governing body of the whole area. He further stressed the need to establish a strategic plan aimed at the safeguarding and promotion of the existing cultural landscape. The recent boom in tourism, in fact, has brought steady economic speculation outside the community, which may likely lead to the displacement of residents away from the five towns (Moggia, 2018).

Destination management strategy

The governance of the Cinque Terre site as a tourism destination is complex and fragmented (MIBACT, 2016). Since its establishment in 1999, the Cinque Terre National Park Authority has acted as the Destination Management and Marketing Organization (DMO) for the destination. On the eve of the 2011 flooding, its functions included the management of the tourist information offices, transportation services within the site, and marketing of the Cinque Terre (Lorenzini, 2011). The Park Authority was also in charge of the development of the tourism action plan, the management of tourist flows, the management of tourism-dedicated facilities, and the promotion of products combining tourist experience, rural economy and terrace maintenance (Lorenzini, 2011; Storti, 2005).

Since 2001, the Park Authority established the *Cinque Terre Card* in partnership with Trenitalia to monitor visitor arrivals at the site from the railway stations of Monterosso and Riomaggiore (Parco Nazionale delle Cinque Terre, 2016a). The authority also worked, with limited success, to establish an environmental quality certification system for hospitality businesses at the site and to assess the tourist carrying capacity of the Cinque Terre site (Lorenzini, 2011; Patrucco, 2008). Despite the assessment being completed in 2007, the authority never released the results of the study, nor did they develop a revised destination strategy that considered the steady growth in environmental stress caused by tourism in the Cinque Terre (Patrucco, 2008).

Following the flooding, authorities prioritised the clearing of roads in key tourist areas in Monterosso and Vernazza and were successful in restoring the main route connecting the Cinque Terre towns in time for the beginning of the 2012 tourist season (Povoledo, 2012). The Park Authority maintained its role as DMO and pursued a new strategy to promote tourist arrivals to the Cinque Terre site. In 2014, the Park Authority and the La Spezia Port Authority agreed to create a visitor centre dedicated to cruise passengers seeking to go on excursions in the Cinque Terre, and to collaborate in the management of one international event within the site. The Park Authority also launched a pilot project as part of the INTERREG Programme *Martittimo 2014–2020* to promote environmental sustainability among local tourism SMEs and their competitiveness and appeal among international visitors (ENEA, 2018). In 2015, the Park Authority and the provincial Chamber of Commerce established a destination management partnership to promote the green economy, sustainable management and biodiversity among relevant tourism businesses within the Cinque Terre (Alboretti, 2015).

The Cinque Terre National Park Authority is adamant in promoting environmentally driven practices of responsible tourism. In 2013, the Park Authority established a collaboration with the *Associazione Italiana di Turismo Responsabile* (AITR) and the *Alta Scuola di Turismo Ambientale* to educate local entrepreneurs and develop innovative tourism products oriented at niche environmental tourism markets (LegaCoop, 2013). In the view of the Park Authority, this initiative can enhance the sustainability of tourist flows within the fragile Cinque Terre site and ultimately lead to successful integration between the economy and the local environment (LegaCoop Liguria, 2013). More recently, the Park Authority reintroduced the environmental quality certification system for local hospitality, leisure and tourism-related businesses that proactively contribute to the promotion of sustainable development (Parco Nazionale delle Cinque Terre, 2016b). The certification praises those businesses that promote local goods and the traditions of the Cinque Terre to visitors and consumers throughout their journey in the site (Parco Nazionale delle Cinque Terre, 2016b). In the view of the Park Authority, certified businesses play a significant role in the pursuit of integrated local management and in the achievement of economic, environmental and social sustainability in the Cinque Terre (Parco Nazionale delle Cinque Terre, 2016b).

The major activity of the Cinque Terre National Park Authority for the management of visitors is that of the *Cinque Terre Card*. The new partnership with Trenitalia announced in 2014 allows visitors to integrate the park ticket with the railcard and access several trails within the Cinque Terre site (Parco Nazionale delle Cinque Terre, 2016a). The card represents the main source of income for the Park Authority, with revenue reinvested in tourist information, maintenance of trails, and provision of Wi-Fi during the visit. The park also uses part of the revenue to restore dry terraces and hire professional guides to access remote trails. Nevertheless, there are critics of the partnership with Trenitalia, particularly with regards to the relatively small share of the ticket price (25%) that goes to the Park Authority (Mastrandrea, 2016).

Following the 2011 flooding, the Park Authority has the power to suspend the sale of the *Cinque Terre Card* to better manage visitors. The current intention of the Park Authority is to grant access to the Cinque Terre exclusively to card holders and drastically reduce the annual visitor flow from 2.5 million to 1.5 million (Deiana, 2018). This mechanism, however, has found some opposition among local businesses, which emerged during the focus groups organised by the Ministry for Culture, Arts and Tourism (MIBACT, 2016). Local authorities and the Park Authority, in particular, consider restricted access as the only solution to the steady increase of visitors following the 2011 flooding (Camera di Commercio di Genova, 2017). In the words of former Park Authority

Director, Vittorio Alessandro, 'restricted booking positively benefits the appeal of the site and enhances the host-guest relationship towards responsible tourism in environmentally vulnerable destinations' (Alessandro, 2016a). In turn, this measure also enhances practices of responsible tourism within the frame of vulnerability and risk reduction in natural areas.

In 2015, the Cinque Terre National Park Authority was awarded the *Carta Europea per il Turismo Sostenibile* (CETS) for the implementation of a collaborative sustainable destination plan with relevant local and European stakeholders. Through collaboration, the Park Authority is seeking to define a medium-term strategy and a coordinated management plan for the Cinque Terre site that adheres to the ten principles outlined in the Charter (Parco Nazionale delle Cinque Terre, 2014a). The Park Authority is currently leading a project to assess the ecological impact of tourism in the Cinque Terre site, support sustainable business practices, and promote new trails targeting lucrative niche markets (e.g. wine tourism) (Parco Nazionale delle Cinque Terre, 2014a). The Park Authority has established partnerships with local sustainable businesses and promotes their products and services through their portal (Parco Nazionale delle Cinque Terre, 2014a). Adherence to the Charter is expected to establish successful sustainable management practices within the Cinque Terre site and enhance the protection of natural and cultural heritage through sound sustainable tourism services (Parco Nazionale delle Cinque Terre, 2014a).

The recovery of the Cinque Terre is still continuing but is not without controversies. On the one hand, UNESCO and ICOMOS recommend the development of 'contingency plans directly aimed at tourists and hikers ... to be applied in case of disasters' (UNESCO, 2012: 23), 'alongside the development of sustainable tourism strategy ... with the overall aim of strengthening the long-term sustainability of the cultural landscape' (UNESCO, 2013: 143). The draft Site Operational Plan acknowledges the need to prioritise environmental safeguards and cultural promotion over consumer-oriented policies and develop an integrated strategy for the site (MIBACT, 2016). However, data from the Ministry of Culture, Arts and Tourism suggests that there is very poor stakeholder integration, especially among rural and tourism businesses (MIBACT, 2016). The fragmentation between stakeholders is emblematic in the case of the *Via dell'Amore* trail between Riomaggiore and Manarola, with the Park Authority challenging the decision of the local authorities to outsource the management service of the trail to a private entity (Alessandro, 2016b).

Discussion

The vulnerability of the Cinque Terre to hydrogeological hazards was well-documented prior to the October 2011 flooding. This study argues that the steady decrease of agriculture and viticulture in the terraces greatly contributed to the vulnerability of the Cinque Terre site. This aspect was highlighted in other studies in the Cinque Terre (e.g. Cevasco *et al.*, 2014) and underpins the works of Calgaro *et al.* (2013) on the importance of the ecological dimension in assessments of destination vulnerability. This study also illustrates how the regional authority approach has done little to stimulate the retention and enhancement of abandoned terraces. The latter has been deemed as uneconomic in a recent government-funded cost-benefit analysis (Galve *et al.*, 2016), which underpins contemporary research on the influence of market principles in post-disaster recovery (Amore, 2016; Gotham & Greenberg, 2014). The findings of this study, finally, show that there are important flaws in the current land-use framework for the Cinque Terre site. The 2011 flooding unveiled the governance shortcomings in the site, and the long recovery is a testimony to the fragmented policy environment. This aspect underpins previous research in post-disaster destination governance (Amore & Hall, 2016; Larsen *et al.*, 2011).

The current Cinque Terre destination strategy positions economic sustainability and prospective niche tourism demand as strongholds in the development of innovative, high-quality services. Despite the plea from local stakeholders, there is no explicit statement on the need to reduce the visitor flows as a priority to reduce the vulnerability of the Cinque Terre to anthropic pressure. This aspect underpins Hall's (1998) critique of the prioritisation of economic interests ahead of sound environmental protection. Based on the findings collected and the analysis of reports and documents available, it can be stated that the Cinque Terre fell short of pursuing sustainable development principles recommended in tourism policy and planning (Dredge & Jenkins, 2007; Hall, 2008). The implementation of the destination management strategy in the Cinque Terre following the 2011 flooding, more importantly, downplays the ecological vulnerability of the site and the likelihood of floods in the future. The current strategy for the site deploys a 'business as usual approach', which is the mainstay of most of the tourism policy practices highlighted in the literature section. Ultimately, this reinforces Patrucco's (2008) sustainability paradox in the management of the Cinque Terre by the Park Authority.

Evidence from the Cinque Terre contradicts the conceptualisation of resilience and sustainability as complementary elements in destination development discourse (Cochrane, 2010). The lack of integration between the land-use planning and the destination management strategy in the case of the Cinque Terre is testimony to the shortcomings in contemporary policymaking highlighted in the literature (Lew, 2014). The post-flooding destination governance of the Cinque Terre has heightened the vulnerability of the local ecosystem and the local community. This trend underpins the findings from previous research in post-disaster contexts (Calgaro *et al.*, 2013). The debris clearance in key tourist hotspots in 2012 and the agreement with cruise operators in 2013 put tourism gains ahead of community wellbeing. Similar post-disaster contingency planning in tourism can be found in Thailand (Calgaro *et al.*, 2013) and the United States (Gotham & Greenberg, 2014).

Undoubtedly, the Cinque Terre National Park Authority has embarked on a laudable initiative with the allocation of ticket sale revenues to the retention and recovery of abandoned terraces and the promotion of services and products combining agriculture, tourism and landscaping. Nevertheless, the scale of the project is very small if we consider the over 6700 km of terrace system within the site and the small revenue shares from ticket sales (25%). Also, delays in the delivery of an integrated operational plan for the Cinque Terre site and in the creation of a buffer zone in accordance with the UNESCO-ICOMOS recommendations are testimony to a destination governance failure (Amore & Hall, 2016), which is currently far from being solved. Overall, it can be stated that the Cinque Terre is far from being considered a resilient destination as conceptualised in the literature (Amore *et al.*, 2018; Hall *et al.*, 2018). This study, therefore, disagrees with previous research on the Cinque Terre as a successful case for protecting cultural and natural heritage (Carlarne, 2007).

Conclusion

This chapter has provided a critical analysis of policy documents and destination strategies put in place in the Cinque Terre following the October 2011 flooding. This study argues that governance failures in post-disaster contexts are likely to increase the vulnerability of destination-relevant stakeholders, hinder their adaptation to hazardous events, and negatively affect the recovery of destinations at large. Moreover, it advances the currently limited understanding of destination recovery of the Cinque Terre with insights from relevant tourism literature in destination sustainability and resilience.

There are, of course, a series of limitations in the study. First, delays in the delivery of the new operational plan and the buffer zone partly limit the application of the literature to the Cinque Terre case study. Second, the site is far from being fully recovered, meaning that more research is needed once the whole site is fully operative. Third, there is scope to integrate the findings of this study with further data from qualitative interviews among managers and directors of the Cinque Terre site. Arguably, the chance of participants taking part in interviews is likely to increase once judiciary investigations on the Cinque Terre National Park are over.

Further research of this kind is needed to enhance understanding of tourism planning practices and assess whether local authorities embark on the sound sustainable and resilient destination-level policies advocated in the literature, particularly in areas that are recognised for their vulnerability to hydrogeological hazards. There is a need for more critical studies framing the rhetoric on sustainable development and governance fragmentations as factors preventing the delivery of effective sustainable policies for resilient destinations. More research focusing on the Cinque Terre is also needed to foster policy learning and support local authorities' quest for a sustainable development agenda, as advocated by the Mayors of Monterosso and Vernazza in the recent round table with the Ministry for Culture, Arts and Tourism (Moggia, 2018).

References

Agnoletti, M. (2014) Rural landscape, nature conservation and culture: Some notes on research trends and management approaches from a (southern) European perspective. *Landscape and Urban Planning* 126, 66–73.

Alboretti, C. (2015) Intesa tra Parco Nazionale delle Cinque Terre e Camera di Commercio della Spezia. *Altrimondi News,* 7 July. [online] Available at: http://altrimondinews.it/2015/07/17/parco-delle-cinque-terre-e-camera-di-commercio-insieme-per-una-economia-sostenibile/

Alessandro, V. (2016a) Cinque Terre e turismo: Il presidente del Parco risponde alla polemica sul 'numero chiuso'. *GreenNews.info,* 19 February. [online] Available at: http://www.greenews.info/rubriche/top-contributors/cinque-terre-e-turismo-il-presidente-del-parco-risponde-alla-polemica-sul-numero-chiuso-20160219/.

Alessandro, V. (2016b) A proposito della Via dell'Amore nel Parco delle Cinque Terre. *Greenreport.it,* 19 April. [online] Available at: http://www.greenreport.it/news/aree-protette-e-biodiversita/proposito-della-via-dellamore-nel-parco-delle-cinque-terre/

Amore, A. (2016) The governance of built heritage in the post-earthquake Christchurch CBD. In C.M. Hall, S. Malinen, R. Vosslamber and R. Wordsworth (eds) *Business and Post-disaster Management: Business, Organisational and Consumer Resilience and the Christchurch Earthquakes* (pp. 200–218). Abingdon: Routledge.

Amore, A. and Hall, C.M. (2016) From governance to meta-governance in tourism?: Re-incorporating politics,interests and values in the analysis of tourism governance. *Tourism Recreation Research* 41 (2), 109–122.

Amore, A. and Hall, C.M. (2017) National and urban public policy agenda in tourism. Towards the emergence of a hyperneoliberal script? *International Journal of Tourism Policy* 7 (1), 4–22.

Amore, A., Prayag, G. and Hall, C.M. (2018) Conceptualising destination resilience from a multi-level perspective. *Tourism Review International* 22 (3–4), 235–250.

ANSA (2018) Processo 5 Terre: Bonanini in carcere. *ANSA,* 15 July. [online] Available at: http://www.ansa.it/liguria/notizie/2018/07/15/processo-5-terre-bonanini-in-carcere_5a737464-7300-4b5f-940f-a9468ead656e.html

Bartelletti, C., Giannecchini, R., D'Amato Avanzi, G., Galanti, Y. and Mazzali, A. (2017) The influence of geological–morphological and land use settings on shallow landslides in the Pogliaschina T. basin (northern Apennines, Italy). *Journal of Maps* 13 (2), 142–152.

Becken, S. (2013) Developing a framework for assessing resilience of tourism sub-systems to climatic factors. *Annals of Tourism Research* 43, 506–528.

Bernstein, S. (2002) Liberal environmentalism and global environmental governance. *Global Environmental Politics* 2 (3), 1–16.

Biggs, D., Hicks, C.C., Cinner, J.E. and Hall, C.M. (2015) Marine tourism in the face of global change: The resilience of enterprises to crises in Thailand and Australia. *Ocean & Coastal Management* 105, 65–74.

Bournemouth Tourism (2017) *Bournemouth and Poole Tourism Strategy 2017–2022.* Bournemouth: Bournemouth Tourism.

Bramwell, B. and Lane, B. (1999) Sustainable tourism: Contributing to the debates. *Journal of Sustainable Tourism* 7 (1), 1–5.

Buultjens, J., Ratnayake, I. and Gnanapala, A.C. (2014) From tsunami to recovery: The resilience of the Sri Lankan tourism industry. In B.W. Ritchie and K. Campiranon (eds) *Tourism Crisis and Disaster Management in the Asia-Pacific* (pp. 132–148). Wallingford: CABI.

Calgaro, E. (2010) Building Resilient Tourism Destination Futures in a World of Uncertainty: Assessing Destination Vulnerability in Khao Lak, Patong and Phi Phi Don, Thailand to the 2004 Tsunami. PhD, Macquarie University, Sydney.

Calgaro, E., Dominey-Howes, D. and Lloyd, K. (2013) Application of the *destination sustainability framework* to explore the drivers of vulnerability and resilience in Thailand following the 2004 Indian Ocean Tsunami. *Journal of Sustainable Tourism* 22 (3), 361–383.

Calgaro, E., Lloyd, K. and Dominey-Howes, D. (2014) From vulnerability to transformation: A framework for assessing the vulnerability and resilience of tourism destinations. *Journal of Sustainable Tourism* 22 (3), 341–360.

Camera di Commercio di Genova (2017) *Il Turismo Sostenibile per lo Sviluppo della Liguria.* Genoa: Camera di Commercio di Genova.

Carlarne, C.P.(2007) Putting the 'and' back in the culture-nature debate: Integrated cultural and natural heritage protection. *UCLA Journal of Environmental Law & Policy* 25 (1), 153–223.

CCDR Alentejo (2014) *Uma Estratégia de Especialização Inteligente para o Alentejo.* Évora: Comissão de Coordenação e Desenvolvimento Regional do Alentejo.

Cevasco, A., Pepe, G. and Brandolini, P. (2014) The influences of geological and land use settings on shallow landslides triggered by an intense rainfall event in a coastal terraced environment. *Bulletin of Engineering Geology and the Environment* 73 (3), 859–875.

Cevasco, A., Brandolini, P., Scopesi, C. and Rellini, I. (2013) Relationships between geo-hydrological processes induced by heavy rainfall and land-use: The case of 25 October 2011 in the Vernazza catchment (Cinque Terre, NW Italy). *Journal of Maps* 9 (2), 289–298.

Cochrane, J. (2010) The sphere of tourism resilience. *Tourism Recreation Research* 35 (2), 173–185.

Comune di Vernazza (2018) *Gestione Sostenibile dei Flussi Turistici in un Sito UNESCO Italiano.* Vernazza: Comune di Vernazza.

D'Onofrio, R. and Trusiani, E. (2018) Strategies and actions to recover the landscape after flooding: The case of Vernazza in the Cinque Terre National Park (Italy). *Sustainability* 10 (3), 742–757.

Dahles, H. and Susilowati, T.P. (2015) Business resilience in times of growth and crisis. *Annals of Tourism Research* 51, 34–50.

Deiana, S.D. (2018) *L'Ente Parco propone di limitare l'accesso di turisti alle Cinque Terre per preservare il fragile equilibrio di sentieri e borghi. Un provvedimento che farà discutere.* [online] Available at: https://www.lifegate.it/persone/stile-di-vita/troppi-turisti-nelle-cinque-terre-proposto-il-numero-chiuso

Dredge, D. (2015a) *Short-term Versus Long-term Approaches to the Development of Tourism-related Policies.* Paris: OECD.

Dredge, D. (2015b) Tourism-planning network knowledge dynamics. In M.T. McLeod and R. Vaughan (eds) *Knowledge Networks and Tourism* (pp. 23–41). Abingdon: Routledge.

Dredge, D. and Jenkins, J.M. (2007) Introduction to tourism policy and planning. In D. Dredge and J.M. Jenkins (eds) *Tourism Planning and Policy* (pp. 3–32). Hoboken, NJ: John Wiley & Sons.

Dredge, D. and Jenkins, J.M. (2012) Australian national tourism policy: Influences of reflexive and political modernisation. *Tourism Planning & Development* 9 (3), 231–251.

ENEA (2018) *ENEA coinvolge il Parco delle Cinque Terre quale area pilota del Progetto STRATUS per l'implementazione di un Marchio di Qualità Ambientale rivolto alle imprese turistiche legate al mare.* [online] Available at: https://ambiente.sostenibilita. enea.it/news/enea-coinvolge-parco-cinque-terre-quale-area-pilota-progetto-stratus-limplementazione-un

Fondo Ambiente Italiano (FAI) (2016) Apre al pubblico Podere Case Lovara in Liguria. *FAI.* [press release]. Milan: [online] Available at: https://www.fondoambiente.it/news/apre-al-pubblico-podere-case-lovara-in-liguria

Galve, J.P., Cevasco, A., Brandolini, P., Piacentini, D., Azañón, J.M., Notti, D. and Soldati, M. (2016) Cost-based analysis of mitigation measures for shallow-landslide risk reduction strategies. *Engineering Geology* 213, 142–157.

Great Barrier Reef Marine Park Authority (GBRMPA) (2007) *Great Barrier Reef Climate Change Action Plan 2007–2011.* Townsville, QLD: GBRMPA.

Ghaderi, Z., Mat Som, A.P. and Henderson, J.C. (2014) When disaster strikes: The Thai floods of 2011 and tourism industry response and resilience. *Asia Pacific Journal of Tourism Research* 20 (4), 399–415.

Gotham, K.F. and Greenberg, M. (2014) *Crisis Cities: Disaster and Redevelopment in New York and New Orleans.* Oxford: Oxford University Press.

Hall, C.M. (1998) *Introduction to Tourism: Development, Dimensions and Issues* (3rd edn). Melbourne, VIC: Addison-Wesley Longman.

Hall, C.M. (1999) Rethinking collaboration and partnership: A public policy perspective. *Journal of Sustainable Tourism* 7 (3–4), 274–289.

Hall, C.M. (2008) *Tourism Planning: Policies, Processes and Relationships* (2nd edn). Harlow: Prentice Hall.

Hall, C.M. (2009) Degrowing tourism: Décroissance, sustainable consumption and steady-state tourism. *Anatolia* 20 (1), 46–61.

Hall, C.M. (2010) Crisis events in tourism: Subjects of crisis in tourism. *Current Issues in Tourism* 13 (5), 401–417.

Hall, C.M. (2011) Policy learning and policy failure in sustainable tourism governance: From first- and second-order to third-order change? *Journal of Sustainable Tourism* 19 (4–5), 649–671.

Hall, C.M. (2016) Putting ecological thinking back into disaster ecology and responses to natural disasters. In C.M. Hall, S. Malinen, R. Vosslamber and R. Wordsworth (eds.) *Business and Post-disaster Management: Business, Organisational and Consumer Resilience and the Christchurch Earthquakes* (pp. 269–292). Abingdon: Routledge.

Hall, C.M. and Jenkins, J.M. (1995) *Tourism and Public Policy.* New York, NY: Routledge.

Hall, C.M., Prayag, G. and Amore, A. (2018) *Tourism and Resilience: Individual, Organisational and Destination Perspectives.* Bristol: Channel View Publications.

Hall, C.M., Safonov, A. and Naderi Koupaei, S. (2022) Resilience in hospitality and tourism: issues, synthesis and agenda. *International Journal of Contemporary Hospitality Management*, ahead-of-print. https://doi.org/10.1108/IJCHM-11-2021-1428

Haxton, P. (2015) *A Review of Effective Policies for Tourism Growth.* Paris: OECD.

Healey, P. (2003) Collaborative planning in perspective. *Planning Theory* 2 (2), 101–123.

Higgins-Desbiolles, F. (2006) More than an 'industry': The forgotten power of tourism as a social force. *Tourism Management* 27 (6), 1192–1208.

International Council on Monuments and Sites (ICOMOS) (1996) *World Heritage List: Portovenere/Cinque Terre (Italy), No 826.* Paris: ICOMOS.

Jopp, R., DeLacy, T., Mair, J. and Fluker, M. (2013) Using a regional tourism adaptation framework to determine climate change adaptation options for Victoria's surf coast. *Asia Pacific Journal of Tourism Research* 18 (2), 144–164.

Klein, N. (2015) *This Changes Everything: Capitalism vs. The Climate.* New York: Metropolitan Books.

Larsen, R.K., Calgaro, E. and Thomalla, F. (2011) Governing resilience building in Thailand's tourism-dependent coastal communities: Conceptualising stakeholder agency in social–ecological systems. *Global Environmental Change* 21 (2), 481–491.

Legacoop Liguria (2013) *Decolla in Liguria l'Alta Scuola di Turismo Ambientale con il sostegno di Legacoop.* [online] Available at: https://www.legaliguria.coop/decolla-in-liguria-lalta-scuola-di-turismo-ambientale-con-il-sostegno-di-legacoop/

Lew, A.A. (2014) Scale, change and resilience in community tourism planning. *Tourism Geographies* 16 (1), 14–22.

Lew, A.A. and Cheer, J.M. (eds) (2017) *Tourism Resilience and Adaptation to Environmental Change: Definitions and Frameworks.* Abingdon: Routledge.

Lew, A.A. and Hall, C.M. (1998) The geography of sustainable tourism: Lessons and prospects. In C.M. Hall and A.A. Lew (eds) *Sustainable Tourism: A Geographical Perspective* (pp. 99–203). New York: Longman.

Lorenzini, E. (2011) The extra-urban cultural district: An emerging local production system: Three Italian case studies. *European Planning Studies* 19 (8), 1441–1457.

Mastrandrea, A. (2016) Dopo l'alluvione le Cinque Terre hanno bisogno di un turismo sostenibile. *Internazionale,* 25 October. [online] Available at: https://www.internazionale.it/reportage/angelo-mastrandrea/2016/10/25/cinque-terre-alluvione-turismo-sostenibile

Ministero dei Beni e delle Attività Culturali e del Turismo (MIBACT) (2016) *Porto Venere, Cinque Terre e Isole (Palmaria, Tino e Tinetto) Piano di Gestione per il sito UNESCO.* Rome:. MIBACT.

Moggia, D. and Marchese, F. (2012) *Le Cinque Terre: piano integrato di ricostruzione deconomica e sociale.* Tafter Journal, 1 August. [online] Available at: http://www.tafterjournal.it/2012/08/01/le-cinque-terre-piano-integrato-di-ricostruzione-economica-e-sociale/

Moggia, E. (2018) *Un unico centro di prenotazione e più servizi per i residenti.* Citta della Spezia News, 15 May. [online] Available at: http://www.cittadellaspezia.com/cinque-terre-val-di-vara/attualita/un-unico-centro-di-prenotazione-e-piu-servizi-per-i-residenti-259758.aspx

Mondini, G. and Bottazzi, C. (2006) L'analisi della Domanda Turistica nei processi di gestione dei paesaggi culturali. *Aestimum* 49, 15–29.

Moreno, A. and Becken, S. (2009) A climate change vulnerability assessment methodology for coastal tourism. *Journal of Sustainable Tourism* 17 (4), 473–488.

Mowforth, M. and Munt, I. (2015) *Tourism and Sustainability: Development, Globalisation and New Tourism in the Third World.* Abingdon: Routledge.

Organization for Economic Cooperation Development (OECD) (2012) *OECD Tourism Trends and Policies 2012.* Paris: OECD.

Parco Nazionale delle Cinque Terre (2003) *Norme e Indirizzi di Piano.* Portovenere: Parco Nazionale delle Cinque Terre.

Parco Nazionale delle Cinque Terre (2014a) *Adesione alla Carta Europea per il Turismo Sostenibile nelle Aree Protette.* Portovenere: Parco Nazionale delle Cinque Terre.

Parco Nazionale delle Cinque Terre (2014b) *Carta Europea del Turismo Sostenibile.* Portovenere: Parco Nazionale delle Cinque Terre.

Parco Nazionale delle Cinque Terre (2016a) *Cinque Terre Card* [online] Available at: http://www.parconazionale5terre.it/dettaglio.php?id=34423

Parco Nazionale delle Cinque Terre (2016b) *Ente Parco Nazionale delle Cinque Terre: Piano della Performance.* Portovenere: Parco Nazionale delle Cinque Terre.

Patrucco, D. (2008) Il paradosso turismo sostenibile/sostenibilità ambientale: il Parco Nazionale delle 5 Terre come case study. Paper presented at the *III Convegno Nazionale sul Turismo Sostenibile,* Amatea, 13–14 September.

Pavlova, I., Makarigakis, A., Depret, T. and Jomelli, V. (2015) Global overview of the geological hazard exposure and disaster risk awareness at World Heritage sites. *Journal of Cultural Heritage* 28, 151–157.

Povoledo, E. (2012) In Liguria's coastal hills, a storm's fury brings a struggle for restoration. *The New York Times* 3 January, A8.

Regione Liguria (2013) *Relazione sullo stato dell'ambiente in Liguria – Anno 2013 – Suolo: Difesa da rischi naturali.* [online] Available at: http://www.cartografiarl.regione.liguria.it/SiraRsaFruizionePubb/TemaRsa.aspx?page=1&Anno=2013&Codtrel=RSA&Sezione=11&Tema=SUOLO:%20DIFESA%20DA%20RISCHI%20NATURALI

Regione Liguria (2015) *Direttiva Alluvioni 2007/60/CE e D.lgs 49/2010 – Classi di rischio alluvionale ed elementi territoriali esposti.* [online] Available at: http://srvcarto.regione.liguria.it/geoviewer2/pages/apps/download/index.html?id=1725

Regione Liguria (2016) Relazione sullo stato dell'ambiente in Liguria – Anno 2016 – Suolo: Difesa da rischi naturali [online]. Retrieved from http://www.cartografiarl.regione.liguria.it/SiraRsaFruizionePubb/TemaRsa.aspx?page=1&Anno=2016&Codtrel=RSA&Sezione=11&Tema=SUOLO:%20DIFESA%20DA%20RISCHI%20NATURALI.

Regione Liguria (2017) Relazione sullo stato dell'ambiente in Liguria – Anno 2017 – Suolo: Difesa da rischi naturali [online]. Retrieved from http://www.cartografiarl.regione.liguria.it/SiraRsaFruizionePubb/TemaRsa.aspx?page=1&Anno=2017&Codtrel=RSA&Sezione=11&Tema=SUOLO:%20DIFESA%20DA%20RISCHI%20NATURALI

Regione Autonoma del Friuli Venezia-Giulia (RFVG) (2014) *Piano del Turismo 2014–2018 della Regione Autonoma Friuli Venezia Giulia.* Trieste: RFVG.

Storti, M. (2005) *Il Paesaggio Storico delle Cinque Terre.* Florence: Florence University Press.

Strickland-Munro, J.K., Allison, H.E. and Moore, S.A. (2010) Using resilience concepts to investigate the impacts of protected area tourism on communities. *Annals of Tourism Research* 37 (2), 499–519.

Terranova, R., Zanzucchi, G., Bernini, M., Brandolini, P., Campobasso, S., Clerici, A., . . . Zanzucchi, F. (2006) Geologia, geomorfologia e vini del Parco Nazionale delle Cinque Terre (Liguria, Italia). *Bollettino della Societa` Geologica Italiana,* 15 (6), 115–128.

Tourism Industry Association of New Zealand (TIANZ) (2015) *New Zealand Tourism Strategy 2015.* Wellington: TIANZ.

Tourism England (2010) *A Strategic Action Plan for Tourism 2010–2030.* London: Tourism England.

Tyrrell, T.J. and Johnston, R.J. (2008) Tourism sustainability, resiliency and dynamics: Towards a more comprehensive perspective. *Tourism and Hospitality Research* 8 (1), 14–24.

United Nations Educational, Scientific and Cultural Organization (UNESCO) (1997) *Convention Concerning the Protection of the World Cultural and Natural Heritage. World Heritage Committe, Twenty-first Session, Naples, 1–6 December 1997.* Paris: UNESCO.

United Nations Educational, Scientific and Cultural Organization (UNESCO) (2012) *Mission Report: Portovenere, Cinque Terre, and the Islands (Palmaria, Tino and Tinetto) (Italy) (C 826) 8–12 October 2012.* Paris: UNESCO.

United Nations Educational, Scientific and Cultural Organization (UNESCO) (2013) *Convention Concerning the Protection of the World Cultural and Natural Heritage. World Heritage Commission: Thirty-seventh Session, Phnom Penh, 16–27 June 2013.* Paris: UNESCO.

United Nations Educational, Scientific and Cultural Organization (UNESCO) (2017) *Convention Concerning the Protection of the World Cultural and Natural Heritage. World Heritage Committee: Forty-first Session, Krakow, 2–12 July 2017.* Paris: UNESCO.

United Nations International Strategy for Disaster Reduction (UNISDR) (2005) *The Hyogo Framework for Action 2005–2015: Building the Resilience of Nations and Communities to Disasters.* Bangkok: UNISDR.

United Nations International Strategy for Disaster Reduction (UNISDR) (2015) *Sendai Framework for Disaster Risk Reduction 2015 – 2030*. Bangkok: UNISDR.

United Nations World Tourism Organization (UNWTO) (2009) *UNWTO Tourism Resilience Committee Considering Impact of Economic Crisis on Tourism Industry*. [online] Available at: http://climate-l.iisd.org/news/unwto-tourism-resilience-committee-considering-impact-of-economic-crisis-on-tourism-industry/

United Nations World Tourism Organization (UNWTO) (2011) *Governance for Sustainable Tourism Development*. Madrid: UNWTO.

13 Conclusion: Tourism, Cyclones, Hurricanes and Flooding: An Emerging Research Agenda

Girish Prayag and C. Michael Hall

As outlined in Chapter 1 (Hall & Prayag), the tourism industry, including tourists, can be severely impacted by cyclones and hurricanes. These weather-related events can lead to flooding, but floods are not necessarily linked to only cyclones and hurricanes. Collectively, existing studies on the impacts of disasters show that the damage caused by hurricanes, storms and cyclones can take three forms. First, strong winds can cause considerable structural damage to buildings and infrastructure but also affect the agriculture industry. Second, any associated rainfall can result in extensive flooding, and in sloped areas can lead to landslides and slumps. Third, the high winds pushing on the ocean's surface can cause the water near the coast to rise above the usual sea level, resulting in storm surges (Granvorka & Strobl, 2013). Storm surges can result in severe property damage in coastal areas, salt contamination of agricultural and residential land, and contribute considerable coastal erosion (Granvorka & Strobl, 2013). However, hurricanes, cyclones and floods can also have some positive effects on ecological systems, such as flushing of silted swamps and rivers and replenishing food chains (Fritz *et al.*, 2007). As with the impacts of many disasters, they can also lead to refurbishment of both general community and tourism specific infrastructure, thereby potentially improving tourism infrastructure and services in the long run (Faulkner & Vikulov, 2001). The shared experience of such disasters can also strengthen community bonds, while creating better coherence between the tourism industry and the local community (Faulkner & Vikulov, 2001). As outlined in this book, several consequences of cyclones, hurricanes and flooding have been identified requiring tourists, tourism businesses and destinations to prepare for, cope with, and recover from these events (see Chapter 2 for an overview). This chapter discusses the findings from previous chapters in relation to the existing literature and identifies some of the current gaps in knowledge that can guide researchers in progressing the research agenda on cyclones, hurricanes and floods in the tourism field.

Chapter 3 (Bischeri) raises issues related to the design of strategies that enable communities to recover fully from disasters. In particular, the author notes the lack of studies examining architectural practices that can contribute to disaster resilience, with specific reference to cyclones. Recovery and resilience are closely linked as suggested in previous studies (Hall *et al.*, 2018, 2022; Orchiston, 2013; Möller *et al.*, 2018). This chapter argues that architecture has a close relationship with community recovery and offers the idea of a resilientscape by highlighting, for example, how landscape can be used as a mitigation tool. The importance of community involvement and input in designing resilientscapes is emphasised. It is surprising, however, how little of the tourism resilience literature examines the design issues raised in this chapter in relation to building community or even tourism sector resilience. Brown *et al.* (2017) in their systematic review of the literature on resilience of the hotel sector found that how hotel design and the design of the entire hospitality system contribute to resilience are not areas that have been adequately researched. The importance of choosing the right location, coupled with system design to warn and minimise risk, and how these components fit within the broader disaster management and risk reduction plans at organisational, community, and destination level must be further investigated. Brown *et al.* (2017) identify the Hotel Resilient Programme as an example of a design and certification programme that can make this sector more resilient.

Moving from community recovery and resilience post-disaster, Chapter 4 (Cahyanto) examines the needs of visitors during a hurricane advisory. Evacuation is a leading mitigation strategy for reducing human losses, and the chapter highlights the importance for policymakers and destination management organisations (DMOs) to consider risk factors, risk communication, and risk prevention intention as drivers of risk prevention behaviours of visitors. Often tourists do not adopt self-protective behaviours because they are unfamiliar with the destination (Burby & Wagner, 1996). The chapter found that visitors consider, for example, the likelihood of getting hit by a hurricane, mode of transportation, possibilities to leave, infrastructure accessibility (e.g. highways) and travel party size, among others, as influencing their intention to evacuate. The chapter also identifies the lessons learned from Hurricane Irma, and these should help destinations to develop better disaster management plans. This chapter builds on the substantial knowledge on information seeking behaviours of visitors regarding hurricane evacuation (Cahyanto *et al.*, 2016), their risk assessments and perceptions (Matyas *et al.*, 2011), cognitive and affective responses (Villegas *et al.*, 2013), and practices that can improve communication to tourists for hurricane evacuation (Cahyanto & Pennington-Gray, 2015; Chan *et al.*, 2020). In addition, studies on the effect of hurricanes on community resilience to environmental change exist (e.g. Forster *et al.*, 2014) as well as on the impacts of hurricanes on visitation to national parks in the United States (Woosnam & Kim, 2014). The consensus that emerges is that destinations, tourism businesses and tourists are becoming increasingly vulnerable to strong hurricanes as a result of both the siting of tourism infrastructure and resort location, and the effects of climate change (Scott *et al.*, 2012; Scott *et al.*, 2019).

Destination managers have to invest in hurricane communication messages that target a wide array of tourists, and receptiveness of content of the message by different groups must also be assessed (Cahyanto *et al.*, 2016). While there seems to be a substantial body of research on hurricanes and cyclones in relation to visitor behaviour, this cannot be said for flooding. There is still a substantial gap on risk assessment, perceptions, and behaviours of visitors prior to, during and after flood related events. Despite the importance of providing the right information and timely communication being highlighted in previous studies (Mair *et al.*, 2016; Möller *et al.*, 2018; Mason *et al.*, 2019; Chan *et al.*, 2020), the design elements of the message and their effectiveness have not been investigated among tourists. In the marketing literature, there is substantial evidence to suggest that design elements of any form of communication and the different types of marketing appeal used influence the decision-making processes of consumers (Johar & Sirgy, 1991; Prayag & Soscia, 2016). Yet studies that examine the design of communication materials for disaster management remain scarce despite several studies reviewing the effectiveness of post-disaster marketing campaigns (Chacko & Marcell, 2008; Orchiston & Higham, 2016; Mason *et al.*, 2019).

Chapter 5 (Kiss & Chang) investigates the impacts of typhoons on the tourism industry in Taiwan. Disaster preparedness, especially tourism disaster management strategy, is a significant part of the tourism industry in Taiwan. The chapter identifies the best practice for various sectors, including their hazard management policies. Using the lens of proactive and reactive strategies, the chapter examines hazard reduction, readiness, response, and recovery strategies. The authors found that practices across the sectors were more or less the same due to the well-developed hazard management system by the government. This stresses the importance of leadership at the highest level to ensure that disaster plans are supported by local communities. A systematic review of the tourism risk, crisis and disaster literature by Ritchie and Jiang (2019) highlighted the need for more research on proactive disaster management strategies of organisations and destinations. The chapter also notes that insurance policies are important as a mitigation strategy for tourism businesses, and the role of collaboration between various stakeholders in the recovery phase facilitates faster recovery. The issue of collaboration is examined in more depth in Chapter 8 (Jiang & Ritchie). Yet many small tourism businesses face challenges in securing adequate insurance coverage for disasters. As found in the study by Ghaderi, Mat Som and Henderson (2015), after the Thai floods, small tourism businesses lacked strong leadership, resources and coordinated effort to overcome the post-disaster challenges and neglected getting insurance coverage for floods. The role of leadership in tourism businesses and destination management organisations pre- and post-disaster is another area that needs further research (see also Ghaderi *et al.*, 2021; Jiang *et al.*, 2021).

Chapter 6 (Fitchett, Hoogendoorn & Van Tonder) follows on a similar topic as Chapter 5 (Kiss & Chang) and examines the impacts of cyclones on the tourism industry in the South-West Indian Ocean using three case studies. This is an improvement on existing methodologies used to research disasters. As observed by Ritchie and Jiang (2019) in their systematic review of the crisis and disaster literature, most studies employ the single case study approach. Also, unlike Taiwan (Chapter 5), where hazard management strategies are well developed, this chapter highlights the challenges faced by developing countries such as Madagascar and Mozambique where disaster warning, preparedness and recovery strategies are inexistent or poorly implemented. Besides the financial loss, damage to infrastructure and personal possessions can place severe strains on small tourism enterprises. The chapter highlights the vulnerability and lack of adaptive capacity of small tourism businesses. Research on disaster preparedness, mitigation, response and recovery strategies used by small tourism businesses is particularly lacking (Hall *et al.*, 2018; Orchiston, 2013; Ritchie & Jiang, 2019). Often small tourism businesses lack the financial resources, awareness and capacity to prioritise planning and preparedness (Orchiston, 2013; Brown *et al.*, 2017). This further increases the vulnerability of the tourism industry and the destination. The chapter also analyses comments on TripAdvisor by tourists on cyclones and found that these are rarely mentioned by tourists, but tourists do mention climatic conditions such as flooding, severe and prolonged rainfall, high wind, rough waves and storm surges. This theme is explored further in Chapter 9 (Möller), where the role of social media in crisis communication is discussed.

Chapter 7 (Sun & Milne) provides an understanding of the effects of cyclones on tourism demand in the context of South Pacific SIDS (Small Island Developing States). Tourism is an important driver of economic growth and employment in these islands, notwithstanding that these islands are also very vulnerable to climate change, and hence, prone to disasters (Hall, 2015). Based on data from the Vanuatu International Visitor Survey (IVS), the authors show that tourism demand decreases following Cyclone Pam, but volunteers arriving in the country to help with the recovery effort buffer the drop in overall demand. After this cyclone, tourists relied more on their family members and contacts to find out more about the destination rather than relying on official websites. The importance of personal compared to official information sources post-disaster remains an area that must be investigated further to improve communication to tourists. The analysed data in this chapter confirms that overall satisfaction levels of visitors post-cyclone were higher than pre-cyclone, thereby providing evidence that the visitor experience can improve post-disaster. The importance of social media as a tool for recovery is also highlighted, which is a similar recommendation to what was suggested in Chapter 5 (Kiss & Chang). Studies investigating the impact of disasters on tourism demand abound in the literature (see Ghartey, 2013; Granvorka & Strobl, 2013; Wang, 2009). Previous studies, for example, have investigated the economic effects of hurricanes from 1963 to 2008 on Jamaica's tourism industry (Ghartey, 2013). Ghartey (2013) showed that hurricanes result in local currency appreciation and decline in real tourist expenditure. However, the fall in tourist arrivals is only temporary, which is confirmed in almost all studies on tourism demand. The appreciation of the real exchange rate is due to the fall in demand for foreign currencies as residents direct financial resources to domestic reconstruction activities. At the same time, the supply of foreign currencies can increase as the larger diaspora and international organisations donate more financial assistance to the affected country (Ghartey, 2013). Yet the effects of other types of disasters such as floods and bushfires on tourism demand are areas that need further attention.

Chapter 8 (Jiang & Ritchie) uses the case study of Cyclone Marcia in Central Queensland, Australia as the backdrop for understanding collaboration and actions in tourism disaster management. The chapter provides evidence of how effective collaboration can lead to faster recovery. The authors examined specifically the types of collaborative structures and what collaborative actions are important for successful recovery. They conclude, among others, that the collaboration structure should span across multiple management levels and sectors, leading organisations (such as DMOs) should play an important role in securing resources for the recovery, and external stakeholders are as important as tourism stakeholders. The chapter offers several collaborative actions before, during and after the disaster that can facilitate destination recovery. As noted in another work by the same authors (Ritchie & Jiang, 2019), response and recovery remain the most researched stage of disaster management in the tourism field. This chapter builds on a previous study by Jiang and Ritchie (2017; Jiang et al., 2021) that, for example, identifies competing demands and poor relationships as key barriers to collaboration, while communication and trust are the key elements for effective collaboration. The extent of collaboration between stakeholders affects both preparedness and evacuation. As shown by Faulkner and Vikulov (2001), disasters can be a significant leveller in the sense that larger tourism operators can lose more compared to smaller tourism businesses, with both types of businesses potentially facing cash flow problems. This may spur collaboration for the recovery of the tourism industry and the community. The broader disaster management literature also shows a range of individual and organisational factors that affect the degree of preparedness and evacuation. For example, individual factors include gender, prior experience with a disaster, perceived likelihood of another disaster, and education, while organisational factors include size of the establishment, degree of horizontal and vertical integration, and company culture, among others (Burby & Wagner, 1996). These individual and organisational factors require further investigation from the lens of tourists and tourism businesses respectively to further understand preparedness and evacuation, as suggested by the study of Cahyanto et al. (2016).

Chapter 9 (Möller) delves deeper into the role of tourists in the disaster communication process following Cyclone Winston in Fiji. While many of the previous chapters tend to emphasise communication as important before, during and post-disaster, often the industry perspective is prioritised with very little understanding of what tourists actually need, as emphasised in Chapter 4 (Cahyanto). Mair et al.'s (2016) review of the disaster and crisis management literature showed that the tourism industry lacks crisis management plans, communication and proactive responses. Using the lens of the tourism riskscape, this chapter analyses the spatial contexts of disaster communication through social media. The chapter examines the views of both tourists and destination stakeholders, which departs from existing studies that tend to examine only one stakeholder. The author found that tourists used social media as tools for showing action and response post-disaster. The tourist role blurs into that of the volunteer and disaster-relief aid worker, which requires further investigation as this blurring of roles could inform the development of different typologies of tourist behaviour post-disaster. The chapter argues that social media becomes a unifying force between tourism stakeholders by strengthening bonds between tourists, local staff and the local community. In a related study, Möller et al. (2018) investigate the same tropical cyclone in Fiji and analyse Facebook tourism and crisis communication. They apply the social mediated disaster resilience (SMDR) model to understand how social media can be integrated in resilience building activities and its potential for increasing hotel resilience. This integration of communication strategies and resilience building activities should be researched further by quantifying the extent to which social media contributes to individual, organisational and destination resilience.

While some of the previous chapters discuss flooding as a consequence of cyclones and hurricanes, Chapter 10 (Toubes et al., explores the impacts of marine and coastal floods on the tourism industry using a case study of Miño River, Spain. As the chapter highlights, more research is needed on inland rain-derived floods to analyse the potential direct and indirect impacts on tourist activity. In particular, impacts of floods on heritage sites, natural spaces, tourist facilities and local infrastructure must be ascertained for better mitigation and recovery strategies. The chapter identifies several impact and resistance parameters that should be considered in the assessment of damage caused by floods on the tourism industry. Existing studies on the impacts and consequences of flooding on the tourism industry examine issues such as the coastal squeeze and coastal tourism (Lithgow *et al.*, 2019), building tourism business resilience (Usher *et al.*, 2019), industry vulnerability, preparedness, warnings, evacuation, and mitigation related to flash floods (Cohen, 2007). As Cohen (2007) notes, tourism development can change the ecological conditions of a local area in such a way that it increases its vulnerability to flooding. This nexus of tourism-development, ecological degradation, and vulnerability to flooding and other types of disasters needs further empirical clarification. Others have sought to examine the behaviour of visitors post-flooding (e.g. Walters *et al.*, 2015) by focusing on motives of visitation and destination image perceptions. Floods can have long-term indirect impacts on tourist behaviour, destination choice, the communication and promotion channels used, the local community, local jobs and public budgets (Araújo-Vila *et al.*, 2019). While visitor behaviour post-disaster is a growing area of research in the tourism field, some disasters, such as hurricanes and earthquakes, have been prioritised at the expense of others, such as floods, volcanic eruptions and bush fires.

Disasters can alter both residents' and visitors' sense of place. In this vein, Chapter 11 (Adie) examines the post-disaster decision making processes of second-home owners on Fire Island following Hurricane Sandy, through the lens of place attachment. Second-home owners in coastal areas are particularly vulnerable to the negative impacts of flooding, hurricanes and tsunamis. Very often second-home owners have a strong sense of identification with the location and community in which the second-home is located. According to the findings from this chapter, post-disaster recovery activities such as rebuilding are very much driven by the bonds between second-home owners and the community through long-established friendships with other second-home owners and locals. This perhaps also exemplifies the importance of networks and social capital for post-disaster recovery. While the tourism literature examines issues of social capital in the disaster context from the organisational (e.g. Chowdhury *et al.*, 2019) and community perspective, what factors create social capital from a tourism perspective and the role of the tourist in this creation remain to be ascertained. As argued in Chapter 9 (Möller), following a disaster, the tourist role can shift to volunteer and disaster-relief aid worker. This implies that the tourist can also contribute to building social capital, but this remains relatively unexplored in the tourism disaster management field. Also, given that communities can draw from different types of capital, including social, natural, human, financial, cultural, built and political, to manage change (Ahmed *et al.*, 2004), these factors must be investigated holistically in the tourism context.

Chapter 12 (Amore) addresses the issue of sustainable development and resilience in the Cinque Terre following the floods of 2011. This chapter critically examines post-disaster planning and strategies aimed at reducing destination vulnerability and highlights the conflicts among tourism stakeholders in prioritising recovery strategies. From an analysis of public documents, it was found that ineffective land-use planning, which included the lack of impetus by local government to retain and enhance abandoned terraces in the Cinque Terre and the lack of stakeholder integration among rural and tourism businesses, are factors that did not strengthen destination resilience post-flooding. Resilience has been conceptualised from different perspectives, and therefore it is not surprising that different types of resilience, such as economic, social, human and environmental, are needed for effective recovery post-disaster. An emergent research strand examines destination resilience as a concept (Amore *et al.*, 2018; Becken, 2013; Hall *et al.*, 2018, 2022; Lew, 2014; Prayag, 2018), but further research needs to clarify the concept itself and its relationship to other types of resilience. Resilience has been viewed as a disaster recovery strategy and can be used as a preventative measure to avoid undesired outcomes (Slocum & Kline, 2014). However, poor stakeholder engagement in the rebuild phase, as argued in this chapter, led to the community being unable to take responsibility and control over their post-disaster development pathways. This hints at issues of trust and communication that hamper effective collaboration as suggested in Chapter 8 (Jiang & Ritchie). Slocum and Kline (2014) highlight the importance of community learning post-trauma to reduce the vulnerability of communities and strengthen their resilience. However, as they point out, strong leadership and cooperation between multiple stakeholders are necessary for any resilience building initiatives to work, a theme that emerges from the various chapters in the book.

Collectively the case studies illustrate some of the economic, socio-cultural and environmental impacts of cyclones, hurricanes and floods on the tourism industry. However, there are several other important themes not covered by the various chapters, and which also reflect some substantial gaps in the wider literature. One important issue is the impact of such disasters on employees. As highlighted in previous studies on the effects of hurricanes on hotels, the biggest challenges remain in the area of human resources post-disaster (Lamanna *et al.*, 2012). Given that hotels rely on service personnel for effective service delivery, hurricanes can severely impact access to employees, and hence the ability to implement effective disaster recovery as shown in case studies on Hurricane Gustav in New Orleans (Lamanna *et al.*, 2012). While hotels have to prepare for the potential physical damage caused by cyclones and hurricanes, the likely loss of lifeline services and the possibility of business closure for an extended period of time must also be contemplated. Such disasters can also lead to employee turnover, both voluntary and involuntary. In the months following Hurricane Katrina, employment in the hospitality industry was down by 80,000 (O'Neill, 2005). While employees and their engagement levels are often considered as part and parcel of both mitigation and disaster recovery strategies, they do not always have their say in disaster planning. In disaster plans, employees should be cross-trained for not only disaster recovery activities but also for building organisational resilience. Employee resilience can contribute to organisational resilience post-disaster (Hall *et al.*, 2018; Prayag, 2018).

A key part of managing recovery of tourism destinations is restoring the destination image and reputation which can be affected by negative or inaccurate media coverage (Khazai *et al.*, 2018). This is illustrated in the study by Chacko and Marcell (2008) investigating the visitor profile, destination image and positioning statements of New Orleans as a tourism destination following Hurricane Katrina. Despite the tourism infrastructure sustaining only minor damage, the road to recovery for the destination was tougher due to sensationalist media coverage of the disaster and the persisting negative images given that the media continually undermined any positive images about the city. The literature notes the importance of using opinion leaders to disseminate positive recovery messages to offset negative publicity from mass media. Mair *et al.* (2016) note that destination image is a topic that has received some attention in the post-disaster tourism literature, but longitudinal studies of the evolution of destination image in this context remain an under-researched area. Also, as shown in previous studies (Ryu *et al.*, 2013), after Hurricane Katrina post-disaster destination image was more negative compared to the pre-disaster image. However, repeat visitors had more favourable perceptions of the destination than first-timers. Understanding how destination image and reputation change post-disaster may assist in destination recovery and serve as input in crisis management plans. Khazai *et al.* (2018) propose the Tourism Recovery Scorecard (TOURS) as a crisis communication tool for benchmarking and monitoring progress on post-disaster recovery of tourism destinations. This tool must be tested in other locations and other types of disasters. Chacko and Marcell (2008) recommend the use of effective advertising in any recovery marketing efforts. Some studies have examined dark tourist behaviour following Hurricane Katrina, arguing that visits to disaster sites allow a better understanding of the impact of the disaster on local communities and can challenge the way tourists think of the place and their sense of belongingness (Pezzullo, 2009). Dark tourism tours can also offer opportunities for education, civic identification, and cultural change (Pezzullo, 2009). Nevertheless, there are substantial issues of ethicality surrounding disaster tourism and its potential to exploit vulnerable populations that must be researched further.

A further important theme that begs to be researched is the well-being of visitors during the disaster and post-disaster stages (Ritchie & Jiang, 2019). While this theme is relatively well researched from the community point of view, the long-term impacts of disasters on tourist well-being require further investigation, particularly with respect to the longer-term implications for travel behaviour and destination choice. Arguably, such concerns also flow over to broader concerns regarding destination resilience and well-being, and the capacity of destinations and the people, organisations, and environments within them. As a result, greater attention likely needs to be paid to the learning processes that surround high magnitude weather events and flooding so that future events can be anticipated, appropriately mitigated, or, if that is not possible, adapted to (Hall, 2018). Yet the possibilities of positive learning can sometimes appear limited given the potential costs to some stakeholders of change (Chan *et al.*, 2020; Hall *et al.*, 2022). However, as noted at the start of this book, many destinations are increasingly having to face the challenges of global heating and the effects it will have on the frequency and intensity of weather events and flooding. In such a context, it is therefore to be hoped that some of the cases in this book provide valuable insights into both short- and longer-term responses to the materially and behaviourally damaging effects of cyclones, hurricanes and flooding.

References

Ahmed, R., Seedat, M., Van Niekerk, A. and Bulbulia, S. (2004) Discerning community resilience in disadvantaged communities in the context of violence and injury prevention. *South African Journal of Psychology* 34 (3), 386–408.

Amore, A., Prayag, G. and Hall, C.M. (2018) Conceptualizing destination resilience from a multilevel perspective. *Tourism Review International* 22 (3–4), 235–250.

Araújo Vila, N., Toubes, D.R. and Fraiz Brea, J.A. (2019) Tourism industry's vulnerability upon risk of flooding: The Aquis Querquennis complex. *Environments* 6 (12), 122.

Becken, S. (2013) Developing a framework for assessing resilience of tourism sub-systems to climatic factors. *Annals of Tourism Research* 43, 506–528.

Brown, N.A., Rovins, J.E., Feldmann-Jensen, S., Orchiston, C. and Johnston, D. (2017) Exploring disaster resilience within the hotel sector: A systematic review of literature. *International Journal of Disaster Risk Reduction* 22, 362–370.

Burby, R.J. and Wagner, F. (1996) Protecting tourists from death and injury in coastal storms. *Disasters* 20 (1), 49–60.

Cahyanto, I. and Pennington-Gray, L. (2015) Communicating hurricane evacuation to tourists: Gender, past experience with hurricanes, and place of residence. *Journal of Travel Research* 54 (3), 329–343.

Cahyanto, I., Pennington-Gray, L., Thapa, B., Srinivasan, S., Villegas, J., Matyas, C. and Kiousis, S. (2016) Predicting information seeking regarding hurricane evacuation in the destination. *Tourism Management* 52, 264–275.

Chacko, H.E. and Marcell, M.H. (2008) Repositioning a tourism destination: The case of New Orleans after Hurricane Katrina. *Journal of Travel & Tourism Marketing* 23 (2–4), 223–235.

Chan, C.S., Nozu, K. and Cheung, T.O.L. (2020) Tourism and natural disaster management process: Perception of tourism stakeholders in the case of Kumamoto earthquake in Japan. *Current Issues in Tourism* 23 (15), 1864–1885.

Chowdhury, M., Prayag, G., Orchiston, C. and Spector, S. (2019) Postdisaster social capital, adaptive resilience and business performance of tourism organizations in Christchurch, New Zealand. *Journal of Travel Research* 58 (7), 1209–1226.

Cohen, E. (2007) Tsunami and flash-floods—contrasting modes of tourism-related disasters in Thailand. *Tourism Recreation Research* 32 (1), 21–39.

Faulkner, B. and Vikulov, S. (2001) Katherine, washed out one day, back on track the next: A post-mortem of a tourism disaster. *Tourism Management* 22 (4), 331–344.

Forster, J., Lake, I.R., Watkinson, A.R. and Gill, J.A. (2014) Marine dependent livelihoods and resilience to environmental change: A case study of Anguilla. *Marine Policy* 45, 204–212.

Fritz, H.M., Blount, C., Sokoloski, R., Singleton, J., Fuggle, A., McAdoo, B.G., Moor, A., Grass, C. and Tate, B. (2007) Hurricane Katrina storm surge distribution and field observations on the Mississippi Barrier Islands. *Estuarine, Coastal and Shelf Science* 74 (1–2), 12–20.

Ghaderi, Z., Mat Som, A.P. and Henderson, J.C. (2015) When disaster strikes: The Thai floods of 2011 and tourism industry response and resilience. *Asia Pacific Journal of Tourism Research* 20 (4), 399–415.

Ghaderi, Z., King, B. and Hall, C.M. (2021) Crisis preparedness of hospitality managers: Evidence from Malaysia. *Journal of Hospitality and Tourism Insights* 5 (2), 292–310

Ghartey, E.E. (2013) Effects of tourism, economic growth, real exchange rate, structural changes and hurricanes in Jamaica. *Tourism Economics* 19 (4), 919–942.

Granvorka, C. and Strobl, E. (2013) The impact of hurricane strikes on tourist arrivals in the Caribbean. *Tourism Economics* 19 (6), 1401–1409.

Hall, C.M. (2015) Global change, islands and sustainable development: Islands of sustainability or analogues of the challenge of sustainable development? In M. Redclift and D. Springett (eds) *Routledge International Handbook of Sustainable Development* (pp. 55–73). Abingdon: Routledge.

Hall, C.M. (2018) Climate change and its impacts on coastal tourism: Regional assessments, gaps and issues. In A. Jones and M. Phillips (eds) *Global Climate Change and Coastal Tourism: Recognizing Problems, Managing Solutions, Future Expectations.* (pp. 48–61). Wallingford: CABI.

Hall, C.M., Prayag, G. and Amore, A. (2018) *Tourism and Resilience: Individual, Organisational and Destination Perspectives.* Bristol: Channel View Publications.

Hall, C.M., Safonov, A. and Naderi Koupaei, S. (2022) Resilience in hospitality and tourism: Issues, synthesis and agenda. *International Journal of Contemporary Hospitality Management*, ahead-of-print. https://doi.org/10.1108/IJCHM-11-2021-1428

Jiang, Y. and Ritchie, B.W. (2017) Disaster collaboration in tourism: Motives, impediments and success factors. *Journal of Hospitality & Tourism Management* 31, 70–82.

Jiang, Y., Ritchie, B.W. and Verreynne, M.L. (2021) Developing disaster resilience: A processual and reflective approach. *Tourism Management* 87, 104374.

Johar, J.S. and Sirgy, M.J. (1991) Value-expressive versus utilitarian advertising appeals: When and why to use which appeal. *Journal of Advertising* 20 (3), 23–33.

Khazai, B., Mahdavian, F. and Platt, S. (2018) Tourism Recovery Scorecard (TOURS)–Benchmarking and monitoring progress on disaster recovery in tourism destinations. *International Journal of Disaster Risk Reduction* 27, 75–84.

Lamanna, Z., Williams, K.H. and Childers, C. (2012) An assessment of resilience: Disaster management and recovery for greater New Orleans' hotels. *Journal of Human Resources in Hospitality & Tourism* 11 (3), 210–224.

Lew, A.A. (2014) Scale, change and resilience in community tourism planning. *Tourism Geographies* 16 (1), 14–22.

Lithgow, D., Martínez, M.L., Gallego-Fernández, J.B., Silva, R. and Ramírez-Vargas, D.L. (2019) Exploring the co-occurrence between coastal squeeze and coastal tourism in a changing climate and its consequences. *Tourism Management* 74, 43–54.

Mair, J., Ritchie, B.W. and Walters, G. (2016) Towards a research agenda for post-disaster and post-crisis recovery strategies for tourist destinations: A narrative review. *Current Issues in Tourism* 19 (1), 1–26.

Mason, A., Flores, L., Liu, P., Tims, K., Spencer, E. and Gire, T.G. (2019) Disaster communication: An analysis of the digital communication strategies used by the medical tourism industry during the 2017 Caribbean hurricane season. *Journal of Hospitality and Tourism Insights* 2 (3), 241–259.

Matyas, C., Srinivasan, S., Cahyanto, I., Thapa, B., Pennington-Gray, L. and Villegas, J. (2011) Risk perception and evacuation decisions of Florida tourists under hurricane threats: A stated preference analysis. *Natural Hazards* 59 (2), 871–890.

Möller, C., Wang, J. and Nguyen, H.T. (2018) #Strongerthanwinston: Tourism and crisis communication through Facebook following tropical cyclones in Fiji. *Tourism Management* 69, 272–284.

O'Neill, J.W. (2005) Hurricanes and values. *Lodging Hospitality* 61 (15), 40–42.

Orchiston, C. (2013) Tourism business preparedness, resilience and disaster planning in a region of high seismic risk: The case of the Southern Alps, New Zealand. *Current Issues in Tourism* 16 (5), 477–494.

Orchiston, C. and Higham, J.E.S. (2016) Knowledge management and tourism recovery (de)marketing: The Christchurch earthquakes 2010–2011. *Current Issues in Tourism* 19 (1), 64–84.

Pezzullo, P.C. (2009) 'This is the only tour that sells': Tourism, disaster, and national identity in New Orleans. *Journal of Tourism and Cultural Change* 7 (2), 99–114.

Prayag, G. (2018) Symbiotic relationship or not? Understanding resilience and crisis management in tourism. *Tourism Management Perspectives* 25, 133–135.

Prayag, G. and Soscia, I. (2016) Guilt-decreasing marketing appeals: The efficacy of vacation advertising on Chinese tourists. *Journal of Travel & Tourism Marketing* 33 (4), 551–565.

Ritchie, B.W. and Jiang, Y. (2019) A review of research on tourism risk, crisis and disaster management: Launching the annals of tourism research curated collection on tourism risk, crisis and disaster management. *Annals of Tourism Research* 79, 102812.

Ryu, K., Bordelon, B.M. and Pearlman, D.M. (2013) Destination-image recovery process and visit intentions: Lessons learned from Hurricane Katrina. *Journal of Hospitality Marketing & Management* 22 (2), 183–203.

Scott, D., Gössling, S. and Hall, C.M. (2012) *Tourism and Climate Change: Impacts, Adaptation and Mitigation*. Abingdon: Routledge.

Scott, D., Hall, C.M. and Gössling, S. (2019) Global tourism vulnerability to climate change. *Annals of Tourism Research* 77, 49–61.

Slocum, S. and Kline, C. (2014) Regional resilience: Opportunities, challenges and policy messages from Western North Carolina. *Anatolia* 25 (3), 403–416.

Usher, L.E., Yusuf, J.E.W. and Covi, M. (2019) Assessing tourism business resilience in Virginia Beach. *International Journal of Tourism Cities* (in press) https://doi.org/10.1108/IJTC-02-2019-0019

Villegas, J., Matyas, C., Srinivasan, S., Cahyanto, I., Thapa, B. and Pennington-Gray, L. (2013) Cognitive and affective responses of Florida tourists after exposure to hurricane warning messages. *Natural Hazards* 66 (1), 97–116.

Walters, G., Mair, J. and Ritchie, B. (2015) Understanding the tourist's response to natural disasters: The case of the 2011 Queensland floods. *Journal of Vacation Marketing* 21 (1), 101–113.

Wang, Y.S. (2009) The impact of crisis events and macroeconomic activity on Taiwan's international inbound tourism demand. *Tourism Management* 30 (1), 75–82.

Woosnam, K.M. and Kim, H. (2014) Hurricane impacts on southeastern United States coastal national park visitation. *Tourism Geographies* 16 (3), 364–381.

Index

Printed in the USA
CPSIA information can be obtained
at www.ICGtesting.com
LVHW011136150324
774517LV00040B/1625

9 781845 419462